"Highly Recommended....

UP FROM DEPRESSION is a lucid, non-technical interpretation of one of the most common emotional disorders which afflicts, without discrimination, a large segment of our population. It is admirably suited to meet the informational needs, misunderstandings, and anxiety of the lay public, and provides 'common-sensicle' suggestions as to what to do when depression strikes." —*Irving Blumberg,*
N.Y.S. Committee Against Mental Illness;
N.Y.S. Association for Mental Health

". . . a splendid book for the laity which should be very helpful to all those persons who have a close relative who has become depressed."

—*Modern Medicine*

"For anyone who has a depressed relative, this book can be invaluable." —*Newsday*

"Written for the intelligent layman, this book contains much sound, helpful advice on the problem of depression." —*MD Medical Newsmagazine*

". . . this book is recommended for friends and relatives of all psychiatric patients."

—*New York State Journal of Medicine*

UP
FROM
DEPRESSION

An eminent psychiatrist tells you what
depression is, how to recognize its
symptoms and what to do when depression strikes at a member of *your*
family.

Leonard Cammer, M.D.

PUBLISHED BY POCKET BOOKS NEW YORK

POCKET BOOKS, a division of Simon & Schuster, Inc.
1230 Avenue of the Americas, New York, N.Y. 10020

ISBN: 0-671-65865-4

First Pocket Books printing August, 1971

25   24   23   22   21   20   19   18

POCKET and colophon are registered trademarks
of Simon & Schuster, Inc.

Printed in the U.S.A.

ACKNOWLEDGMENTS

I AM deeply grateful to those of my colleagues and co-workers who gave so generously of their time and effort in reading the manuscript of this book and in making constructive suggestions toward its improvement. Certainly this work is all the better for the attention they bestowed upon it. I mention them as follows: Seymour Berg, M.D., H. Ezell Branham, Jr., M.D., Eva M. Claytor, B.A., Hans B. Drexler, M.D., Eugene N. Dye, M.D., Morton H. Hand, M.D., David J. Impastato, M.D., H. Peter Laqueur, M.D., Matthew T. Moore, M.D., Albert M. Ross, M.D., Harvey M. Ross, M.D., Andrew Salter, Nathaniel Shafer, M.D., and Hans K. Wehrheim, M.D. I also want to express my appreciation to the friends, patients, and the relatives of patients who read all, or parts of, the manuscript and sent me their carefully considered impressions. They, too, have helped immeasurably.

Finally, I extend thanks to my wife, Beatrice Cammer, whose close writing collaboration with me gave shape and clarity to the many problems discussed in these pages. The book and I are most pleasantly in her debt.

LEONARD CAMMER

New York, New York

Contents

PART TWO: OVERCOMING DEPRESSION

TO THE READER

EVERY ONE of us is depressed at times and this is perfectly normal.

We may fall into a mood, live through the "Monday blues," have a gloomy spell, or be morose because of a head cold. Feelings like these are common in our daily lives. So is the dejection that may overcome a person after being refused a business loan, or even the sadness that one is left with after seeing a movie with a grim theme.

As you read this you may be reminded of a time during some critical phase of your own life when you reached a low point and said, "I guess I'm just depressed." And you were interpreting your feelings correctly, although you probably dismissed them after a while and bounced back. We take such mild passing blues for granted and even as natural in the course of living—*provided that they do not interfere in our daily tasks*.

However, this book is not about blue moods. Its thesis is real depression, a serious and widely prevalent disorder of which the average person knows little or nothing; and though it yields readily to treatment it is an illness that goes untreated most of the time. Yet its impact on the family can be incalculable in emotional distress, social and economic chaos, and sometimes in the tragic loss of the depressed person who dies by his own hand.

I am convinced that all of this could be averted if relatives knew what depression actually is. Often, a family member will surmise the illness but not grasp its deadly significance. Only recently, a daughter who brought her despondent mother to me said: "I *thought* she was depressed, but I didn't know what to do. She had so many complaints and the doctors said there wasn't anything really wrong with her. Now I realize her nervousness is depression, but I still don't understand it—why it happened or where it came from. Can anything be done about it, Doctor?" If this daughter had had some precise knowledge of depression she would have known what steps to take. As it was, a risky period of suicide potential elapsed before anything was done for her mother's condition.

I recall, too, the situation of a wife so shocked by her husband's depression that she was immobilized. "It came out of the blue. There were days when he seemed like a walking corpse. I couldn't think . . . or dare talk of it. I didn't know which way to turn." And yet when this woman was armed with the full truth about depression she did a splendid job of dealing with her husband's illness. She shed her anxieties and collaborated so fully in his treatment program that she deserved a badge of merit for her share in his recovery.

Looking back at many patients, I can attribute their return to health in large part to the relatives' participation in the recovery process. Indeed, the numerous question-and-answer sessions that I have conducted with many families on this subject have produced the material in these pages. I believe that in turn this information will dispel the unknowns of depression for you.

Throughout this writing I have held to one main goal— to provide facts that will enable you to deal with and understand your relative's condition, when he or she is being treated as an outpatient, in a hospital, at home during and after treatment, or before you ever seek professional consultation.

Treatment can do a great deal for the person, but the added "extra" must come from you. If this book succeeds in knocking down the wall of hearsay that surrounds depression and in releasing the family from its anguish when one of its members suffers this illness, and if it helps to bring the depressed person back to a normal way of life, then it is doing its intended job.

PART ONE

UNDERSTANDING DEPRESSION

CHAPTER ONE

What Is Depression?

PERHAPS YOU are reading this book because a relative of yours has gone into a slump. It may be your mother, uncle, sister, or any other person in the family and you have probably wondered for weeks or months what was wrong. I am sure, too, that you have tried to coax the person out of the low mood, that you have suggested going for walks or to the movies, and that you have invited friends to call, in the hope of cheering him up.

But nothing seems to get through. Your relative is still removed from everyone, and as you watch him in his endless gloom you feel that life has brought him to a standstill. You recall that this once happened to a friend's sister. It made little impression on you at the time, but now that it is hitting home you puzzle over it and try to guess what triggers such a peculiar mood. Furthermore, if you are like many people I have known you may start to believe that *you* caused this condition, that in some way it is your fault.

"WHAT'S HAPPENING TO US?"

Discontent now stirs your household. All in the family are at loggerheads. Each is impatient about what should or should not be done, and quarrels break out. If there are children around, they too absorb the unrest and get cranky and unmanageable. In short, you are seeing how an entire family can fall apart when one of its members slips into melancholia, with no one to decide on a course of action.

At this point you may be shaken and baffled. How long can it go on? And what is really wrong?

Your Relative Is Ill with Depression

Yes, *ill,* because depression is not a mysterious visitation of gods or demons, as many believed in ancient times. It is just as much an illness as kidney or heart disease or any other physical disorder that you might name.

But, paradoxically, this may be a cause for optimism. As an enigma that you cannot solve, it frustrates you. As a definable illness, it can be dealt with. And though it is a depressive one ("a mental thing," may be your first despairing thought), do not decide that it is the end of the world. Most depressed people do get well, because they can be successfully treated. With one proviso: they need the family's help as an integral part of the recovery process.

Depression Is Not an Outgrowth of Modern Times

This illness was known to man from the beginnings of recorded history. The Bible is replete with descriptions of the grief-stricken, and of the agonized feelings of men and women who lost their faith in God and themselves, and hope for the future.

In the fourth century B.C., Hippocrates, the Father of Medicine, described four temperaments of man, one of which was the *melancholic* (the depressive). We still use the term *melancholia* to characterize the hopeless, despondent condition of the depressed person.*

People knew of depression in the Middle Ages too, although, as in ancient times, they construed it to be a spell cast by some wicked force. Only toward the end of the eighteenth century did studies in newly established institutions and hospitals for mental disorders uncover the *medical* nature of mood disturbances.

Today we can sum up depression as the result of

---

* The three other temperaments were the phlegmatic, the sanguine, and the choleric. Hippocrates believed that all four were caused by abnormal fluxes of (1) black bile (the melancholic personality mentioned above); (2) phlegm (the phlegmatic personality); (3) blood (the sanguine personality); (4) white bile (the choleric personality).

certain biologic and social forces that, in a complex setting, act detrimentally on the person's nervous system function. The depressed activity in turn adversely changes the person's behavior, feeling tones, and thoughts. This totality of abnormal function constitutes a depressive illness.

Depression Plays No Favorites

When you are told that your brother-in-law, let us say, is depressed, do not retort quickly, "Oh no, not John. He's too intelligent. He wouldn't let his nerves get him." Or if it is your Aunt Jane, whom you adore, "Impossible. She's so gay and full of high spirits. She'd never be depressed over anything."

This is not true. Depression can strike anyone—a housewife, cabdriver, businessman, schoolteacher, gambler, actress, bricklayer, saleswoman, Phi Beta Kappa student, longshoreman, and so on. And it appears in stable and mature persons, neurotics, and children. Moreover, it can occur at any level of the economic, social, or intellectual scale, and in every kind of personality. To deny the condition, then, will not blow it away.

Depressive illness falls into several categories which I will discuss in later chapters. Right now I will briefly outline its general pattern.

Depression Starts with the Blues

In my introductory words I touched on ordinary blue feelings that occur in everyone at times. But when these blues linger and cannot be shaken off, and if they interfere with continued normal living, they may be leading to a true depression.

As the Blue Feelings Take Hold

The sadness that pervades the person can in itself be the essence of depression. He or she becomes aware of feeling desolate and may despair aloud, "Why do I fall into these black moods?"

Even when the depressed person does not recognize the unnatural feeling tones, there is still a sense that something is wrong and pulling him down. He will verbalize it: "I have such a heavy heart."

The heavy heart signifies utter weariness. A person in this condition may drag about all day and wonder how to push through it. Or, if the depression is intense, he or she will not get going at all. The sluggishness is plain to be seen as the person bogs down at any little obstacle. His thinking faculties seem dulled and he blanks out in conversation. At the same time he complains, "I'm so jittery and restless."

The Mental Pain of Depression

This is a unique emotional quality compounded of anguish and despair, self-disgust, and intense guilt with anger and fear. Mental pain may also express itself as agitation and hopelessness. The sufferer wishes that he had never been born or could return to nonexistence.

The Physical State of Depression

Many body responses accompany depression but these are almost always *functional* (see Chapter 7 for a fuller explanation of this term). Your relative may complain of aches and pains in the bones or joints, feelings of nausea, dizziness, stomach ache, pressure in the head, or a variety of other physical symptoms, which, however, do not point to an illness that shows up on physical examination. Still, something *is* wrong physically, even though the X-ray does not catch it, because depression can symptomatize an active disorder of *nervous function*.

Said another way, the nervous system, which is physical and part of the body, may not be working as it should. The neural circuits and pathways are disturbed and inhibited because the brain chemicals do not operate with the balance required for normal emotional harmony.

However, whether you visualize depression as an emotional or as a physical disturbance is purely academic. Technically, you would be right either way or both ways. What is more pertinent is that everyone tends to think of, and refer to, depression as a *nervous* condition, that is, a "nervous breakdown." Haven't you found yourself uttering just these words?

DEPRESSION AND NERVOUS BREAKDOWN

Let me use an analogy here. When someone says, "I had a virus," he or she usually means anything from the common cold or sinusitis to a bout of diarrhea. In the same way, the colloquialism "nervous breakdown" can signify almost any kind of emotionally upsetting experience.

I have heard a patient describe the mild depression she endured when her engagement was broken as a *"terrible nervous breakdown."* Another patient, who suffered a severely psychotic* (though short) depression with collapse, told me that it was "a *little* nervous breakdown . . . not too bad."

It seems to me that when the average person says "nervous breakdown" he really means an emotional illness that was serious enough to disrupt work and the continuity of living. In this respect he is quite correct. A depression that removes someone from his or her responsibilities does indeed connote a nervous breakdown. Nevertheless, this term remains too vague to be useful, because it tells so little. Instead, I am going to suggest a better way for you to understand what happens in the nervous breakdown that culminates as a depression. Let me show you how the person's tensional- (nervous-) energy system operates.

The Tensional (Nervous) Energy of Depression

Each of us can move, think, work, feel, and so on, because the body receives a constant supply of the energy it needs through the intake of food.

---

* *Psychosis* is the medical term for severe mental disorder. Hallucinations, delusions, and a loss of contact with reality characterize a psychosis. It may also include deep depression. But do not let the word *psychosis* (or a manifestation of it in a relative) frighten you. You may have heard that a person with a psychotic depression will be "institutionalized" for many years. Perhaps that was true a generation ago, but not today. Treatment can now overcome such an episode. It is worth remembering that the larger percentage of people recover from it in a relatively short time, regardless of how distressing the actual episode appears when the person is in the throes of it.

This is *caloric* energy, and the muscles produce it.

But before this happens, the brain and nervous system, coordinating with glandular secretions and other chemical processes, must activate these muscles with *tensional* energy.

The process can be likened to the workings of the automobile. Gasoline is the caloric fuel, but an electrical system with generator, spark plugs, and a timer provides the controlled energy that fires the fuel. Both systems must operate together in harmony.

Every second of the day we all discharge (expend) a certain amount of tensional energy. This is normal. Not one of us could function without tensional energy, or even if it fell below a certain level peculiar to each individual. In order to go, we must, so to speak, have a warmed-up motor and be set in gear. The crux of the question about tensional energy, then, becomes: How much of it do we generate and how well do we utilize it?

Some people maintain and distribute their daily quotas of tensional energy wisely and accomplish all their tasks. They wind up a usual day with just average tiredness. However, a person may generate a normal amount of tension but expend it *unwisely* and become depleted too fast.

Another person, who has a normal tensional threshold, may find that prolonged periods of stress, as in a harsh, grinding struggle for survival, are oppressing him; he gradually uses up enormous amounts of tensional energy to cope with the struggle and ends with a chronic fatigue.

A third individual may build up *too much* tensional energy and never learn to discharge it properly. He might develop many kinds of psychosomatic symptoms at first; but later, in the process of coping with the symptoms, he too exhausts himself.

Over a period of days, weeks, or months all such persons lose more and more tensional energy through the uncontrolled or wasteful use of emotion, or by bottling it up only to have it spill over as physical ailments. Ultimately, they are sapped of emotional reserve and strength; or, as I have defined it in another book, they develop an *exhaustion of adaptive energy*.

Everyone requires this adaptive energy in order to

adjust to life situations as they arise. Once the person has lost or exhausted adaptability he or she becomes depressed. (See Chapter 5 for further comments on adaptive energy).

Therefore, depression may mean that the person's entire being has failed to adapt to life's stresses. This is not to say that he is to blame. Rather, his tensional energy exchange system no longer operates smoothly and the result is depression. The machinery has broken down; hence, "nervous breakdown."

THE INTERRELATIONS OF ANXIETY, FEAR AND ANGER

In its most basic sense, then, depression in your relative means that he or she is suffering from a nervous disorder.

However, this illness includes three other responses; they are *anxiety, fear,* and *anger.* Most persons tend to lump these emotions with depression and use the term "nervousness" or "too much tension" to describe the whole uncomfortable feeling. For example, a woman who consults me initially does not state, "I'm depressed, Doctor." Instead she may say, "I'm so nervous, I'm afraid to go out alone" (the fear). "I dreaded the trip coming here. I called my son to bring me because I'm upset all the time" (the anxiety). "The smallest thing frightens me" (the fear and the anxiety again). "And then I'm mad at myself and everybody else for it" (the anger).

Her son confirms this. Finally, when these complaints are sifted, an underlying depression (and exhaustion of her adaptive reserve) is exposed.

In getting to recognize and understand depression, it is vital that the interrelated emotions not mislead you. This is why you should know their role both in their normal and in their excessive use.

Normal Anxiety, Fear and Anger

Ordinarily, the emotions that the nervous system generates are normal and useful to all of us. Each provides a special way to protect us in stressful conditions and to ensure our survival. Thus, whenever a threat of some kind is directed against our life or security, one of these emotions will impel us to act in some way to overcome the threat.

Anxiety, in its healthy form, mobilizes us to make decisions and take constructive action. A person might feel anxious about holding his job and anticipate being fired. Normally, he responds to this anxiety by taking work home, studying the job problem, or in some way improving his competence and skill. Anxiety thus helps guarantee his employment.

Fear works for us too. It causes us to retreat until the danger passes. An individual may be afraid to use his car in heavy traffic if he believes that he will panic and lose control. He then stays off a crowded freeway until he is more practiced in driving. Fear may also keep a person from acting impulsively in areas where he is threatened by immaturity or lack of knowledge. He can then gain time until he is more experienced.

Anger too protects us. In many life situations we find that we must battle for our safety and rights. Anger quickens our senses for this. A soldier may not realize that he becomes angry with the enemy in order to deal with the danger to himself, but actually his anger is mobilizing his adaptive energies for self-preservation.

But the Person May Overreact

We may develop too much anxiety, too many fears, and far too great an anger for our own good. This happens when the situation becomes a threat to the person and he cannot deal with it.

Illness of any kind is just such a threat. If it is depression he will respond to it as to any other illness—with anxiety, fear and anger that often swell to ungovernable proportions.

How the Anxiety, Fear and Anger are Expressed in Depression

Anxiety shows up as restlessness and bouts of panic. The person constantly anticipates the worst and gets uneasy and jumpy at any minor event. Always on tenter-hooks, his body also expresses anxiety symptoms in sweaty palms, headache, palpitation, and so on.

Fears are manifested when he refuses to be left alone and then, contrarily, shrinks from participating in a social group. Fear of failure is also voiced. "I ought to quit my job before I'm fired," or, "I'll give up the business. I'll lose it anyway."

Anger comes out as a rage at being ill. The person wants to hit or cut himself. He explodes with irritability and sarcasm, blaming everyone for his distress and per-haps striking out at them physically. He may even decide that "they" are banded together to persecute and destroy him and have devised a plot to this purpose.

Mainly, it is important for you not to be confused by the anxiety, fear and anger, and not to conclude that your relative is simply acting out a temper tantrum or playing the prima donna. I am not saying that you can identify and tick off these three emotions as easily as you would items one, two, and three on a grocery list. Their subtle-ties can deceive you. But if you watch closely you will finally note the depression lurking beneath, especially when you see that despite the person's erratic and un-pleasant behavior he is also sad, drained, and inert, that he berates and depreciates himself, and that he can no longer relate to the world.

THE ASSOCIATED FEAR OF INSANITY

When someone is depressed, not only feelings are dis-torted but thoughts as well. He or she dwells on taking an overdose of sleeping pills or jumping off the roof. Or the person ruminates all day and night about minor stresses that "won't get out of my mind." He is aware that the persistence of these thoughts is unnatural. He broods about them, perhaps alone in the dark, and finally follows through to what seems the only conclusion—"I must be going insane." He is not convinced of the insanity *as yet,* because he realizes that he still knows who he is, the time of day, the place he lives in, and the identity of those around him. But he is now afraid that the maddening thoughts will, in the end, drive him insane.

Do Not Expect Your Relative to Tell You This

He may seem secretive but this is not so. He is simply afraid to express the sense of doom that overpowers him, first, because he thinks he will be laughed at or called insane and then be "institutionalized"; second, because a superstitious dread warns him that if the thoughts are verbalized they will be transformed into real happenings and will then capture and control him.

Other ideas torment him, too. "If I'm going insane, maybe it will be passed on to the children." Unfounded as such fears may be, they aggravate the guilt feelings that develop with depression. A chain reaction then ensues— from depression to fear to guilt and into deeper depression.

However, a depressed person does not "go insane." But the fear of doing so can, in itself, be a *symptom* of depression.

DEPRESSION AND HEREDITY

Whenever an illness strikes and the sufferer cannot understand its nature, he or she may begin to think that the disease was inherited. This is especially true of emotional illness, including depression, which has always loomed up as the most frightening of disorders. Several reasons account for this. In the past, when little was known of its causes, people linked emotional illness with heredity and then with evil. The logic went something like this: If a person was productive and well he must have inherited good qualities; if he was disturbed emotionally he had inherited bad qualities. His mental illness was then equated with evil. Hence, the depressed and immobilized person was stigmatized as an evil person and shunned as such.

Since no effective methods existed until recent times for the treatment of these disturbances, the stigma hung on. Small wonder, then, that when a person believed he had inherited depressive illness and was "incurable" he felt his fate to be sealed. So did those around him.

Heredity and Genetics

The study of genetics developed as recently as the late nineteenth and early twentieth centuries. Only in the past few years have we begun to explore the molecular chemistry of genes, which determines the genetic code. This code gives us accurate information about the heredity of many traits, characteristics, and human *susceptibilities* as they are determined when the sperm and egg unite.

Thus, we know that a person may inherit a susceptibility to certain disorders such as obesity, allergies, sensitivities to drugs, and so on. But will these susceptibilities flourish in growth and maturation? Not necessarily. The fact that your grandmother, mother, or aunt had diabetes does not mean that you must have it too. The same holds true of many other illnesses, *including depression.* We have no clear evidence that depressive illness is directly inherited. A progenitor may have suffered from it, but this does not argue that you will also be afflicted with it. I say this because we now know that even susceptibilities inherited at birth can be modified. It is true that biologists still debate the question of which is more important to the person, his inherited nature or the nurturing environment. Ultimately, studies in genetics will inform us precisely of the "putty" we are made of. In the meantime, if anyone you know is unusually concerned about his or her depressive episodes as these may affect the children, that person should discuss this with the family doctor.

In the light of our present knowledge, however, no one should develop undue anxiety about the heredity of depressive illness. The evidence seems to indicate that the environment can more than compensate for hereditary proneness to depression and other illnesses. Too many good things are working for the person today. Social and scientific advances protect him, add to his constitutional assets, and help stabilize his function for better survival against any sort of disorder, no matter what his susceptibilities. Also, people are learning to communicate more openly about the mental and emotional problems that beset them. As a result, civil agencies and private employers have come to recognize that depression can overcome anyone. They also understand the person's need for relief from stress when the illness sets in. Many employers are inclined to cooperate in its treatment by granting time off and holding the job open. Thus, such illness need not be hidden any longer as a shameful secret; it can be dealt with and disposed of without the added burden of concealment.

CHAPTER TWO

The Seriousness of Depression

WHEN I say that depression is serious I do not mean that it is irreversible. The depressed person can recover. But I do mean that you should always take depression seriously, because those who experience this illness may plumb such depths of misery that they will grasp at any measure to ease their mental pain. For example they may (1) attempt suicide; (2) stupefy themselves with alcohol; (3) drug themselves into oblivion; (4) withdraw to an isolated way of life.

HOW YOU RECOGNIZE THE TENDENCY TO SUICIDE

I will tell you something bluntly, because many persons try to hide from the thought as if this might erase it.

To an alarming degree, the end result of depressive illness is suicide. This is the most direct way I know of saying that depression may be a fatal illness. It can and does lead to death, self-inflicted. Every day you will find newspaper items of a housewife who seals the kitchen and turns on the gas oven, of an actress who swallows too many sleeping pills, of a businessman who hangs himself. Since depression occurs in children, adolescents, adults, and older people, you can see that suicide knows no age limits.

If you ever suspect that your relative is capable of destroying himself and possibly has stepped to the brink of it, act on your suspicions. You may be closer to the truth than you think.

Unfortunately, many myths circulate about suicide and dull the average person's alertness to it. I hope you will note these inaccuracies well, as I describe them below.

15

The Fallacies and Facts of Suicide

FALLACY: When someone threatens suicide, doesn't this mean that he is just talking and won't really commit the act?

THE FACT: On the contrary, the depressed person almost always "cries out" for protection against his or her impulse, either directly or in disguised form. Eight out of every ten persons warn others of their suicidal intentions beforehand. "Talking about it" is one way in which the person notifies you that his suicide is imminent. Many persons would be saved every day if others understood what they were trying to say. But if the message is missed and help is not forthcoming, the act of suicide takes place.

FALLACY: Isn't the person who says he'll kill or hurt himself just faking? Doesn't he simply want attention and to manipulate those around him?

THE FACT: Every depressed person requires attention and uses all psychologic devices possible to serve his or her needs. If these devices are ignored or denied, even though the person is using them to attract notice or to manipulate, despair may overwhelm him. In rejecting such a person one is daring him to act. More often than not he will. And unhappily, the man who pulls a trigger with the gun at his temple cannot change his mind.

FALLACY: Is it true that someone who has attempted suicide once won't try it again?

THE FACT: No. Here, lightning can strike twice or more times in the same place. Many suicides reveal a history of at least one previous attempt. The second frequently succeeds.

FALLACY: A deeply religious person wouldn't kill himself, would he? Doesn't suicide contradict his faith?

THE FACT: Ministers, rabbis, and priests suffering

from depression have taken their own lives. Devoutness or orthodoxy in any faith will not deter a person from destroying himself when he is depressed.

FALLACY: Isn't a person who tries to commit suicide mentally deranged?

THE FACT: While almost anyone who takes his life is depressed, he may not be psychotic or "mad." The person can be entirely oriented to reality but unable to deal any longer with the burden of depression and the remorseless rise of tension. They disturb his judgment and distort the worth of life. While some "make an end to it" on impulse, others will coldly devise plans to find deliverance in death.

Other fallacies also find credence among the more gullible, but the facts about self-destruction are the stark reality.

Number of Suicides

For the total population, suicide constitutes the tenth leading cause of death in the United States alone. For college students it is the second leading cause. In the adolescent group (ages fifteen to nineteen) it ranks third, and among all young adults (ages twenty-five to forty-four) it is fourth.

Reports from the United States Department of Health, Education and Welfare reveal that well over 20,000 persons annually die by their own hand—about one person every twenty minutes. Moreover, unofficial estimates indicate that every year at least an equal number of others kill themselves, but because our culture considers suicide to be disgraceful, irreligious, or contestable grounds for insurance benefits, the cause of death is concealed. It is probable that deaths from suicide more correctly approximate 40,000 to 50,000 each year.

You should also know that for every person who succeeds in killing himself, five to ten times as many make a real attempt that fails. Reports show that some two million persons alive today in the United States have already made at least one such attempt. It hurts to realize that these two million represent a pool from which many suicides will be drawn in the ensuing years.

Like other statistics, these may seem an abstraction to you and remote from your depressed relative. But when you translate them into individual human values you will realize how many fine and productive persons could have been saved had the signs of suicidal intent been recognized.

Therefore, it would be a good thing to note this cardinal rule in dealing with a depressed person: *Someone should stay with him at all times or find a means of protecting him so long as he retains the desire to die.*

What Brings the Person to Suicide?

Any one of several dilemmas. You may not yet have recognized that your relative is depressed. However, you can detect the suicidal intent if you are alert to any of the following conditions affecting the person.

HAS THERE BEEN A RECENT LOSS?   It may be that a loved one, a thing, an opportunity, or even the intangible stuff of prestige has been wrenched away. Its significance is overwhelming, and the person feels that he can never reconcile the loss. He cries, "How can I go on from here?" and secretly plans not to go on at all.

IS INTENSE STRESS CAUSING A CHRONIC FATIGUE? Perhaps one series of disasters after another has dogged the person, and the struggle to fight them off now takes its toll. Overcome by physical, mental, and moral exhaustion, he or she is unable to pull out from under. This person may then present a definite suicidal risk.

ARE LONELINESS AND REJECTION APPARENT?   Your relative may express the emptiness that goes with a lonely way of life. He implies that the world holds no place for him, nobody wants him, and only a fool would think that this could change. So why fight it? But do not dismiss this as a passing notion, because it can be his way of telling you that he is looking for death.

DOES THE PERSON SEEM LOST AND UNSURE?   There

may be no overt signs of depression. But suddenly you sense the uncertainty and self-doubts, the inability to measure up to normal confidence levels, the feelings of total inadequacy for any task. Here you must listen to him carefully, because he is revealing a central plan—to whip up the courage to "end it all."

IS HE AT THE "WHAT'S THE USE" THRESHOLD? Perhaps he has been an active, accomplished person but has gradually begun to dwell on the futility of life. You notice that nothing holds any appeal, that everything seems to have gone stale for him. You wonder why. It seems so out of character. But these depressive thoughts of monotony and tedium may be a signal that he or she is heading for self-destruction.

In Chapter 7, I will discuss many other symptoms of depression, but those I have just outlined typify suicidal preoccupation and are the most easily detected.

HOW YOU RECOGNIZE THE TENDENCY TO ALCOHOLISM

The anguish of mental pain that I defined for you in Chapter 1 is unrelenting. It maintains a guerrilla warfare against the person until the need for relief dominates all else.

Killing the Mental Pain

The most common "painkiller" for mental distress is alcohol. This was as true in the past as it is today. Alcohol is not a natural substance, but every civilization has discovered a fermentation process that will produce this intoxicant. Used almost universally, it is the oldest of all tranquilizers. Thus, a depressed person may turn to alcohol quite naturally to escape his mental hell. It does offer relief but its danger is twofold.

FIRST, ALCOHOL ADDS TO THE DEPRESSION. Although it deadens the mental pain, it also depresses the nervous system. In its total effect it *adds* to the depressive illness.

SECOND, ALCOHOL COVERS UP. When the family finally notices the alcoholism they may let the primary illness (the depression causing the alcoholism) slip by them.

A thirty-six-year-old suburban housewife I knew grew severely fatigued from the strain of overmanaging her children and household. She was unable to keep up with her rigid work schedule, and her resultant tension gradually settled into depression. She discovered that one or two drinks before bedtime induced the sleep she badly needed. Then a drink before dinner helped her in preparing the meal. After that, a few more killed off her evening nervousness. Finally, she found that a swallow or three at lunch calmed her nerves for the afternoon. At the end of six months she was consuming almost three-fourths of a bottle of hard liquor daily. But it was another three months before her husband and children noticed that "mother drinks." At last she was brought to the family doctor. While the alcoholism seemed the predominant issue, psychiatric consultation soon exposed *a primary depression,* for which she was successfully treated. The drinking stopped abruptly, and she returned to her normal responsibilities.

Not every alcoholic starts as a depressed person. There are many other reasons for resorting to drink, but depression of some kind can be a main cause. When your relative medicates himself with alcohol he is camouflaging his depression. Diagnosis and treatment are thus delayed, sometimes too long for a cure to be effected.

HOW YOU RECOGNIZE THE TENDENCY TO DRUG ADDICTION

Everything I have just said about the hazards of alcoholism applies equally to the possibility of drug abuse. Virtually all drugs can be obtained on the market today, legally and illegally. Depressed persons often visit two or three doctors and, hoping for the magical cure, get prescriptions from them all. They end by taking excessive amounts of drugs, believing that if one pill is good, two are better and three or more the best.

Self-Medication

You must exercise the utmost vigilance when a relative tells you that he or she is taking a "wonder pill" passed along by a friend. "It peps me up and makes me feel like a million." You ask yourself: Why is this pepping-up needed? And what's in that pill? Perhaps you go along with it, hoping it will not last more than a day or two. But after several weeks you learn that the drug is still being taken and more of it. You may even be asked for money so that it can be bought on the illegal market. It is then that you realize that something is very wrong.

The Pill Poppers

Among the drugs that the depressed person turns to are *sleeping pills*. They are the most widely used and abused, because insomnia and restlessness are major symptoms in depression; and since the person also feels tired and draggy, he or she will turn to the regular intake of *pep pills*. These give a temporary lift, but at the same time may induce a jittery reaction. Then, along with the pep pills, *tranquilizers* are taken to relieve the daytime nervousness, some of which has been aggravated by the pep pills. (See Chapter 10 for a full discussion of these drugs.)

The tense and depressed person thus becomes a "pill popper." He feels most secure when gulping down pills, the tranquilizers and pep pills by day, the sleeping pills at night. But imagine what this does to the nervous system! Suppose we stepped up the voltage of an electric motor and at intervals cut in a resistance coil. How could we expect this electrical system to perform smoothly? The motor would run in fits and starts and after a while burn itself out. Similarly, when the equilibrium of the nervous system is jerked about in this way, it too will exhaust itself and the underlying depression will rapidly fulminate.

Getting "Hooked" on Drugs Because of Depression

Once your relative has taken to self-medication with no

one checking on the dosage, he or she runs the risk of addiction. This is especially true of the *opiates* (heroin, morphine, codeine, and similar narcotics), of the *stimulants* (amphetamines and other pep pills), and of the *tranquilizers* (barbiturates, the newer sedatives and "mind" drugs).

I know of numerous men and women who became severely addicted to sleeping pills and morphine (or other opiates) for relief of symptoms because their depressions were never diagnosed. And apart from those who are addicted, many others resort to LSD ("acid"), barbiturates ("goofballs"), marijuana ("pot," or "grass") and amphetamines ("speed," or "pep pills") for the "kicks." If you discover that some member of your family is taking such drugs, get medical consultation about his or her emotional stability. And do not be surprised if you learn that depression of some kind is at the bottom of the drug problem.

HOW YOU RECOGNIZE THE TENDENCY TO SOCIAL WITHDRAWAL

By its very nature, depression drives a person into isolation. He or she is often slowed down in body and mind, and simply cannot communicate with those in the environment.

It is too bad that most family members do not comprehend the meaning of withdrawal. So much heartache could be avoided if they did. Some get angry at the withdrawn person and retaliate by ignoring him. Or the more interested ones will do their best to pull him back into active social life. But neither tactic accomplishes anything, because the depressive element that is causing the retreat is not seen.

For example, if the person says that he wants only to be left alone the family will be glad to make themselves scarce. In the next breath, however, the person will say that he is afraid and wants to be with someone. You may try to respond to this, but when you keep him company he sits in a heavy silence. No matter how you entreat him not to shut you out and how much love and warmth you spread over him, he turns away. You finally conclude that he is unreachable, and with some uneasiness you go about your own business. Your empathy cannot be evoked.

The Meaning of Empathy

Empathy for depressive illness is a feeling that one must cultivate. You may be anxious about your relative and very *sympathetic*—that is, you feel *for* him or her. But this is not the same as being *empathetic*. *Empathy*, a word used in psychologic medicine, means the ability to feel as the other person feels and to understand that feeling—to identify emotionally and put yourself in the other person's place.

It is far easier to do this for physical illness such as pneumonia or a heart ailment, because these are "familiar" to you. Or if the patient has a broken arm you "see" the disability—that is, you can touch the plaster cast encasing it and "know" the discomfort of the injured limb. This is empathy, and it leads to solicitude and tender care.

But when an individual is removed from everyone because of a depression that no one understands or even recognizes, the temptation for most people is to throw up their hands. Worse, they become offended because the depressed person will not "confide" in them. One mother told me in the patient's presence: "He just moves away from us and acts as if we're not there. He knows we love him. Why does he have to hurt us this way? You don't know what I've been going through, Doctor." If only she knew the suffering *he* has been going through!

When You Turn Away from the Problem

The depressed person senses that he is a burden to the family. But he is a burden to himself too, because he is helpless to rectify his condition and is ashamed and humiliated by it. His only recourse then is to drift farther away.

When such withdrawal continues, the depression can destroy many family relationships, especially those of husband and wife, or parent and child. What people cannot understand they cannot tolerate. Sooner or later, depressive behavior arouses hostility in them and a rift is born. No one feels close to the depressed person any longer. Each pursues his or her own way of life, and this augments the separateness. When the withdrawal lasts too long it creates a scar in the relationship that is not easily removed, even when the depression has cleared up. The person and his family will then be forever sensitized to each other's antagonism.

This is why it is essential to know that withdrawal is not a deliberately perverse character trait, but a symptom in itself. I venture to say that if the average family perceived it in its true depressive context and saw the interaction taking place, they would voice their insights something like this: "No wonder he's removing himself from us. He feels that he's a millstone around our necks and he knows we feel that way too. It must be awful for him. Let's see if we can't find a way to help. Maybe we owe it to him."

CHAPTER THREE

What You Should Know About Endogenous Depressions

I HAVE found it useful to classify depressions into three principal categories:

1. Endogenous depressions
2. Reactive depressions
3. Neurotic depressions

In this chapter I will deal with the first category. (The second and third will be discussed in Chapters 4 and 5.) As a preliminary I want to mention three essential factors that bear on all depressions: the intensity; the duration; the quality.

The *intensity* varies. It may be *mild, moderate,* or *severe.* The general rule is that mild depressions, while distressing, can be overcome rather quickly. Moderate and severe depressions are almost always classified as serious and should be managed with medical help.

The *duration* of a depression may be *acute, recurrent,* or *chronic.* An acute depression, no matter what the reason, comes on quickly and may endure only a week, or as long as four months. It can clear up spontaneously without treatment. A recurrent depression is an acute episode that reappears at different intervals, with normal periods (called "remissions") in between. A chronic depression arises more gradually and lingers for an indefinite time, even up to two or more years, with ultimate remission.

The *quality* of a depression can be *retarded*—that is, the person's function is slowed down. Or it can be *agitated,* with the person in a state of general nervous excitement.

As you study the various depressions in the following pages you will come across the modifying terms I have just defined. Try to remember them, because they may be valuable clues to the patient's condition.

ENDOGENOUS DEPRESSIONS

This word, pronounced en-*dodj*-i-nus, means "internally generated." Endogenous depressions result when the brain and nervous system (part of the *internal* person) become disorganized in some way and can no longer function normally. The doctor may call this kind of depression an *organic* or *physical* disturbance of nervous function, which indeed it is. In the following sections different varieties of endogenous depression are described.

Involutional Melancholia at the Menopause
(Change of Life)

Perhaps you have just encountered involutional melancholia in one of your relatives. And maybe your first thought is: How could this happen to someone in *our* family? Right here it may reassure you to know that of all depressions, this is the most common type seen in doctors' offices and yields the most readily to treatment.

In women it appears at about the ages of forty-five to fifty-five; in men, at about sixty to sixty-five. Although involutional melancholia creates so much chaos in the home, especially where either parent is suffering through the menopause, families rarely pursue treatment for it quickly enough or with the vigor that the illness deserves. Considering the excellent therapeutic methods of today, the distress at the involutional period is unnecessary. Perhaps some men and women, the latter especially, meet the menopause with the martyrdom of past tradition, as they would an implacable enemy. Yet they could be freed of its symptoms and, above all, of the agitation and depressive moods that wear them down.

Involutional Depression in Women

The person I am about to describe may strike a chord of recognition in you. She may be wife, mother, aunt, or some other female relative.

Let us say that in the past few months she has seemed nervous and the doctor has told you that she is going through her menopause. You wonder whether this is why she is so irritable of late and ready to snap your head off when her routine is interrupted the least bit. Everyone in the family is beginning to steer clear of her. She cries a lot, wrings her hands, and constantly complains of her "nerves," of burning sensations at the back of her neck, and of a tightness "that's like a band around my head."

You wish you knew whether moving away from the old neighborhood where she lived for twenty years is causing it. She tells you that she has not been the same since. She hates this new apartment and locale, and bitterly declares that she cannot sleep here, not even with the capsules prescribed by the doctor. There were no such noises overhead or street sounds at the old place, she insists. (Not true, you know; they were worse there.) You also suspect that if she were not blaming the move it would be something else. Six months ago she might have said that it was because her aged senile mother died. And if her recently divorced daughter returns home with her small child she will give that as the reason.

Still, whatever it is, you can see that she is distraught. In fact, she is developing ideas of persecution and believes that everyone is conspiring against her. You begin to realize that, apart from the menopause, something else is seriously wrong and you must find the answer. Continuing this way is hell on earth.

Involutional Depression in Men

When a man passes through the menopause the physiologic events that go with it take place more imperceptibly than in a woman. But if, as a result of these changes, involutional depression appears, he will show the same symptoms of agitated disruption.

In this illness both men and women tend to lose sexual interest, but the man often displaces this loss with suspicions of his wife's fidelity. He monitors her telephone calls and checks on her mail. At this late date in the marriage these jealousy reactions will confound the most serene and devoted of wives. Very often, hoping to keep peace, she warns everyone to stay away, not even to telephone her.

The turmoil and hopelessness of involutional melancholia may key the person to such a pitch that he will attempt to find relief through suicide.

What Causes Involutional Depression?

Let us remember first that the menopause can or should arrive as a normal experience for everyone. Most men and women do *not* have depression at this time of life.

Why do some? No one knows exactly what elicits the intense agitated depression of the menopause. Much clinical evidence points to changes in body hormones as the mechanism that triggers an imbalance in the nervous system to produce depression. The preconditions of a rigid personality function also play a role. For example, the "perfectionist" person (who cannot adjust to change or make compromises as the need arises) will crack rather than bend when one stress too many appears. The alteration in hormones at the menopause is just the stress in point, and the person can no longer maintain stability. In the ensuing weeks there is a gradual exhaustion of the supply of nervous energy as the person tries to adapt. Involutional depression then finds fertile ground, and the person goes into a "nervous breakdown." (See Chapter 1, section on Tensional Energy of Depression; also Chapter 5, section on Exhaustion of Adaptation.)

Manic-Depressive Illness

In appearance, manic-depressive illness is the most bewildering of all to the family, so I will explain it at some length.

First, let me tell you about the word *manic*. This is simply a medical term that refers to the *high,* or over-stimulated, feelings which the person expresses. They are the opposite of depressed emotions. When the person is manic, he or she feels *too* good or, shall we say, "hopped up." From now on, I will refer to this manic phase of the illness as the "high" period, and a few pages along I will define it in greater detail.

Please study Figure 1 (pages 30–31) which charts six variations of manic-depressive illness. You will notice that in its most classical form (Graph C), depressive or low moods alternate with abnormally high feelings. Sometimes the high phase precedes a depression. A full cycle consists of a high and a low period. Average cycles (measured from one depression to another) recur at intervals of six months to five years or more.

You will also see in Figure 1 that there are recurring periods of acute depression or acute mania (Graphs A and B), of chronic depression or chronic mania (Graphs D and E); and of mixed and unpredictable cycles (Graph F). Graph A indicates that depressive episodes may recur with *no* high period in between. We call this manic-depressive, *depressed.* Graph B shows cycles of high episodes recurring with no depressed periods in between; these are called manic-depressive, *manic.* To you these terms may seem clumsy, but to the clinician they accurately specify the cycle process that he must treat.

When Does Depression in This Illness Begin and Recur?

The onset of the first depression appears at about age thirty, although it can occur as early as age twenty or as late as age forty. Men and women are equally susceptible to the illness. Each episode may seem to repeat the first, but a succeeding one may be either milder or more severe in its intensity.

I noted in the first section of this chapter that acute episodes may be as short as a week or continue for as long as four months. If they become chronic they may last a year or more before remission. The remission may last for two to fifteen years (or, it is hoped, indefinitely). I have known persons who went through only two epi-

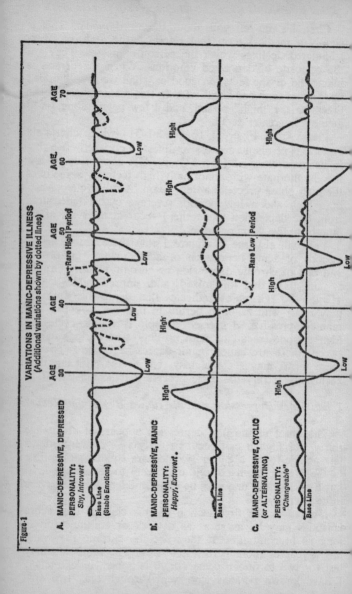

Figure-1

VARIATIONS IN MANIC-DEPRESSIVE ILLNESS
(Additional variations shown by dotted lines)

A. MANIC-DEPRESSIVE, DEPRESSED
   PERSONALITY:
   Shy, Introvert

B. MANIC-DEPRESSIVE, MANIC
   PERSONALITY:
   Happy, Extrovert.

C. MANIC-DEPRESSIVE, CYCLIC
   (or ALTERNATING)
   PERSONALITY:
   "Changeable"

D. MANIC-DEPRESSIVE, CHRONIC DEPRESSED

PERSONALITY:
Chronic Worrier

Occasional
Normal

Rare High

Occasional
Deep Low

Base Line

E. MANIC-DEPRESSIVE, CHRONIC MANIC
(also called HYPOMANIC)

PERSONALITY:
"Human Dynamo"

Occasional
Very High

Occasional
Very Low

Base Line

F. MANIC-DEPRESSIVE, MIXED CYCLIC

PERSONALITY:
Happy, Extrovert

Base Line

sodes of recurrent acute depression and others, more rarely, who suffered ten or more recurrences. The remitting nature of these episodes is precisely the pattern that gives this illness its special identity.

The First Depressive Episode in Manic-Depressive Illness

When the initial depression starts, you may be faintly aware that your relative has been sleeping poorly and feeling tired. You did not notice when it began, but after several weeks of it you realize that something is wrong. He (or she) wakes up every morning around four or five o'clock, miserable and blue. He cannot get back to sleep, and this makes him irritable. Once he is up, it is quite a haul to get him off to work. He tells you that the day ahead seems so long. His feelings puzzle him and he wants to fight them off, so he forces a smile and promises that he will snap out of it. When he returns that evening his spirits have lifted a bit and he may go out to visit. You are encouraged. But next morning he is in the dumps again. This pattern repeats itself daily and looks as if it will never let up.

If the symptoms remained at this level, a moderate depression would be diagnosed. With treatment, the person would recover without too much difficulty. However, when the symptoms grow more extensive, the depression is severe. At this stage he will lose interest in work and, later, in his appearance. Testy and annoyed with everyone, he says that he feels robbed of energy. You give him vitamins, prescribe rest, and keep people away. It does not help. He also complains of a fluttery stomach, nausea, pains in the head, and dizzy spells. On physical examination, blood tests and X-rays check out as normal; the doctor may then suggest that he is "run down and nervous." As a last effort, you take him on a trip "to get away for a while."

On vacation he shows little interest in people, food, or recreation. He is low in spirit all the time and cannot make up his mind about the smallest thing—what to wear or to eat, whether to sit, to walk, or to read. When he begins to wonder aloud whether everyone is against him and at the same time cries and berates himself as "a flop in life," you decide that he is better off at home.

You are right. At this point he is showing a full-blown, acute, and agitated (in some cases, retarded) depression. The illness may have taken several weeks or more to develop, but now it has reached a climax.

With proper and intensive treatment, there is more than a reasonable hope of full remission in a short time (four to six weeks). If untreated, the depression may stay at this level anywhere from three months to two years, unless the condition so worsens that it potentiates suicide.

When the Second Depression Appears in This Illness

If you are like most people, you will block out the possibility of a recurrence after the patient's recovery. This is only human, because no one wants to live with a sword poised over his head. However, should the depression recur, your first reaction may be to sigh and think: Well, here we go again.

Not exactly. This time, with experience and knowledge, you will recognize the earliest symptoms right away. Having seen your relative through one depression and its successful treatment, you will take the required steps promptly. This eliminates the time lag of guessing and may well be a primary factor in abbreviating both the illness and the course of treatment.

What Is Meant by the Term "Manic Episode"?

Refer again to Figure 1. Earlier, I mentioned that a high (or manic) episode may occur prior to a depressive one or may follow it. Both can take place in regular or mixed patterns (Graphs C and F).

A typical high episode appears suddenly. It seems that almost overnight, certainly within a few days, the person is surcharged with an overload of ideas. He sleeps only a few hours, but wakes up feeling fine. True, he does not eat well, but this is because he is "too busy" to eat and is finding "more important things to do." On the move constantly and bursting with plans, he tries to involve you in his enthusiasms about his exciting projects. He spends money munificently and he erupts with wild optimism and exuberance to anyone on any subject.

HE CANNOT BE SLOWED DOWN. When you try to inhibit or criticize him he will get angry, perhaps violent. If you point out that his ideas are preposterous, he laughs at your "stupidity." He will rebel and resist all efforts to control him. Medication? Ridiculous. See a doctor. Why should he? *He's* not complaining. Far from it. Everything is "simply great." He is healthier than any of you or the doctor himself. Life is fabulous!

And you stand by, steam-rollered.

Such forms of elevated feelings, with the individual always overactive, are called *hypomania* (*hypo-* meaning "less than"; hence, less than full mania). Here medical help is mandatory, because the person may suddenly plunge into acute depression. This sharp conversion from a high "good" feeling to the depths of despondency signals danger. After living at such altitudes of exhilaration the person cannot bear his sadness. His nervous system will not tolerate this abrupt drop in tensional energy, and he may commit suicide before you have time to realize that his spirits have plummeted from a high to the very depths of low.

However, not all high episodes convert to depression. Some last for weeks or months and settle into chronicity at the elevated level.

What Causes Manic-Depressive Disorder?

There is a popular impression that this illness is inherent in personality development. That is to say, if someone is happy, bubbling, and extroverted, he or she inclines to manic-depressive illness. There are no grounds for this. If you look at Figure 1 again, you can see from the graphs that the shy, introverted person may also be as prone to variations of manic-depressive illness as the extroverted type. Or neither type will be prone to it.

In my opinion the manic-depressive cycle represents, primarily, a physical and metabolic disturbance of the nervous system. The great quantity of research in brain function over the past fifteen years has shown that chemical changes and abnormal brain metabolism combine to interfere with neural circuits, thus slowing down or speeding up nervous activity. This produces depression or excitation, depending on the phase of the cycle; and in turn, it distorts the person's reasoning, agitates his behavior, creates fluctuations in the feeling tones, and throws his mental and physical being into disequilibrium.

Is There a Normal High or Low?

Yes. You may know someone who gets a bit moody at one time, or peppy and euphoric at another. But this does not mean that he or she is heading for manic-depressive illness. Biologic rhythms occur in nervous function just as daily and seasonal rhythms occur in the weather. Thus, any kind of mood shift is normal within relatively wide limits.

Even with previous histories of manic-depressive illness, different persons may level off at their own lows or highs. One individual may run to a pleasant, subdued personality function, another to the ebullience of the "human dynamo" whose towering feats of accomplishment are legend. This states the broad spectrum of norms into which such persons often stabilize without ever veering off again into an episode of either too low or too high.

However, if your relative is the sort of person who sometimes feels uneasy about his emotional processes, urge him to consult with his physician or psychiatrist occasionally, if only to relieve his anxiety.

Depression with Psychosis (in Schizophrenia)

In Chapter 1, I defined a *psychosis*. You have probably heard of *schizophrenia* (pronounced skiz-o-*free*-nee-a), which is a psychotic illness. Now, however, I want to direct your attention to the type of schizophrenia that contains depression. Here, depression is a symptom which helps reveal the existence of the psychosis.

Perhaps a young daughter in the family is giving some

cause for concern. Unexpectedly, she has come home from college in a funk, announcing that she has dropped out of school. She stays in the house, mopes, and shows no interest in dating, sports, or her friends; she does nothing, and her apathy and indifference are marked. Pale and hollow-eyed, she trails around the house, looking sad and bedeviled. With some alarm you wish she would get over her blues and "stop acting like Camille."

Your perceptions of her, as far as they go, are correct; but put another way, she is showing a retarded (sloweddown) depression.

The Psychosis Appears

Symptoms of another kind start to surface. These indicate the primary illness, schizophrenia. She complains that "everything is a blur and disconnected. It's all tied up inside of me." Familiar objects and persons appear strange and distorted to her. Hallucinations may develop; she will hear voices or see things that are not there. She may also reveal delusions of persecution. Or fantasies of grandeur capture her mind. Sleeping all day and staying awake at night, she inhabits an inner world that excludes everyone. You might describe it as one mother did: "She sits there, Doctor, but I don't know where she is, really. She's not in the room and she's not in this world."

Now, further symptoms of the *depression* appear. The girl cries and reviles herself savagely, then sinks into despair. At the same time she is less and less able to distinguish between real and unreal. Both the depression and the schizophrenia are interwining as one illness.

Yet, while the schizophrenia is by far the primary process and has produced the thought disturbances, poor judgment, and inability to control behavior, the severe and intense depression presents the graver problem; *schizophrenic depressions account for the largest proportion of suicides in males and females between the ages of fifteen and twenty-five*. If the depression is not given immediate attention it may be too late to treat the schizophrenia, because I can assure you that the person may no longer be alive for treatment.

A total program for this kind of depression will also include treatment of the schizophrenic process itself.

Post-Partum Depression (Following Childbirth)

Many women experience a letdown after giving birth to a child. This is not unusual. You may have thought of it as pure fatigue, especially when the labor was prolonged and the delivery difficult. The letdown feeling may even dip into mild depression which clears up after a week or so— a very normal reaction.

However, if these post-partum blues persist or increase in intensity, there may be trouble ahead.

The Moderate Phase

It may be your wife that I am talking of here. After your child was born, you noticed the mild depression I mentioned above, but this did not worry you. You arranged for a nurse or a relative to help and thought that that would solve the matter. However, several weeks have elapsed at home and your wife seems no better. In fact, she is worse and looks more droopy and forlorn than ever.

In addition she becomes frantic because she does not experience the sweet maternal sensations she had expected. Make no mistake, she would like to be close to her baby, but her feelings are divided against themselves. She cannot find the emotional strength or desire to feed the child or give it any kind of motherly care. And to manage her home again is an ordeal beyond her.

She weeps a lot, refuses food, and quivers at the ring of the phone or doorbell. As in most endogenous depressions she awakens too early and lies there, tense and ruminating. What if she accidentally drops or smothers the baby? She is afraid even to touch it, because of her strange thoughts and fearful impulses. She cannot trust herself to manage the smallest action, and every ten minutes she flies to the telephone to hear your supportive words.

At this stage the depression is moderately serious; if recognized for what it is, it can be treated effectively with no further damage done.

When the Depression Progresses and Becomes Severe

Now she becomes increasingly edgy and irrational. She will cry out that you do not love her, that you are ignoring her. She storms at your neglect. These ideas grow into paranoidal delusions. She will insist that you want to get rid of her or that people are spreading lies about her and saying that she is a sexual pervert. In response to these twisted thoughts she may strike out at you, at her parents, and at her friends, convinced that everyone is the arch-enemy.

At this crucial juncture the depression must be aborted as quickly as possible with intensive treatment; the alternative is long-term chronic illness that may take many months to dislodge.

What Causes Post-Partum Depression?

Apparently the young mother is sensitive to the changes in body chemistry and glandular metabolism brought on by the pregnancy and birth. To be sure, such changes are natural and expected. But they may also represent a stress for a particular person that exceeds the degree of this individual's nervous system tolerance, thus touching off a major disturbance in mental function. (There is another type of post-partum depression that sometimes appears, but I will reserve discussion of this illness until we reach Neurotic Depression in Chapter 5.)

Will Post-Partum Illness Appear with the Next Child?

It may, but it need not. Initially, it can show up after the first, second, or third child and at any age in the mother. Most times it occurs after the first child is born or in the susceptible woman who has reached her mid-twenties or early thirties. Still, there is no reason to feel that one depression like this necessarily betokens another. It does not tend to repeat itself, although some cases of recurrence are seen with subsequent pregnancies. There is no telling. However, I generally recommend to a mother who recovers satisfactorily from the first episode and remains in good health that she proceed with her plans for another child and disregard the previous complication.

Depression Due to Aging (Senility)

Today, with increased longevity, older people are faced with many problems for which they are not prepared. They retire, develop chronic illnesses, and encounter difficult social changes as children grow up and leave home, old friends pass away, and the need to move to a new environment arises. In addition, they undergo body changes; and just as aging alters the skin or other parts, it affects the brain and nervous system. Hardening of the arteries and other blood-vessel changes reduce circulation to the brain, a condition which often produces endogenous depression.

As You Notice the Depression

You may be one of the millions of adult children who see their parents succumbing to the aging process. In your case it may be your father. You accept his failing memory and other evidences of a "little senility." But one day it seems to you that he is becoming completely deranged. Where, before, he was a bit irascible, he now shouts at you and is abusive. If you telephone him he orders you to visit more often, but when you get there he greets you with a tongue-lashing; you are mismanaging your personal affairs, he yells, and your general conduct is stupid and selfish. Or he calls on heaven to witness that he was cursed with faithless children. Sometimes you think he is confusing you with another person as he rages that you are out "to try to cheat me of all I've got." "Who, me?" you almost ask, looking over your shoulder. When you leave him you are wrung out. On top of this he will not touch food and he bursts into tears without warning. He is also showing a rapid weight loss and you may worry about a malignancy. But, however guardedly you voice your concern, any expression of it throws him into still another paroxysm of fury.

Or It May Be Your Aged Mother

Of late she keeps whimpering that she has outlived her usefulness and nobody cares about her any more. When you fondly dispute her self-depreciation she gets excited and reviles you as a hypocrite. (This in itself is uncharacteristic, since she has always been a quiet, gentle woman.) Nothing pleases her any more. She is impatient with living and mocks the love of her children and grandchildren as lies. Any tiny deviation from routine sends her into a tailspin. However, her moods can change in a moment. On a down-swing, when the mental pain of her depression is too much she weeps for herself. Sobbing that she is alone and neglected, she presents an unhappy spectacle of rapid decline.

It is sad to watch a parent in this state. I have seen many elderly patients in such condition. Their internal changes in brain function have resulted in depressive illness. This in turn has damaged their relationships, even with those closest and dearest to them. But, heartbreaking as this kind of disorder looks, one can give thanks that today it is remediable. Treatment for the elderly person who suffers from endogenous depression often results in long recovery periods. His or her return to normal, with the emotions stabilized, can be a highly dramatic event— one that often surprises a family who had given up all hope that their parent would ever be well again.

Toxic Depressions Caused by Drugs

All drugs and chemicals affect the body and mental function. This is why they are prescribed. But you or anyone can show an unexpected sensitivity to a drug. For example, you may know that an aspirin can cause a stomach upset; or that certain drugs, even those on prescription, may make you sweat, get dizzy, or flush. If you drink too much coffee, tea or "cola," the caffeine in them may overstimulate your kidneys or cause your heart to beat fast. Such reactions to drugs are *side effects*. As a rule they are annoying but harmless. However, in some cases they can be severe and we then call the side effect a *toxic* reaction. (See further discussion of side effects in Chapter 10.)

Should a drug effect result in brain or nervous system toxicity, extreme depression may appear.

Symptoms of Toxicity

Perhaps one of your family has been taking too much of a sedative. (See section on drug addiction in Chapter 2.) The person is listless and indifferent to his surroundings. He cannot concentrate on any one thing and has lost vitality. He grumbles, stops seeing friends, and looks drawn and washed out. If the drug is one of the newer tranquilizers, he may also show restlessness and agitation. This may mean that a toxic depression has emerged. But whether the individual shows a slow-down or overcharge of function one thing is obvious—he is "doped up."

The drug toxicity may also produce odd and illogical thoughts which interfere with judgment. For example, a man may suddenly marshal all his strength, despite the distress of the illness, and decide that he must go bowling. What if the bowling alleys *are* closing in ten minutes? He knows that they will open for him. Or at midnight he will announce that he must call his brother long distance to argue about a trifling ten-year-old debt, one that he himself had long since discounted. You try to talk him out of it and suggest that the call is foolish, that the next day he will be sorry for it. He brushes your advice aside and yells, "Don't tell me what to do. You're just plain crazy."

Ordinarily, simple toxicity will clear up in twenty-four to forty-eight hours after the body eliminates the drug. However, sometimes the depressive toxic effect remains long after this, because the nervous system is too disrupted to recover from it immediately. The person then requires antidepressant treatment.

Depressions Caused by Infections

Endogenous depressions may result, not only from infections of the brain and nervous system proper, but from generalized body infections as well.

When the infection is in the brain and nervous system proper, as in meningitis or encephalitis, one sees high fever, coma, and delirium. This is the acute phase of the brain infection. Once it is over, however, and the patient is on the road to *physical* recovery, the family heaves a sigh of relief and gives thanks to the powers that be.

But to everyone's dismay the person may then become extremely melancholic because the infection also threw the nervous system out of balance. The patient will cry steadily without being able to say why. His or her mental and physical function slows down, although in some cases agitation and restiveness appear. Such a condition may last for several months after the infection subsides, before it is recognized for what it is—depression.

When generalized infection invades the body, through a virus for example, it can create toxicity to the brain and nervous system, and the person may be left with a depression which can last from one to two months.

I recently saw this aftermath in someone I knew, an energetic woman of fifty who was always cheerful with a keen sense of fun. Now, convalescing from a serious viral illness, she felt "weak as a kitten" and utterly despondent. Her fright about her condition intensified the low mood. She was clearly in a retarded depression which should have lifted when the generalized infection was gone; but since it persisted, antidepressant care was finally required to get her well.

I suspect that many such viral infections, which have been epidemic in recent years, affect the person's nervous system and trigger a low-grade retarded depression that is not easily thrown off. These mood disturbances should be treated early and not allowed to take root.

Depressions with Glandular Disorders

You may be aware in a vague way that glandular secretions (hormones) affect normal function. Maybe you have known someone with "glandular troubles." But perhaps you do not realize what happens to the person's *emotions* because of these difficulties.

Suppose it is an individual with a low *thyroid* function.

You may have noticed that he tends to be apathetic. In fact, everyone considers the person a dullard because the thinking process is slow and there seem to be memory blocks. Actually, though, this man or woman may be of normal intelligence, but suffering from a retarded depression associated with a hypothyroid condition.

At the opposite pole is the person with an overactive or toxic thyroid (*hyper*thyroidism) who may be depressed and agitated at the same time. You can see that he or she is perpetually tense, constantly on the go in a nervous kind of way and given to flare-ups of temper at the smallest thing.

There is also the woman whose irregularities of *ovarian hormonal balance* create premenstrual tension, a common-enough nervousness that appears a few days before the period. But if this condition is excessive, the irritability and mild depression that she shows can be difficult to live with throughout this trying interval.

In another case, secretions from the pituitary gland (at the base of the brain) and the adrenal glands (which lie on top of the kidneys) may be poorly balanced. If you have ever been involved in the treatment of someone who is afflicted with this condition, you may have learned that abnormal secretions from these glands can also create severe depression. Associated with it will be certain physical symptoms of high blood pressure, hirsutism (increase in body hair), dry skin, headaches, and fainting spells.

The Illness and the Cure

Many of these glandular conditions can be stubborn, but some are improved by purified drugs similar to natural hormones. These drugs compensate for hormonal deficiencies and may also help clear up a depression.

But here is the paradox. Some hormonal drugs, such as those contained in birth-control pills and in different cortisone preparations, may *cause* depression and nervous disorders if the person takes too much or is sensitive to them. I have seen this happen many times, and just recently in a case where hormones, which were prescribed for the change of life, brought about a depressive episode. While it is not common for a depression to result from a glandular disorder or, conversely, from the cure, nevertheless it may occur in special cases and can be severe and prolonged if not taken in hand early.

Depressions Following Injuries

Have you ever known someone who was involved in an auto crash or who experienced injury by some other means? He or she probably suffered from what we call "shock." In shock states the circulation of the body and brain slows down and the blood pressure drops. At the same time, other chemical changes in the body produce a general collapse of nervous function. The person seems stupefied, and you can see this plainly.

Because of the damage to the nervous system, a depressive episode often follows a shock state. The depression, usually retarded, lasts only so long as the nervous system is impaired. Once the latter heals, the depression should clear up. But while it exists, it requires psychiatric care.

Postoperative Depressions

You may be anxious about an aunt who is convalescing after an operation. The doctor has assured you that the surgery was successful. Still, your aunt eats poorly and does not seem to care whether she ever gets well or not. The doctor worries about this attitude, which delays healing and impedes recovery. You wonder why, with so much to look forward to, she is so dispirited about the future.

Well, let's remember that the surgery itself was not exactly fun. In spite of new techniques in anesthesia and operative procedures, your aunt was exposed to a great physical stress. Many people emerge from this stress so debilitated that the exhaustion of nervous energy culminates in endogenous depression. This complication dilutes the surgical cure.

On the other hand, a cheerful frame of mind leads to good intake of food, sound sleep, and improved muscular function. All of these give impetus to the healing process.

With depression, the person's body and nervous system slacken. Convalescence then drags out far beyond the time warranted by the surgery. I have known of cases wherein postoperative depression was not detected and the patient died. The surgeon and other attending doctors could find no *medical* reason for the death. It is my belief that such a patient "commits suicide" simply because the depression wills him or her to die in the postsurgical period.

One can deduce the depressed mood when the patient will not eat, sleeps fitfully, but peculiarly enough, *complains very little*. Nothing matters, not even pain or discomfort. He or she seems to submit to death as if thinking, "My life is over. It makes no difference what happens to me now."

Depressions Following Changes in Body Structure

Men and women who lose a part of their bodies, either through accident or illness and surgery, may become acutely depressed under any of the following conditions: First, when loss of the body part carries a personal meaning that evokes a strong emotional reaction to it; for example, surgery or accident may alter the genital, or sexually identified, organs and give the person a sense of castration. Second, loss of the body part may interfere with the individual's trained way of earning a livelihood, as in the case of a pianist who loses a hand. Third, the change in body structure may interfere with other functions, thus leaving the person partially or totally invalided. And fourth, the need for an alteration in the body may come as a severe and intolerable blow to the individual's self-image. When he or she is unable to cope with any of the foregoing conditions, and when satisfactory or compensatory alternatives are lacking, the person becomes acutely depressed.

Depressions with Acute and Chronic Conditions

Every illness, whether short or long, acts as a stress on the body and nervous system. A woman may suffer from a chronic ulcer; ultimately her "nerves" become ragged with the suffering and the need to diet. She gets "fed up." Others may find the pain and limitations imposed by arthritis, chronic gall-bladder disease, heart trouble, or a lung or kidney disorder an insupportable stress.

I recently treated the depression of a man in his forties whose occupation as a tool and die maker satisfied him and whose family life was better than most. He did not mind working long, hard hours, but the persistent discomfort of a chronic spinal compression with sciatica constantly nagged at him. Worn down into depression by his physical symptoms, his interest in life diminished, but most crucially he grew indifferent to the active treatment of the sciatica. He had had enough of it. "Living is too tough if I have to crawl through this suffering every day," he told his wife.

Suppose this person were your responsibility. Probably you would not understand why he did not pursue the very medical care that could remove most of the pain. But once depression takes hold, it often blunts the person's drive to get well, and not until it is treated will he be remotivated and energized to obtain the intensive medical or surgical attention so much needed.

The Depression of Physical or Mental Fatigue

You may be familiar with the catchwords that describe different categories of persons who are caught in the struggles and competition of our culture today. This partial list will refresh your memory.

The nervous housewife
The debt-ridden worker
The pressured executive
The harried small businessman
The oppressed civil servant
The deprived slum dweller
Any victim of the age of anxiety

Stress Reactions of Fatigue

The human being can absorb a great deal of stress; but

with too much, the overload peak is reached. No one is exempt. At the breaking point, depression may appear. If fatigue has stretched the person beyond endurance limits, you will see that he or she is too tired to think, move, eat, make love, converse, or even enjoy a bit of good news.

Now this is entirely unlike the normal weariness that follows an ordinary day's work. We also differentiate it from the fatigue of riding a bicycle in the park, or dancing the evening through, or cleaning the basement on a Sunday for the fun of it. In these situations, one can still enjoy a good meal, a movie, or some distraction, and the tiredness disappears after a rest or a night's sleep.

No, the nervous exhaustion that I speak of here emerges from chronic stress—the grinding friction of an incompatible marriage, unrelieved slum living, the harshness of an unkind boss, the tyranny of corporate employment, the insensitivity of bureaucratic control, chronic warfare, social turmoil, and so on. Acute depression of nervous function is then inevitable. Such fatigue reactions technically represent an exhaustion of adaptive reserve; but they also create a chemical imbalance in the brain and nervous system that is identical with an endogenous depression. For rapid recovery, only a comprehensive program of physical treatment combined with surcease from the stress stimulus will return the person to a stable emotional level.

Stress Reaction in Caring for a Depressed Person

Paradoxically, many well-meaning, empathetic relatives, in their zeal to render complete care, may become depressed themselves by exceeding their physical and emotional capacity to nurse the depressed person. Driven by love, devotion, or even a strong sense of duty, they drop their personal interests, ignore all other obligations, deprive themselves of needed sleep and rest, and worse, identify so closely with the depressed person that they too, "experience" the anguish of his suffering. Soon, all of this leads to an exhaustion of *their* adaptive reserve. Hence, it is a good idea to know your own limitations and not allow yourself to collapse into martyrdom. Whenever possible, it is best to *share* the many burdens that present themselves so that when the patient recovers, as most do, you, the relative, will have saved some of yourself for the family's return to a normal way of life. In the first few pages of Chapter 17 I discuss some aspects of just this problem and how to delegate responsibilities to other friends and relatives.

CHAPTER FOUR

What You Should Know About Reactive Depressions: Grief

A SENSE of loss is the substance of reactive depression. The person feels that permanence is demolished and the patterns for survival and security are scattered to the winds. The loss, whether real or symbolic, looms so great to the person that he responds by mourning it inconsolably, certain that he can never fill the empty space that it has left. This mourning or grief is the reactive depression.

Depression Caused by a Loss Through Death

To illustrate, I will assume for the moment that someone close to you was bereaved of her husband. There was no question of your empathy; it was fully aroused. You could not imagine how anyone would ever surmount such a tide of sorrow, how life could ever be the same for her.

After the first shock she had seemed numb and slowed-down in function. To perform any task required a monumental effort. Then she grew silent and withdrawn, although at times you saw flurries of agitation. Her sleep was sporadic, but you learned that occasionally it was somewhat refreshed. But this did not last. As the day wore on, she went back to remembering, and the sadness and tears appeared again.

Now, however, it is two years or more and she still keeps her shades drawn and refuses to leave the house alone. Even with all the sleep she gets, she never feels rested. At times you wonder whether she is "playing to the gallery," but you instantly erase the thought as disloyal. You wish, however, that she would stop looking only to you. You arrange for theater tickets, pick her up in your car (at much personal inconvenience), bring her to your home, and try to entertain her. But she is fixed on one subject—her broken heart and ruined life. What can she do with herself? Where can she go? She seems to be saying that she was not only bereaved but *betrayed* by the loss.

You finally admit to yourself (in spite of sentiment and twinges of guilt) that you are thoroughly weary of listening to her. How much more of it can you take?

When Should This Kind of Grief Reaction Cease?

Many religions and cultures set a traditional mourning period, from twenty-four hours to a year or so. This stipulation by each society confirms the human need to end the grieving; it says that it must not be interminable.

However, in some cases the loss may assume such proportions that the person can never find a compensatory substitute, and lives on in the grief; and this chronic, low-grade depression may continue a lifetime if untreated. I am sure that you have seen parents who were bereaved of a child, whose pining continued, with little abatement, through the years.

The difference between a normal grief reaction, which passes in due course, and the prolonged and intense response to bereavement that never leaves off lies in the individual's personality before the loss. In one case the dominant trait may be the dependency of the person, as in the widow described above. In another it is a rigid and perfectionist character structure from which extreme guilt for the loss ensues. Or it may be an immature and anxious personality that makes the individual dwell on each detail and relive it with every reminder of the loss. With such people, the depression continues to feed on itself, because their capacity to respond to restorative stimuli for self-support has been corroded by previous personality damage.

Depression Caused by Other Losses

Following the loss of material things, an opportunity, a relationship, a job, or even what we call "face," the same pattern of retarded depression can show up as in the death of a loved one.

To take an ordinary occurrence nowadays: a person is robbed, but has adequate insurance coverage. A mild temporary depression may follow the event, but this will vanish rather quickly once the loss is made good. A patient of mine did not fare this well emotionally when his business funds were embezzled by a trusted bookkeeper. He was doubly injured: he lost not only considerable money, but faith in his employees and business associates as well. The bitter philosophy that "no one can be trusted any more" underlined his low mood. Fortunately, this depression did not expand into the extreme suspicion of paranoia, because his accountant partly compensated the loss by translating it into a valid tax deduction. Moreover, his other employees rallied around him so loyally that his belief in people was restored and he soon threw off the depression.

You can probably think of others whose reactive depressions were caused by a loss, such as that of an attractive job for which the person was uniquely qualified; the forfeited education of a school "drop-out"; the overlooked "chance of a lifetime" to buy a certain house; the vanished opportunity to marry "that perfect person"; or the forced surrender of high administrative office with a consequent diminution of status. In retrospect, the individual may scourge himself and spend years in a low-grade depression, mourning and resenting the loss when it goes uncompensated.

Depression Caused by Situational Changes

A severe situational change too can strike with the impact of brutal deprivation, telling the person that his basic way of life is gone. The change may be retirement, divorce (separation), geographic uprooting and work displacement, isolation and loneliness, and so on. To any of these he or she may respond with melancholia.

Retirement

Your husband may have given up his business or job
recently, something he had looked forward to for the
past year. His financial affairs were arranged soundly
and his funds were sufficient. You heard him exult about
the wonderful things he was going to do—fish, work up
other hobbies, and travel. Best of all, he would be finished
with that "damned commuting to work" every day.

Now, with retirement an accomplished fact, he has
grown jumpy and fretful. He misses his work and the
people on the job. Sure, he agrees, the fishing was great
for a while, but "who can fish all the time?" He visits
with the grandchildren, but soon tires of them. Too fid-
gety to sit through a movie, he also scorns the Golden
Agers. "They're old." He says he feels boxed in and has
no goals any more. He is unable to accommodate to his
new routine and he grieves for the loss of the old one.

He cannot concentrate on the newspaper beyond the
headlines, although he "explains" that it is because his eyes
bother him. If you send him on an errand he returns immediately, uneasy at being out alone. He begins to fix on
all sorts of ailments, imperiously directing your attention
to them, and if you betray a second's impatience he talks
pitifully of himself and his aches and pains. You had
thought retirement would be one grand vacation for both
of you. Instead, he is underfoot and a hindrance in the
house. You may even mutter occasionally, "After all *I*
didn't retire." As a last resort you suggest that he return
to work, and he groans, "Who wants an old man like
me?"

You realize that he is going in circles and is depressed
in some way. But you also feel helpless—how to get him
out of this impossible mood and back to his normal self?

Divorce

"My closest friend can't get over her divorce."

This is often true. A woman who is married for a number of years adapts to a certain style and value system of

life that give her security. But separation and divorce fragment this settled adjustment.

Your friend may be someone you have long admired as a generous and competent woman. She had been married about fifteen years when she learned that her husband had fallen in love with someone else and wanted to give up his family for her. Now she goes to pieces, sure that somewhere along the line *she* "flunked" the marriage. The loss of her husband means that belonging, stability, and joy are shattered. Legal negotiations, the backwash of the children's confusion, and her new role as a single woman are added hardships for which she is unprepared.

She is also faced with adapting to new values and different interests. The prospect of coping with such stresses is more than she can bear. She responds to the loss of her past happiness with grief and depression.

Displacement

When someone is uprooted, for whatever reason, he or she discovers that it is more than a mere "get up and go." Harsh losses are involved. Friendships made over a period of years must be left behind—together, possibly, with a lovingly tended garden, a familiar view from windows or patio, and the intimate sounds and smells of a long-settled house. These orientations to time and place relax the person, but with displacement he loses these bonds. Unknowns lie in wait at every turn. Each particle of living must now be anticipated.

I think of an elderly colleague of mine, secure in his home and ties with his friends, who was forced to move to a dry climate for the sake of his wife's health. Their mutual devotion made the sacrifice seem small.

However, once in the new locale the absence of his old surroundings and relationships undid his stoicism. He became sad and wrapped in nostalgia. The depression that emerged from this situational change had all the characteristics of a general grief reaction, one so intense that it finally needed the treatment and sensitive rapport of a nearby colleague. Only when the latter helped him learn how to integrate with the new community and form closer ties within it, did he at last compensate for the loss of his old life.

Loneliness

More persons than you might suppose are "cast out" by family or society. Of the lonely and rejected many are normal, but accident, fate, or some personality or physical characteristic shuts them out as misfits or outsiders. Such a blow to the self splinters the person's intactness, because no one can live as an isolate without paying a price.

To belong to a group with strong identifications constitutes an essential survival need, biologically and socially. The person who does *not* belong reacts with anxiety, fear, and anger at not finding a niche in life. He or she is pushed to the limits of despair. There is, for example, the single girl, rejected at home, who migrates to a large city but cannot find friends. If this gives her a self-image of failure and chalks up life as a loss to her, she may gradually slide into depression and end as one more "unexplained" suicide.

Furthermore, we cannot overlook the numerous persons who endure loneliness without being alone. It may be a child, an adolescent, or a married person who lives in a family setting; but he or she feels repudiated and, in effect, displaced. A youngster may sense the neglect of divorced parents who do not accept him. A wife may feel the cold breath of her husband's indifference when his major interests lie in work or play that excludes her. Or a divorcee, victimized by a psychopathic husband, may return home only to be cold-shouldered by parents who refuse to condone her "mistake." "Don't get us involved. It's up to you to figure your way out of the mess."

For those in this position the present holds no gratification and the future seems a dead loss. Reactive depression may then engulf them.

CHAPTER FIVE

What You Should Know About Neurotic Depressions

THIS CATEGORY of depression is caused by the neurotic (maladaptive) personality of the individual.

Neurotic persons start with an immediate handicap in the maintenance of stability. Unable to tolerate average stresses in day-to-day living, they do not gain strengths in the normal struggle against obstacles. Rather, their emotional fiber is weakened, because in dealing with life they burn up all reserves of nervous energy at every turn. The exhaustion that inevitably follows makes them easy targets for depression.

You may want to object here: "But isn't there some truth to the jokes that circulate about neuroticism? Aren't we all a bit neurotic—a little rattle-brained?" As a piece of whimsy we can say this. But to a psychiatrist, the term *neurotic* contains a technical and clinical significance which the untrained observer may not see.

"THEN WHO IS NOT NEUROTIC?" This would be the right question. It is easier to answer than the other way around, although I intend to reply to both sides of it.

To some extent, psychiatric standards can define a norm. My own gauge of successful personality function that stays reasonably free of neurotic tensions is based on three main requisites:

1. *Adequacy:* the expression of the person's known potential. The nearer he comes to achieving it the closer he is to mental health.
2. *Effectiveness:* the measure of his contribution to society as compared with the cost of his sustenance, since the reckoning of society decrees that each person must earn enough to pay his own way.

3. *Gratification:* the quantum of pleasure or satisfaction the person can procure in the course of life.*

To summarize, the successfully adaptive person, within his social and economic position, fully exploits his strengths and capacities; he supports himself; and he finds an ample amount of fun and pleasure in living.

When personality function lacks one or all of these essentials, neuroticism is implied and depression is a possibility. Not that any hard and fast rule can say that this or that neurotic person will exhaust his or her adaptive reserve and become depressed. But the *tendency* toward it is ever present.

At one time or another you have probably known the counterparts of some of the persons I will now describe. For example, in Chapter 1, you read of those who live with too much anxiety or fear, or with perpetual anger and rebellion, thus becoming candidates for depression. So, too, do the immature who seethe with the conviction that life has cheated them; the inadequate person who feels overwhelmed by a sense of inferiority; the psychopath, clever and charming, who lies, cheats, steals, and cares only for himself and his pleasures but still falls prey to depression when his wits or run of luck fails; the treadmill worrier who constantly trembles at what may happen next; the chronic complainer or hypochondriac; the "psychosomatic" who lives with unrelieved tension and develops such illnesses as stomach ulcers, asthma, migraine headache, colitis, certain kinds of skin disorders, and so on; and the obsessive-compulsive individual whose personality traits include perfectionism.

The Obsessive-Compulsive Pattern: A Classic Model of Neurotic Depression

In my writings and teachings and throughout this book I have used the concept "exhaustion of adaptive energy" to characterize a process that can lead to depression. This concept applies especially to neurotic depression, and one

---

* From L. Cammer, *Outline of Psychiatry* (New York: McGraw-Hill Book Company, 1962).

of its most frequent victims is the obsessive-compulsive person.

Visualize for a moment the rigid and perfectionist type who feels compelled to be "right and proper" at all times. This individual must execute every act in the correct way, *his* way. Let anyone get up from the sofa and the pillows are promptly fluffed "just so." One cigarette in the ashtray and the latter must be emptied. Time and money are budgeted with minute care. The task of today must never be put off for tomorrow, no matter how crucial the reason. (Indeed, you may innocently admire this conscientiousness.) But in abiding by what is right, such persons live by the letter, not the spirit, of the law.

Other traits and mannerisms expose their rigidity. If a thought obsesses them, they may feel compelled to act upon it. For example, they may be unable to sleep unless their shoes are lined up evenly. Or they may always feel the need to buy an even dozen of any item. If they clear out a desk, everything must wait until the corners are scoured with a toothbrush. They return to their parked cars four or five times or more to reaffirm that the emergency brake is on.

But, you may argue, isn't this just an orderly or careful person? No. The test of an obsessive-compulsive neurosis is: 1. Can the person dismiss the intrusive thought (the obsession)? 2. Can he or she move on to the next order of business and skip the compulsive act? Or will anxiety and tension rise as the thought persists or until the action is performed?

Why Exhaustion of Adaptation Sets In

To maintain the demanding schedule that the obsessive-compulsive follows, he (or she) must use enormous amounts of energy. He will say that it is just as easy to do things perfectly. But this means keeping up an alertness that cannot waver for a moment. Thus, such an individual never lets down his guard or relaxes his tight hold on the obsessions and compulsions that make him feel secure. It is this haunting need for vigilance that gradually devours his energy. He may go on for years slowly exhausting himself in this way; or, should a crisis arise which demands a large expenditure of energy, the exhaustion may be sudden and rapid.

Our contemporary culture requires more plasticity than such people can bring to it. Their unbending traits and function will not give when changes in family, work, environment, and society reach out and demand a flexible approach to life. The new situation decrees that they must, but their rigidities say *no*. In this conflict, they lose, and are driven into depressive illness.

As I write this, the sister of an old friend comes to mind. I remember her vividly as a woman who was obsessed with the "spotlessness" of her home and compulsively determined to keep it that way. However, her three teen-age children were out of tune with this perfectionist ideal. She would fight to maintain it, and their lively spirits would undo it. She carped, grew irritable, devitalized, and began to think that the children upset her routine maliciously. Her mistrust expanded into paranoidal thoughts which now included everyone. The rigid patterns of her personality clamped down and choked off any other outlet. Nervous energy was exhausted, and a severe depression set in.

The obsessive-compulsive personality with rigidity and perfectionism is complex. In Chapter 3, I explained that he or she is also prone to depression at the menopause. You will meet this personality type once again when I discuss guilt feelings in Chapter 9.

The Neurotic Type of Post-Partum Depression (in an Immature Person)

Earlier I defined post-partum depressive illness for you as an *endogenous* type which results from a specific physical stress on the nervous system itself (Chapter 3).

At that point I deferred discussion of a second kind of post-partum depression. This I classify here under the neurotic category. Its cause differs from the endogenous type. In the latter, if you will recall, I suggested that chemical changes and hormonal imbalances act as the precipitators. Here, however, the depression occurs because the psychologic response to the stress of becoming a mother undermines the *adaptive reserve* of personality function. In short, the coming of the child heralds *a new life situation* with adult responsibilities to which the young woman cannot adjust. She collapses into a neurotic post-partum depression.

As the Symptoms Appear

It may be your daughter-in-law, who has just had her first baby. From the beginning she is blue and listless and sleeps only off and on. At home, she is indifferent to the infant, her husband, and the help offered her. In another mood, she will suddenly wail that she never really wanted the baby. When reminded of her previous yearning for pregnancy she may shrill at you: "I only said I wanted it to please my husband," or, "Maybe I did want it then, but I must have been crazy. I don't now." At another time she will burst out: "Why did I ever have this child?" and cry bitterly that she would like to "give it back." (This reaction is different from that of the mother who, in an endogenous post-partum depression, wishes desperately that she could relate to her child and grieves that she cannot. The neurotic mother feels that the child's very existence oppresses her.)

If you offer her congratulations on having such a fine healthy infant she will turn on you in anger. She seems a mass of contradictions, because in the next moment she will agree that it is a beautiful baby, but then rail at her ineptness in taking care of it. She also ruminates about the child: What if it should get sick and die? Suppose she were to injure it (you will recall that such thoughts also occur in the endogenous post-partum depression); maybe if she looks at a knife she will use it on the baby; or she might throw the child out of a window.

In short, you are seeing not only depression, *but the instability of neurotic personality function as well,* with its manifold fears and anxieties. In this kind of illness, treatment will be directed at overcoming *both* the depressive symptoms (the low mood of despair) and the disequilibrium in personality function that have brought this young woman to her present disturbed state.

Other Types of Neurotic Depression

While there are many more neurotic types of persons who tend to depression (and in finer detail the subtypes are numerous), it would be impractical to describe them all in this book. Many of their symptoms overlap and duplicate each other. Therefore, in addition to the obsessive-compulsive and the immature post-partum types that I have already presented, I will discuss only those three that you are most likely to encounter in neurotic depressive illness.

Neurotic Depression in the Inadequate Person

The person I will now introduce to you is a young man, age thirty. He left high school before being graduated and never quite made the grade in any capacity. Working in his father's auto-repair shop, he takes advantage of his position. His presence antagonizes the other employees. His father implores a brother to take him on, hoping that this will "make a man of him." Unaware of the boy's pathetic lack of resources, the brother gives him a job. The young man strives earnestly to stand up to it, but its stresses, minor as they are, crush him. Immature, spoiled, or call him what you will, he simply cannot work well in a demanding situation.

Such persons, whom psychiatrists term "inadequate," finally deplete their energy supplies in the struggle to give more than they possess and they are overwhelmed with futility. This condition often augurs the beginning of melancholic illness.

Neurotic Depression in the Chronically Angry Person

Another young man, who is the "baby" of his family, has turned rebellious and angry. He demands fast cars, and when his careless driving bangs them up he shrugs it off. He changes colleges several times, because studying for grades is his last concern. Why work for them? He's much cleverer than his professors to start with, and he'll go much farther in the world once he winds up. He counters your criticism by sneering at you and enlarging on your faults. At any remark about his conduct he lashes out in blind rage.

His hostility and venom earn him active dislike. People shun him and he knows it, but by this time he has lost the power to reverse himself. Pushed to the fringes of society, he is overtaken by a depressive illness. This, together with his anger, may send him to self-destruction, possibly as the victim of a car smash in which he is the driver.

Neurotic Depression in the Fearful Person

Some individuals are so riddled with neurotic fear that it immobilizes them. Perhaps you have met the prototype of this forty-year-old married woman. Living in the suburbs, she manages to drive alone to the local shopping center twice a week, but a trip to the city is out of the question. Were she to attempt it, she would freeze at the wheel when caught in highway traffic. The mere thought of setting out unaccompanied for almost any destination sends her into spasms of fear. In addition, she is always afraid that every twinge or ache that she feels is a menace to her health. Her friends know her for a hypochondriac and a worrier. She can always see ahead to the worst. If her husband must take a business trip she "knows" that she will get sick while he is gone, she "knows" that his plane will crash, she "knows" that something will happen. These fears shut her in and deprive her of normal and useful activities. Her mode of life is tantamount to social withdrawal; it instills in her a defeatism and a sense of deficiency. Psychosomatic symptoms appear first, and are then followed by the exhaustion of adaptive reserve that spells depression.

The Suicidal Gesture in Neurotic Depression

The neurotic's attempt at suicide possesses a telltale quality. It is used to maneuver the household and to center attention on himself by terrorizing everyone with his vow of self-destruction. Even so, the *danger* of the threat is no less real. Do not challenge it; under certain conditions the neurotic person may *momentarily* mean business and carry it out. It should never be laughed at or underestimated.

Given the chance, however, the neurotically depressed person will usually signal his intent beforehand. (He or she is not as fixed on suicide as the person in an endogenous or reactive depression.) Interpreted, the signal means: "Even though I'm going to make a big show of dying I count on you to save me from death."

However, the situation may blow up out of control. A depressed woman, caught up in hysteria, shouts at her son: "If you don't do what I say I'll go up to the roof and jump off." In the heat of the argument he might return: "Then why don't you?" At that moment of conflict her judgment snaps; the angry retort goads her into the fatal act; once having set it in motion she cannot halt the impulse, and when the inciter shouts, "I'm sorry; I didn't mean it," it is over and done with.

Or maybe you have seen someone dash into the kitchen following a tumultuous quarrel, grab a knife, and scream, "I'll kill myself and you'll all be sorry." The scene is crudely offensive, and you wish you could make a quiet exit. But the depressed person must be mollified and the knife removed, because impulsively it may be used as threatened. Similarly, a person nursing a grudge about a rejection or a taunt may try to "revenge" it with an overdose of pills and drowse off just enough to prevent his reaching the telephone or calling out for help.

Flamboyant, hysterical, or childish as the neurotic's suicidal threats may seem to you, they should nevertheless be taken at face value. In the final outcome the gesture can be serious and go all the way.

Depression in Children and Young Adolescents (to Age Sixteen)

In Chapter 2, I said that children and adolescents are also subject to depression which can be endogenous, reactive, or neurotic. In the first two categories the cause pattern is usually the same as in adults. However, in the third category it differs, because the term *neurotic,* as it relates to children, applies more to their struggles for normal social development than to fixed psychologic complexes.

Lacking experience, know-how, strength, and the maturation of their faculties, children cannot handle the conditions of a society geared to adult values and competition. They need protection and, above all, belongingness as they grow and until they can develop the expertise required for grappling with life. However, children are sharply attuned to anything that threatens their security. And with good reason. You might be amazed at how often a child's sense of injury is justified.

When Children Are Pawns in the Adult Game of Life

Children are abandoned, rejected, thrown too early on their own resources, neglected, abused, spurned (even maimed or murdered; we do have the child abuse syndrome in medicine).

Parents also separate and divorce, and the split home base no longer gives emotional support to the child, often when it is most needed—at puberty. Reduced to silence and depression, he or she grieves that "no one loves me," or, "I don't belong to anybody," and ends up by deciding, "I don't care about myself." Thus, the child's exquisite sensitiveness adds a lacerating quality to the depression, because the melancholia is related to phenomena that escape his understanding.

The Youngster's Cry for Help

In a *withdrawal pattern,* the depressed child retreats and is abnormally quiet and seclusive. He hides from play and group activities and becomes occupied with his hurts, hoping that someone will notice. Should direction and authority be used at this point to bring the child out of himself he will meet these with passive resistance and further withdrawal, because then and there he craves a superabundance of love, attention, and assurance. In effect, he is saying, "Now you have to give me every minute of your time and thoughts. You have to *prove* to me that you love me." If you fail this testing, which can last for many months, the child will regress and become more inarticulate and depressed.

The *hostility pattern* of depression shows in anger and mutiny. The child plays truant or presents other disciplinary problems in school. At home he is mulish and fault-finding. Violence may be the next phase. He breaks furniture, his own possessions, and those of others. He picks fights, and no matter how you try to placate him he gets worse. But note this too: his crying, whining, and frank misery expose the depressed nervous function that is keeping him off balance and is accounting for his offensive behavior.

The Feedback to the Child in Depression

As such children are pushed away from any region of security a piteous reaction is established. Rejected by adults and peers, they retreat into gloom or chafe with anger; a label is then stuck on them: "Problem child." The antipathies they sense arouse counterreactions of hostility in them and they grow more unlikable. Dimly they know that their tactics are failing, but as children they lack the social power and adroitness to compromise or to pursue beneficial goals and back them up with firm decisions. Normal perspectives of life fade away as hopelessness sweeps them. No opportunity to change is offered from any source. What damns the child is his lack of useful alternatives. Only isolation or rebellion remains. Eventually the seductive thought of self-destruction appears, both as a release from mental pain and as a form of vengeance against "them."

To a child, however, suicide is not the fearsome reality that it is to an adult. Children do not fully perceive the meaning of death. In their minds it can be turned on and off. A little boy will point his pistol and yell, "Bang, bang! You're dead." A few minutes later he will say, "Okay. Now you're alive." In the same way, suicide too is fantasy. If he says, "I'll die and you'll be to blame and you'll wish you were nicer to me," he is making a poignant attempt to tell you of his plight. But he expects to come alive again. Nevertheless, if his threat is ignored or challenged, however unwittingly, he may be pushed into making good the threat "just to show you."

Parents seldom see depression in their children, much less the red flag of suicide. Usually the alertness of an uncle, aunt, cousin, friend, or of you, perhaps, is required to rescue the child from his depression.

CHAPTER SIX

Chart: A Key to Categories of Depression

AT THE end of this chapter there is a chart which inventories the patterns of endogenous, reactive, and neurotic depression. To sharpen its usefulness I will summarize the main differences for you below.

Different Causes

Endogenous depression is caused by a disturbance of brain and nervous-system structure or function. The depression is generated internally, and the nervous system is physically affected.

Reactive depression (grief) is precipitated by an event outside the person's body. It usually takes the form of a loss that affects his or her total future and well-being.

Neurotic depression is the result of a serious maladaptation in personality function. The depressive illness reflects an exhaustion of tensional energy as the person fails in his struggle to adapt to life's stresses.

Differences in the Blue Feelings

The gradations and quality of blue feelings help you recognize the type of depression.

In *endogenous* depression the sadness is characterized by the sense of emptiness within the person. He feels that something is wrong with *him*. Out of this grow his convictions of unworthiness, poverty, and guilt.

In *reactive* depression the tone of emptiness is there also; but here the person feels it *outside* himself and in the environment. He associates this empty feeling with his loss.

In *neurotic* depression the sadness, or blue note, is suffused with self-pity, impatience, and anger at the world. The emptiness is all-inclusive, both inside the person and in the outer world.

Differences in the Thought Patterns

In *endogenous* depression the person is self-depreciatory, with strong guilt feelings and hopelessness. He may think of himself as the worst of moral sinners. However, his twisted thoughts urge him to project the blame onto others. Paranoid delusions grow out of this projective mechanism.

In *reactive* depression (grief) there may be guilt within the grief if the person believes that his own actions brought on the loss. But, as a rule, he will not think of himself as an evildoer. His sorrow, showing some self-pity, relates to the loss itself; his self-esteem does not diminish. It remains intact.

In *neurotic* depression the person considers himself a victim of his suffering. His thoughts say that he is above criticism. He demands that those around him drop everything and give him immediate relief. He may condemn himself in a tolerant sort of way, but generally he blames others for his unhappiness. In consequence he will accuse and distrust almost everyone and show some trends toward paranoid thoughts.

Differences in the Family's Response

You can sometimes classify your relative's depression with fair accuracy just by observing the family's reaction to it.

An *endogenous* depression evokes irritation and impatience from relatives. This is not heartlessness, but simply lack of recognition. Since endogenous depression stems from *within* the brain and nervous system, its "withinness" is ordinarily beyond the family's comprehension and they back away from the essential problem.

With *reactive* depression, wherein the person grieves

because of a loss, the above is not true. Quite the reverse. This condition invites empathy, because families always understand a loss reaction. They expect the sadness and offer comfort and help in full measure.

In *neurotic* depression family members invariably show a mixture of sympathy, pity, and annoyance. They comprehend the suffering of the neurotic, because within any given familial bond the same values and similar emotionality (and neuroticism) are shared in the struggle with life. But these are also the similarities that lead to conflict. After a while the relatives have "had it" and will make this plain. "Listen, you can't be babied all your life, so snap out of it," or, "I've got my own problems; you take care of yours."

Many other important differences characterize the three categories of depression. They are delineated in the chart, and I suggest that you refer to it freely.

COMPARISON OF DIFFERENT TYPES OF DEPRESSION

	ENDOGENOUS DEPRESSION	REACTIVE DEPRESSION (GRIEF)	NEUROTIC DEPRESSION
Cause	A primary disturbance in the structure and function of brain and nervous system; also toxicity, infection, injury.	A specific, meaningful loss of a loved one, of material things, or of an opportunity; displacement; loneliness.	Exhaustion of adaptation; severe or prolonged stress; inadequacy of personal strivings; unresolved conflicts; chronic anxiety, fear, anger.
History of depression in family	Commonly, other family members have had depressions.	No relationship to depression in family.	Illness can sometimes be related to depression in the family.
Onset	Fairly rapid (1–4 weeks) and seems to come from nowhere.	Sudden, and specifically related to a loss.	Gradual, over several weeks. Seems to build up slowly.
Nature of depression	Usually of agitated type with restlessness and "nervousness."	Tends to be retarded and slowed down.	Mixed: sometimes slowed, other times agitated.
Intensity of depression	Most often severe and with time gets worse.	Mild to moderate, but occasionally severe. Tends to remain steady.	Fluctuates from mild to severe.
Duration of depression	If untreated, may last 3–24 months, then improve; but can remain chronic indefinitely.	If untreated, may last 3–12 months. Improves with time, but may remain chronic.	Varies, depending on personality. Many remain chronic with periods of improvement.

COMPARISON OF DIFFERENT TYPES OF DEPRESSION (Cont.)

	ENDOGENOUS DEPRESSION	REACTIVE DEPRESSION (GRIEF)	NEUROTIC DEPRESSION
Tendency to recurrence	Common, with varied periods of remission.	Only with a new loss.	Frequent relapses and remissions.
Mood	Worse in the morning and tends to be better in the evening.	Constant feeling of sadness. Little variation in intensity.	Unpredictable; person blows "hot and cold." Usually optimistic in morning and depressed toward evening.
Sleep	Falls asleep easily but awakens at 4 to 5 A.M. and cannot fall asleep again.	Difficulty in falling asleep, but then sleeps through.	Fitful. Awakens readily, sleeps, reawakens. Morning sleep is deep.
Arising	Awakens tired and jittery, with no sense of rest. Feels miserable in the morning.	Awakens with some feeling of repose and refreshment.	Awakens with a heavy head, but hopes for a good day.
Eating	Little interest in food, and rapid weight loss.	Sluggish appetite, but can be coaxed to eat something. Mild weight loss.	Varies. Some show loss of appetite; others are compulsive eaters and gain weight.
Crying	Intense, spontaneous, and agitated crying spells.	Steady tearfulness and quiet sobbing associated with ruminations over the loss.	Some crying spells; or the person may say: "If I could cry I'd feel better."

Emotional control	Generally, none. Person needs to be managed at all times.	Person retains enough control to manage self.	Varies from well-controlled to unmanageable.
Self-esteem	Completely lost. Feeling of emptiness in the self.	No loss of self-esteem. Feeling of emptiness in environment.	Fluctuates between high and low.
Anxiety	Present and tends to increase as illness progresses.	Present, but tends to diminish with time.	Constantly present and may rise to panic states.
Expressions of fear	Usually intense; mostly fear of being alone.	Occasional mild fears about "what will happen."	Multiple fears about present and future constantly voiced.
Ability to make decisions	Absent. Almost totally indecisive.	Retains ability to decide on important issues.	Indecisive on important matters. Positive decisions on minor matters.
Ability to concentrate	None, especially when agitated.	Can concentrate some when distracted from loss.	Varies, but mostly poor.
Memory	Poor.	Poor.	Variable and unreliable.
Sense of responsibility	Mostly lost.	Retained.	Usually diffused.
Contact with reality and the surroundings	Usually poor. Distorted judgment, lack of orientation, and inadequate perceptions are common.	Good. Oriented to environment and reality situations.	Varies. Judgment colored by level of hysteria and perceptual distortions.

COMPARISON OF DIFFERENT TYPES OF DEPRESSION (Cont.)

	ENDOGENOUS DEPRESSION	REACTIVE DEPRESSION (GRIEF)	NEUROTIC DEPRESSION
Delusions	Very common. Mostly paranoidal; guilt; ideas of poverty, self-depreciation, unworthiness.	Uncommon. If appear, usually as feelings of remorse or guilt about contributing to the loss.	Varies. If present, usually of persecution, oppression, or guilt; occasionally, of unworthiness.
Tendency to alcoholism	Strong, especially if illness is prolonged.	Some tendency, which disappears when mourning stops.	Strong tendency to drown sorrows in drink.
Fatigue	Chronically tired, but shows some energy when agitated.	Constant weariness is present.	Feelings of "no pep" but occasional bursts of energy.
Attitude to fatigue	Does not care.	Accepts the weary feeling.	Feels shame; embarrassed at failure to mobilize self.
Reserve of strength	Little to none.	Can be mobilized and person pulls self together for periods of time.	Very little, but person may "push" for brief intervals.
Physical symptoms	Many complaints about stomach, bowel function, chest pains, headache.	Few complaints. If present, mostly about stomach and chest.	Innumerable vague complaints such as headache, tightness in chest, indigestion, cramps.
Sexual interest	Complete loss.	Usually diminished, but in some instances may be aroused.	Fluctuates. Generally diminished, but person may try to "prove" sexual competence.

Interpersonal relationships	Disturbed; the person withdraws.	Usually greater feelings of closeness and dependence.	Often destroyed; relationships probably poor all along.
Family attitudes to patient	Removed; treat patient as a nuisance and problem.	Empathetic, warm, and protective.	Mixed feelings; family quarrels with patient,
Suicidal thoughts	Present and intense; also expressions of fear of death.	May be present and intense.	Frequently present, but covered up by desire to live.
Suicide attempts	Common and should be anticipated. Determined suicidal attempts relate to desire for relief from mental pain.	Occasional, but meaningful, suicidal attempts relate to loss of hope.	Frequent suicidal attempts appear to be attention-gathering, but person hopes to be rescued.

CHAPTER SEVEN

General Symptoms and What You Do About Them

VARIOUS SYMPTOMS were threaded through the different kinds of depression that I described to you in the preceding chapters. You may have noted that not every depressed person shows all symptoms. Some are peculiar to only one or to several kinds of depression. Others appear in all depressions, either singly or combined. Every symptom is significant within the context of a particular depression.

Understanding the Symptoms Reestablishes Communication

I say *"re*establishes" because the patient's illness inhibits his thoughts, feelings, and actions, and he is not the "same person." One no longer "knows" him; thus, it is difficult to communicate with him. For example, a previously doting grandfather will now stare at his young grandson indifferently. A woman who would normally meet her husband's affection with equal warmth turns away from him. There are other peculiar reactions. The depressed person may ignore a friendly greeting, or shake with anger when merely invited to sit down to a meal. But not because he wants to act this way.

A depressed individual cannot control himself any more than someone running a high temperature can pull the fever down at will. We develop control of thoughts and emotions just as we learn muscle control in walking, running, dancing, and sitting; with illness we may lose this ability to govern our physical selves. In depression the person loses the ability to govern his *emotional* self and his thinking. Pessimism, paranoia, anger, fear, condemnation, tearfulness, withdrawal, and so on, are all symptoms which the depressed person cannot moderate. Normal regulatory control has been lost, and if you admonish him to "stop crying," or to "pull yourself together," you are conveying your displeasure and telling him that he is incompetent to handle himself. This only serves to reinforce his feelings of gloom and failure.

But when you understand the symptoms, you penetrate the thoughts of the depressed person. Thus, you communicate with each other. This in turn becomes the vehicle for dealing with the symptoms and the illness.

Sadness

Your relative may complain of being gloomy, terribly blue or down in the dumps, dejected, or in a bad mood. The intensities of sadness cover a lot of shadings, from pale blue to deep black, so to speak. But whatever words are used to describe it, they signify basically that the person's feeling tones are lower than normal.

What to Do About the Sadness

When the sadness is a simple entity it may be minor and nothing to worry about. But in true depression, it pervades the entire person; and it is bound up with other symptoms. If you are unable to cheer your relative, to distract or divert him or her, the sadness is a pointer, telling you to look further. You should then watch for other symptoms, which in the aggregate will alert you to a depression that is either in the making or fully developed.

Sleep Difficulties

You may see that the sleep patterns are disturbed, with insomnia dominant. If there is agitation the person *awakens early,* usually around four or five A.M., and cannot get to sleep again.

When the depression is retarded (slowed down), he or she wants *only to drowse* and will sleep the day away.

Or *sleep may be fitful*. The person awakens, falls asleep again and reawakens, always feeling dull and unrefreshed on arising.

How You Deal with Sleep Difficulties

If your relative *awakens too early*, intolerable restlessness claws at him. In his or her own words, "I feel just miserable."

The early awakening is doubly assaultive. Not only does it break up needed rest and force the person to toss about vainly, becoming more and more upset, but also the eeriness of predawn and its utter aloneness frighten him. To counter this, you can initiate your own assault against the insomnia with a definite program.

First, train yourself to get up at the same time that the patient awakens so that you can "start the day" for him. Being with someone dispels his sense of doom. Begin by fixing breakfast and bringing out whatever medications were prescribed for the morning hour. As you sit and chat over the table and especially if you convey your own pleasure at this chance for an early morning tête-à-tête, you are communicating with him and inducing him to relax. He may then go back to bed and fall into another two or three hours of sleep. You have just won a small skirmish with the illness.

I agree that this kind of help is not easy. It does involve a high order of unselfishness. But, because you are reading this book, I am assuming that this is what you want to offer.

Too much sleep will not in itself be harmful. But when no benefit ensues in renewed energy, and you gather that the sleep is an "escape," it is best to restrict it during the day. Set up a small task to create wakefulness. Also, encourage him or her to stay up later at night and to awaken earlier next day. But if this program creates irritability, drop it. Excessive sleep is the lesser evil. As your relative recovers and is more cooperative you can supervise his sleeping habits with less difficulty.

If *sleep is fitful*, medication helps (but only those drugs obtained on prescription, never over the counter). There are also simple measures that you can take to reduce the person's tension. Get him into a warm, restful tub bath before he retires. Read an interesting book to him. Play some favorite music. Equally essential are the following "Don't's" for creating more continuous sleep.

Don't offer "suspense" books for distraction.

Don't serve heavy meals in the evening.

Don't leave the bedroom in total darkness; keep a night light burning to prevent fright and disorientation, should the patient suddenly awaken. He can then release into sleep again more easily.

Don't let bedroom temperatures go to extremes of too hot or too cold. Make sure that he or she wears comfortable, loose garments and sleeps under light, unconfining blankets.

Don't let family arguments obtrude, particularly before bedtime.

Poor Appetite

Depressed persons show an aversion to food. They toy with it, pronounce it tasteless, and say they are not hungry. Some subsist mainly on coffee and cigarettes. In a severe depression there may be total lack of appetite and the person will go for days without eating. This causes a rapid weight loss, anywhere from five to thirty pounds in a matter of weeks; the nutritional deficits then aggravate the depression.

(We have the opposite problem too. Certain neurotic people with depression may develop voracious appetites, become compulsive eaters, and constantly raid the icebox.)

How to Help with Poor Appetite

Here you must know what the person means about his feelings toward food instead of what he says. For example, he may be hungry but deny it to you. Perhaps this is because of his hidden guilt feelings and his need to punish himself. Therefore, if you say routinely, "Eat something; it will help you get well," you are, in effect, contradicting the person's inner desire to be punished. You become an antagonist who will not permit him to suffer as his guilt feelings dictate that he should.

You will do better if you approach him candidly. "Look, I know you're hungry, but you're taking something or other out on yourself. Maybe you're right, maybe you're wrong. But starving won't help, because it won't solve your problem. We'll figure out some other way to handle your bad feelings and thoughts. Food comes first though, so right now we're both going to sit down and eat together."

This is what you have done. You have plucked out the emotional invalid's mental demons, brought them into the light of day, and made it plain that you know they are interfering with his food intake. You have acknowledged that guilt exists, but without passing judgment on it. At the same time you have deferred action on the "needed" punishment. By making the decision to put food on the table and explaining why, you have communicated. Your relative will begin to eat then and there. And in caring for a depressed person one victory at a time is all you reach for.

Do Not Harp on Food

Refusal to eat is not always linked with guilt. More often it symptomatizes depressed nervous function. If you hound the person about food, you vex him or her and yourself too. Find other ways to stir the appetite and to push nourishment. Determine the person's favorite foods and prepare and offer them in small quantities and at frequent intervals. Applaud what was eaten, but make no comment on what was left untouched.

Another thing. The depressed person is supersensitive to the appearance of food because nausea is ever present. Entice the appetite with attractive dishes and table settings. With a casual air suggest that you think he or she is entitled to coddling at this time. You may be contradicted and told, "I'm not worth it. I'm no good." Ignore this and proceed with the meal. Do not show disappointment if the food is just pecked at after all the trouble you have gone to in cooking it. Put it away with the light suggestion: "We'll save it in case you want a bite later on."

Sometimes in a depression the patient regresses to the point where an emotional block prevents his taking food into his mouth. But if it gets there it will be swallowed. Thus, you may have to resort to gentle and patient spoon-feeding for a while.

In brief, when you feed a depressed person you are telling him that you know his poor appetite is a symptom of the illness. You are letting him see *your* insight into his thoughts and feelings. You are identifying with his mental pain and such empathy heartens him. If you can put this over, you are part way there.

Loss of Interest in the Surroundings and Loss of Pleasure Drive

Depression produces a flatness in human responses, and the normally active personality is extinguished. No wonder, then, that interests which were once vital are dulled and pleasure drives are lost.

The sick individual turns a blank face to the former excitements of living. Friendships lose point; community, national, or international events might as well not occur. Indifference to the family and surroundings congeals into withdrawal and seclusion. These changes are most striking in one who always loved activity, whether of sports, hobbies, or social life. Thus, a woman who comments, "When my husband gives up his poker night he must really be depressed," may be diagnosing his condition more accurately than she realizes.

As the spouse, child, or parent, or whatever your relationship, you are part of the patient's surroundings and when you too are the object of his or her indifference you feel hurt. But try to realize that you are being shut out only because the person's mental anguish leaves no room for you or anyone else; he can center only on himself. So when you ask, "Won't you please come out for a walk for my sake?" and there is no reaction, do not be offended. Rather, recognize that he lacks the psychic strength to satisfy your appeal. The sick person just does not care. His illness will not allow him to.

How to Help Restore the Person's Interest and Pleasure Drive

Your main task is to force aside the symptom of indifference and to support any stimulative response through authority (providing it also contains the ingredient of affection). Methodically, and with infinite pains, you direct the depressed person back into former pursuits.

One husband I knew gave earnest thought to the previous areas of recreation that his depressed wife had once enjoyed. Bridge was among them, and he began with that. One day he insisted that she start to attend her weekly bridge game again. After some demurral she agreed, but with apprehension. As she had feared, the evening was a stress for her. She barely managed to push through it. Her husband then evaluated its benefits as compared with the effort to get her going. Noting that she ate a little better the next day and conversed more, he decided that every inch of gain counted and he continued prodding. He was right. Before long she began to accept the bridge sessions. Her face and voice brightened. He saw a shade of pleasure in them. Firmer progress was made on the momentum of this renewed interest. Finally, her husband, the household, and other social activity caught her attention, and the way back to health was no longer uphill.

By impelling her to embrace life again, *any* aspect of it, her husband remotivated her for survival. In psychologic terms, her ego function had been greatly weakened; when he took a strong position about her activities and supported her in them he gave her a lifeline to grab hold of.

I can tell you this. Each time you animate the depressed person, you help him or her to build up a fresh energy supply. This halts the inroads of depression, enlarges the perspectives, refuels the person's interests, and reawakens the pleasure drive.

Loss of Sexual Desire

As the depressed person loses his or her zest for living, sexual appetite disappears as well. Single persons may not notice this symptom, but it is quickly discerned by married couples who have led active sexual lives. When the wife is depressed she becomes indifferent and perhaps unresponsive to sexual stimulation, but may submit passively to intercourse. However, when the man's potency is affected he is frightened by it and develops profound anxiety. He may be informed that his inability to erect is transient, but to him it "proves" that life is finished.

How the Spouse Helps When Sexual Desire Is Lost

Most husbands treat the wife's loss of libido with kindness and accept it as a temporary interruption due to understandable causes. This attitude eases any feelings of guilt or self-depreciation that she may harbor for "failing" him.

If it is the husband who is depressed and he shows a lessened or absent sex drive, the wife's role is more difficult. For example, she sees that he is worrying over it but that he keeps silent on the subject because it mortifies him. Taking her cue from his attitude, she may regard the matter as so delicate that she tiptoes around it, dreading to make any false move.

However, the very opposite is required here—the courage to bring the subject into the open, to assure the husband that she is confident his masculinity will return, and that her patience is inexhaustible in waiting for him to get well and recover from the impotence. True, he will be sensitive to every nuance of her words and should she be heavy-handed and labor the point, he may develop a vague alarm, some paranoia, and think that she is "looking for someone else."

But if she is adept and exercises tact and finesse, she will direct him toward an optimistic trust in his future sexual performance.

There is another pitfall which, if allowed to deepen, often creates separateness between husband and wife. Rarely do married couples realize that despite the lessening of sexual activity in depression, both the man and woman yearn for the affectionate exchanges that bound them together before. While the spouse may not respond as fervently as the other would wish, he or she will still want the evidences of love to continue. What could be worse than eliminating all the intimate words and tender gestures of the past? With nothing to substitute, the depressed person will indeed assume that he is forsaken. When such a barrier of coolness builds up it can be more damaging than the depression itself, because it may persist. Later it will entail a more complex effort at sexual readjustment and disinhibition. Affection should never be allowed to wither away. It must continue as a bridge to such time as sexual intercourse is reinstated as a normal part of the marriage.

Self-Neglect

A depressed individual will often disregard his or her appearance, personal hygiene, and social deportment. Poor grooming is usually an obvious sign of depression. The man will not shave and does not care a damn whether he showers or smells. A woman will wear the same spotted and torn dress and not use makeup or comb her matted hair. She too neglects herself until her body odor is offensive. Soon such persons barely resemble the fastidious individuals you knew before.

How You Help When Self-Neglect Appears

You take over immediately and supervise the person through direct management. Do not mince words. Hints are not enough for a depressed person who is wallowing in self-neglect. This symptom denotes considerable regression and you must therefore get down to the elementary instructions of childhood. Clearly and explicitly, tell your relative that he (or she) must bathe, brush his teeth, and comb his hair. You give him the proper clothes and accessories and, if necessary, stay and help him. Do not hesitate to correct sloppy table manners and other embarrassing behavior. But all of this is done with no taint of asperity or harshness. However firm your directive let your voice caress and your face speak eloquently of your fond regard.

Perhaps you are beginning to think that this "policing" is rather petty as compared with the larger problem of the illness itself. By no means. In maintaining your relative's *outward* appearance and all the civilized niceties that go with it, you compel the respect of others despite the depression. After all, the illness is rough enough on family relationships without body odors and repellent behavior to worsen them. Your watchfulness becomes a morale builder that also prevents the depressed person from sinking into self-disgust. Remember, your relative is going to be well again one day, and when you give him this kind of supervision you help him retain his social status and you save him from embarrassing memories of his crude behavior when he was ill.

Loss of Self-Confidence

Each one of us lives with a different level of confidence. For example, you may have a young sister or niece in her twenties who has always radiated self-assurance and poise. Suddenly she starts to flounder. She cannot decide whether to date a certain young man, and she feels unsure of her office work. She gets a bit frowzy and disparages her own good looks. You can see her confidence flaking away. And it is so unlike her. She was never this way before. You try to remain calm about it, but at the same time you wonder whether you ought not to step in and take her in hand.

How to Help When Self-Confidence Is Lost

With this symptom the *last* thing one does is to tease, lecture, or "kid" the person about his or her shakiness. Nor will it do any good to ignore the problem. Something has gone wrong and it will have to be faced.

Therefore, assert straightforwardly that you can see the startling change that has taken place from a week or a month ago. You acknowledge that to become unsure of oneself and depressed in this way can be a scary ordeal. But do not join in her self-pity. Instead, offer this: "Well, suppose you can't rip through your work the way you did before? Let's talk about the things you still do well. What do you think they are?" You will get the automatic reply, "Not anything any more," that a depressed person invariably gives. But if you are wise you will set this aside and name the situations where performance continues to be good in spite of the person's waning self-confidence. And you will have to keep at it without losing heart, because a return of certainty in the person must be reconstructed brick by brick each day.

For example, a young matron I knew kept bewailing her loss of competence as a wife and mother. Ill with neurotic depression, she insisted that she was useless and would never amount to anything again. She had always tended to fret about every minor crisis, whether it was the misbehavior of the vacuum cleaner, a delayed package, or the plan to paint the house next spring. Fortunately, her husband was an astute man who grasped my advice quickly. As an object lesson in the art of reactivating self-confidence, his handling of the problem is worth noting. It was based on the following principle:

Praise the Person's Efforts and Block Out Doubts

Instead of deploring her neuroticisms, which were more pronounced than ever now, he supported her lovable traits and focused on the assets that continued to operate *for* her even within the illness.

When she called him at his job hourly for assurance or when she persisted with this in the evening, he would counter: "You *did* get the children off to school this morning?" "Yes but . . ." "And yesterday?" "Yes." "And the day before and every day this week?" "Yes." "That's wonderful. And you must have cleaned the house well, because it looks perfect." "Yes, but not as . . ." "And you shopped at the supermarket and bought everything you needed?" "Yes but . . ." "And cooked this delicious dinner?" "Yes but it's not . . ." "You're doing a great job. That's all that matters." Each time and in every area, no matter what her objections, he closed the gap against her self-doubts.

Thus, the essence of help for the depressed person who has lost self-confidence is to shore up strengths and minimize weaknesses. In the above case, the husband was conditioning his wife to take pride in what she achieved and to discount what she did not, until she finally learned to utilize this mechanism herself to its fullest advantage.

Agreed that such constant attention to the person can be tedious and wearying. But is it any more so than preparing an invalid's diet, emptying bedpans, changing dressings, and so on? Especially when it is for someone you love? The decision is always yours, but when you educate the depressed person to a healthier mode of adaptation you are rewarding yourself too, because you are doing one thing more—helping to prevent future depressions in the person.

Loss of Self-Esteem: Its Variations

If a self-respecting and productive person begins to doubt his worth and to depreciate himself you can assume that that individual is depressed.

Self-esteem differs from self-confidence, although they are interlocked.

Self-confidence measures our sense of ability to perform.

Self-esteem defines what we think of this ability and, hence, our own worth. It is our self-image.

If we perform with self-confidence, our personal esteem remains.

But when the confidence level of our total personality function is lowered and not reconstructed quickly enough, our pride is wounded. It is then that self-esteem also disappears, leaving us with a negative self-image.

In *endogenous* depression the individual loses all pride and self-respect. He or she feels that nothing of value is left of the self. Guilt and futility are overwhelming, and the person stands condemned in his own estimate.

In *reactive* depression, where a loss of some kind specifies the cause, *personal* self-esteem may not be affected. Rather, there is a sense of emptiness in the environment, of living in a void. However, if guilt and hopelessness grow out of the loss reaction, personal self-esteem will dwindle at the same time.

In *neurotic* depression self-esteem waxes and wanes. At times great conceit and arrogance are displayed, and they serve as attention-getters. But when you see that this conduct alternates with a grotesque humility and abasement, you will know that, underneath, the person is frightened and depressed and begging for help.

What to Do When Self-Esteem Is Lost

In the previous section you learned that self-confidence is bolstered by emphasis on successful performance in day-to-day events. However, this technique is not a restorative for self-esteem; once self-esteem is gone hopelessness supervenes, indicating that the depression is quite serious. If you tried to assure the person that he or she was capable of some normal activity, it would not help. Such normalcy, even in part, does not exist at this stage, and there would be no response to your encouragement for any undertaking.

In reactivating self-esteem, you appeal to the person's reason, either directly or indirectly, pointing to the illogic of his self-disparagement. You search for *past* performance and present him with it. The trick is to get him to place the correct value on accomplishments prior to the depression. *Your object here is to overcome the hopelessness that denotes suicidal thinking.*

It will not do to make an impassioned speech about what "a great person you are, always were, and always will be . . . in this family we think you're tops." He will note its hollowness and turn from it. Instead, point out that his thinking is unreasonable in the light of all his personal assets and capabilities. Then name them. (Everyone possesses some.) His successes may be in the nature of work accomplishment; the rearing of happy, stable children; a reputation as a Mr. Fix-it or as a stamp or coin collector; a fine name as a trusted friend; local fame as the winner of all the gardening prizes; or anything else you know of that applies in his or her case. To reinforce your words, restate them on paper and place the paper in the person's hands. Every time he expresses self-depreciation urge him to read the facts for himself. There may be no immediate reaction, but soon you will find that he has begun to study what you have written and to think about it.

In addition, call on friends to buttress your own efforts. Have a neighbor ask your relative's opinion on the construction of a fireplace. Invite someone in to solicit his advice on how to manage a young son. Or ask a fellow gardener to seek his appraisal of a new hybrid plant. Whatever area it is, make sure that it is something in which your relative shines.

In doing this you are building up a model of his personality strengths and having him test it out. As its logic and validity take hold, the derogatory self-judgments recede. *Your* value of him and those of others begin to supersede his, and ultimately you induce him to acknowledge them. He now has a more favorable image of himself.

Will this make him well? Not alone, but after a while this process elevates the mood and, together with other treatment methods, consolidates the healing process. Once there is full recovery from the depression, normal self-esteem reasserts itself. But in the meantime you have helped mitigate much of the suffering and feeling of degradation that go with loss of self-esteem.

Preoccupation with Body Function

You have read before in this book that the depressed person's thoughts center on the body, that he complains of physical distress with vague aches and pains, and that repeated checkups by the family physician reveal nothing wrong physically.

However, the doctor has probably added that your relative may be undergoing a "functional nervous disorder." This puzzles you. What is meant by "functional?" Is it good? Better than physical? Or bad? And what is to be done about it?

I will explain this term as it relates to depressive illness and the nervous system.

The Meaning of "Functional Disorder"

First, think of yourself and your own ordinary reactions. Have you ever realized that when you go through an intense emotion of any kind, even a pleasant one, you also experience temporary physical changes with it? Let me remind you: did you ever "laugh yourself sick"? Of course you did. As you laughed, you doubled up, your sides and jaws ached, you could not catch your breath, and you gagged on your own merriment. Also, your heart beat faster and "came up into your throat." You "almost had a convulsion." Quite a few symptoms of an emotional reaction called laughter, wouldn't you say? And all of them functional.

The opposite reaction can also result functionally in physical symptoms. Do you recall once encountering a loathsome and disgusting situation that not only upset your feelings but tied your stomach into a knot of revulsion? Maybe this continued to the point where you actually felt nauseated. Your heart raced, your chest tightened, your arms hung limp and weak, and your whole body felt drained. A sour taste filled your mouth, you went dizzy, and your scalp burned.

Now think of any emotion and you will realize that there are times when you *gasp* with joy, *blush* with embarrassment, *seethe* with anger, *tire* with boredom, *shake* with terror, *tingle* with excitement, and so on.

In brief, such physical symptoms are body *functions* that go hand in hand with the feeling of the emotion. If a doctor were to take an electrocardiogram of your heart or do other tests while you were "laughing yourself sick," your heart would show up as normal. So would your stomach if it were X-rayed at the moment when it "knotted" with revulsion. Thus, we call the sickness with laughter and the knotted stomach at disgust "functional." Such a kink or quirk in physical activity is not an organic disorder in itself. It lasts or "functions" only so long as the emotion persists.

This is true of depression too. The physical symptoms which accompany the depressive emotion *function with, and because of, the emotion*. Hence, they are functional;

as physical manifestations, they represent the temporary disorganization of nervous function that is causing the depression. When the depression clears up, so do the physical symptoms—in the same way that your physical symptoms disappear when your laughter or disgust ceases.

Below, I list the most common physical symptoms which the depressed person complains of and which are a *functional* part of the depressive disorder:

Headache.

Burning sensation or tightness at the top or back of the head.

Dizziness or faintness.

Palpitation or rapid heartbeat.

Blurred vision.

Loss of body control; incoordination with a tendency to drop things or bump into fixed objects.

Trouble with breathing, and tightness across the chest— "I can't draw a good breath."

Constipation or diarrhea.

Pressure in the bladder.

Colicky pains in the abdomen.

Heartburn or nausea.

Stomach spasms or a "sticking" feeling in the pit of the stomach.

Pressure or pains in the chest (which the person may mistake for "heart trouble").

Aches and cramps in the legs and back.

Sweating.

Itching or tingling sensations in the skin.

Weakness in the body; shakiness.

How to Deal with Body Preoccupations

The intensity and persistence of the complaints of physical ailments may convince you that something *must* be wrong. You will need all your courage to believe the doctor when he tells you that your relative does *not* have a bad heart (or stomach or lung disease, or any other physical disorder).

However, once you have accepted the doctor's assurance, do not go to the other extreme. (This frequently occurs.) When your relative grouches about a queasy stomach, do not reply, "But you know now that it's all in your mind." It is not. It is in the stomach. True, the complaint is of something functional and not really of a diseased organ. But it still signifies a painful spasm or clutching sensation, in this case a nervous disequilibrium that is causing not only a depressive illness but the discomfort of aches and pains as well. It is no different from the pain you felt when you laughed so hard. That pain was in your side and not in your mind! It disappeared when your laughter was brought into control. Your relative's aches and pains also will disappear when the depression lifts. That is why your sympathy *and* empathy are very much in order.

Instead of calling the complaint imaginary, you concede that it is real but probably due to the depression. Then give your relative the medicine that the doctor prescribed for it. In all likelihood he or she has neglected to take it. The reason? Perhaps because of that psychologic need for punishment that I mentioned a while back. "I don't deserve medicine to get me well," the patient may say to himself. Or maybe the physical symptom is an SOS to attract your attention to the real suffering, the mental pain.

Therefore, take some of the following measures. Prepare some bland food to soothe the queasiness further. Or, if your relative complains of leg cramps, massage the limb. If it is a throbbing headache, have him lie down while you apply a cold compress. Or if his chest seems tight, get him to lean back and breathe regularly while you count to a hundred. The tightness will ease.

To be sure, all of these efforts may be dubbed "placebos," but inherently they contain the attention and love that a depressed person requires. When you dispense these lavishly, the "physical" complaints tend to fade; the depression too subsides for the time being, because he or she now feels that someone understands.

Lack of Concentration

With this symptom the individual cannot sustain an interest in work or any facet of living. Technically, we call this condition a *narrowing of the attention span*. It is impossible for the person to get beyond the headlines of the newspaper or listen to a complete broadcast. If you ask him a question he may perceive it, but it will take a monumental effort for him to formulate a reply, even for a mere yes or no. When the illness is severe the person seems to wander mentally. He hears your voice, but the ability to absorb your words is missing, because the mental constrictions of the depression have closed off their meaning. They do not register.

How to Help When the Depressed Person Cannot Concentrate

Maintain contact with the patient.

First. Realize that when concentration is poor the normal fluctuations of the surroundings—sounds, atmosphere, movement, and so on—confuse him. He is unable to anchor his relationships to things and people any more. Insecurity sets in. Thus, at frequent intervals and without being asked, you should give your relative solid assurance. Paraphrased in your own way, it can run like this: "Don't worry. I'm right here for you and I will be, so don't hesitate to speak to me about anything at all that's on your mind. That's what I'm around for." Such reiterations cushion the small shocks of his confusion and he then feels safer.

Second. In conversing with him or her, always stand within a direct line of vision. Do not call out from another room where you cannot be seen. Make sure you are face to face with the person, that your movements are observed, and that your eyes meet his. This helps stabilize his attention and relate the substance of what you say to what he sees. It is a visual aid in forcing his awareness to record your words.

Third. After asking a question or making a comment, *wait* for an answer. Throttle any impulse to hurry the person. Allocate a full minute to it (time yourself, because sixty seconds is a long time if you are feeling restive). Once you get him started, replies will come a bit faster. His concentration improves and you can then hold his attention. Now is the moment to involve him in some task that can be accomplished *in your presence.* At the same time keep up the flow of talk. The longer your conversational exchange goes on, the better your results.

If he or she pulls back into a flustered silence, do not press. Let an hour or two elapse, then repeat the procedure. The success of each effort will carry over to the next; gradually the attention span widens, thus leading to greater clarity of mind.

Poor memory is a corollary to lack of concentration, and very often these symptoms must be dealt with together.

Memory Troubles

It may disconcert you to find that your relative cannot recall, try as he will, that the Smiths visited your home only last week; that all of you went to the shore on vacation during the summer; or that your parents celebrated their golden wedding anniversary just a month ago. He or she also forgets trivial things—where certain items were placed such as papers, tools, jewelry, a comb and brush, and so on.

This difficulty in remembering is bound up with the causes for lack of concentration. The block in memory and inability to concentrate occur because the person's nervous energy has been inhibited or dampened. I want you to make a special note of this point for a particular reason: it relates to your relative's recovery from the illness. Once you have been told that he (or she) is well, it may perplex you to discover that he has almost no recollection of many incidents that took place during the depression. You ask why. Does this mean that the illness is lingering on? Not necessarily. The blank in recall probably exists because all through the siege of depression the person could not concentrate. Therefore, no recollections or memory circuits were established *throughout that time*. There can be no remembrances of what took place then, since the incidents were never recorded in the brain to begin with.

How You Help with Memory Troubles

Here too you will need extraordinary patience. Easier said than done? You are right, but if you become exasperated with this symptom you might as well dismiss your relative from your conscience here and now.

Let us say that you refer to a recent episode involving his presence. But he seems to have obliterated it. It just never happened. "What in the world are you talking about?" he asks, with much dubious headshaking. If you turn on him and chide, "But how can you *not* remember? We went with Uncle Joe and got that dented fender at the parking lot," you will not jog the lever of recall one bit. To the contrary, you will suppress it. When you challenge the memory in this way, you imply a ridicule that you may not intend but which nevertheless convinces him that he is worse off than he had dreamed of and is probably losing his mind. One look at the hurt in his face and you will be stricken with remorse. Such harmful emotionalism can be avoided for both of you.

Do it this way. Exclude any scolding. Instead, *reacquaint him with the facts*.

Tell him that you know he is having memory trouble but that later this will clear up. This is a simple message of your understanding and rapport; and by affirming the symptom of the memory trouble you indicate your acceptance of it. Now you have his interest. Go on with something like this: "I guess when the fender was dented you were probably so wrapped up in your own thoughts that you didn't notice. That's why you can't remember it now. But this is what happened." Proceed with the details of the incident, relating them as you would a story that he had never heard before. And for practical purposes he has not.

In another case the conversation may revolve about a trip you made with him and he is hazy about it. You might be tempted to prod: "Don't you remember? How we met the Browns and had dinner with them at Mario's?"

But at this stage of nonrecall your relative has not the faintest notion who the Browns are and eating is so unimportant to him in his depressed state that he could not care less if it were Mario's restaurant or Joe's diner. Therefore, when you see his fogginess, put it this way: "When we were on our last trip we met some people by the name of Brown and had dinner with them," and continue in a relaxed, narrative style. He will nod as you talk, actually enjoying your recital, and to your surprise he may retain most of it.

In smoothing the path for him in this way you will notice that somewhere along the line he starts to take part in the general conversation—hesitantly, yes, but it is a beginning. Now entice him into it a bit more and watch his alertness begin to revive. You are by no means out of the rough yet, because in referring to an event he may suddenly block on a word or a name. Provide it unobtrusively (never in an overt fashion). Or he may make an error and then stop. Let it pass. Allow some inaccuracies. He is so ultrasensitive to making mistakes at this stage that if you overdo your help you will embarrass him. Your role is to refresh his recollections and thereby reactivate the remembering apparatus. For this, you use the subtlety of suggestion. Ultimately this method loosens the grip of the constrictions caused by the depression and achieves a breakthrough to memory return. Therefore, consider yourself lucky when he begins to converse again; he is no longer shutting you out. Rather, he is drawing closer to normal relationships and resuming his former place within them.

Inability to Make Decisions or Use Will Power

In depression your relative may often be unable to make up his mind about the slightest thing. For example, if he accedes to an evening out the first hurdle will be—what suit or tie or shoes to wear? A woman with this symptom will flit back and forth from the blue dress to the green, the black, and again to the blue, ending in a stalemate. In a restaurant such depressed persons dither over every item on the menu. Just whether to salt their food becomes a difficult problem for them. Throughout the day, if two possibilities arise, they will spurn both rather than decide on one. Very often anger stirs them when they sense the demand to be decisive. This emotionalism can blow up into open rage if others fail to assist in settling on a choice. The sense of depression then thickens and the person may almost give up the prospect of ever getting well.

Loss of will may correlate with the indecision. Sometimes relatives size up both these symptoms as neurotic traits which the person could discard "if he wanted to enough," or for which he should seek psychologic treatment. But this appraisal is inaccurate. In most depressions, the inability to make decisions and the loss of will power are not simply personality weaknesses but *symptoms* of the primary depressive illness. He or she will continue to show these deficiencies until the depression is treated and recovery is achieved.

What to Do About the Indecision and Loss of Will Power

The dramatic change in the person who develops these symptoms may startle you, especially if he or she is someone who has played a positive and authoritative role in life. But think of him as one whose decision-making machinery is immobilized. Obviously, you cannot "see" it at a standstill, because it is hidden in the chemistry of the brain. Nevertheless, the brain centers for being decisive are out of commission temporarily, in much the same way that a wrist is limited in motion by a sprain. At this point, then, you must take over the decision making.

Do you remember the fable about the donkey who starved to death because he could not decide which bale of hay to eat? Well, I do not know whether the donkey was depressed, but your relative is. Therefore, when he or she wavers between a desire for orange juice or tomato juice, do not leave the choice open. *You* make the decision and he will assent. Similarly, if he does not know whether he wants to wear a sport or a dress shirt, you decide. Hand him the clothes he is to put on. And with what relief he accepts your choice! Also, do not ask if he prefers going for a stroll or to visit friends. Plan one or the other, and he will fall in with it. If left to his own devices he will be torn by uncertainty. As he gets well this disability vanishes and he will again make his own decisions.

Poor Judgment

Here I urge you to abide by a basic principle: *do not rely on the judgment of the depressed person.* Remember that his nervous function is in disequilibrium; as a result, his thinking is distorted and cannot be depended on.

To respect the judgment of a depressed individual and yield to it is wrong. Such a person is subject to the most treacherous pessimism at times. He (or she) will look frantically for any way out of despair and bring up the most far-fetched causes for it, telling you with passionate conviction that the only thing he needs to get well is to liquidate his business and thus be released from the burden of it; or to quit his job; or to sell his house and move to a new community; or to divorce his spouse. Then, and then only, will the depression go away. Should the family be duped into concurring with such judgments they will soon discover that the depression has not lifted automatically, but has worsened, because now, in addition to being ill, the person has cut himself adrift from all his moorings. Invariably, when he recovers from the depression he cries: "Why did you let me do that? You knew I was sick . . . you should have stopped me even if you had to put a halter on me."

What to Do About the Poor Judgment

The person who has gone through several episodes of depression and has gained insight learns not to trust his own judgment when he is ill. No matter what his field of work is, he will take the prudent course and absent himself from the need to make decisions for the time being. But this is not usual. Generally, it is the family who must take over. This is why your intervention may be crucial when your relative is depressed. I can understand that you may be loath to assume this responsibility. But if you are afraid of it and sit back, hoping that he will be inspired to cope with his problems himself, you are doing him an injustice. Whatever his judgment dictates at this point can end as a grievous error which may oppress him for years to come.

For example, the decisions of a twenty-four-year-old mother who suffered a post-partum depression (untreated) were accepted at face value by her parents. That her judgments were faulty due to an unseen depression never occurred to them. Her husband, a weak, unintelligent man, not prepared for marriage, was ready to abandon her. When his wife withdrew into her depression he seized the opportunity to get a divorce. Apathetic one moment and agitated the next, she gave her consent to his demand for custody of the child. Her parents demurred, but she forbade them to interfere. "Stay out of it," she shrieked, "I know just what I'm doing." Intimidated, they dropped their objections. Without medical care it was almost a year before she emerged from her depression, but once the shock of losing her baby struck her she relapsed and continued to teeter back and forth on the brink of mental illness until it was recognized that she required treatment.

It cost another year of legal wrangling before the child was returned to her custody. Her sick judgment had set off a chain of events which could not be reversed until everyone, including the court, recognized that her decisions had been incompetent and should never have been respected at the time.

In another situation, a forty-eight-year-old post-office clerk who was severely diabetic and required daily injections of insulin was afflicted with his second episode of manic-depressive disorder. This time he also showed paranoid delusions (see Chapter 9) and refused his insulin injections, insisting that they were being given him "to dry up my brains." No one in the family dared cross him, but after he went into severe diabetic coma he was rushed to the hospital as an emergency. Close to death, he needed two weeks of intensive medical care to stabilize his diabetic condition. This gross physical trauma could have been averted had his aberrated judgment been overruled.

The families of patients who go through repeated depressions learn from bitter experience. I recall one man who became severely depressed every four or five years. He owned and operated a small dry-goods store in a good location, and from it he derived a comfortable living. During his first two depressions he developed typical ideas of unworthiness, guilt, and self-depreciation. Both times he sold his store at the beginning of his breakdown, each time for a fraction of its worth, convinced that the pressure of work had caused his emotional disorder. On recovery he recognized that his judgment had been poor and he bought back, but at a premium.

However, with the third depression, his wife lost no time when he began to talk of selling again, "this time for good." She promptly arranged for someone else to manage the shop. Meanwhile, she also obtained immediate psychiatric care, instead of waiting and hoping that the depression would evaporate of its own accord.

When judgment is warped, the primary need is to protect the interests of the depressed person. Not that this is always easy. He (or she) will make outrageous objections and resort to epithets and threats. You may be told that you are ruining him financially or socially and butting in where you are not wanted. Nevertheless, this is the time to stick to your guns, because once the patient is well you will be thanked for rescuing him from himself. "I guess I didn't realize what I was doing. Imagine what a fix I'd be in now if not for you." I have heard this sort of thing scores of times.

Agitation

With this symptom the person may be overactive in varying degrees but restlessness and tension are predominant. He or she may pace the floor, fidget, go from room to room, stare unseeingly out of the window, try to sit for a while, or jump up and start on things that are never finished. I daresay that you would describe your relative, in his over-all performance at this time, as "very nervous."

Such persons, depending on their degree of agitation, speak of their "insides churning," of "an ogre in my tank," of the peculiar sensation that gnaws at the pit of the stomach, and of an "iron band" clamped across the chest. Ordinary house noises set their teeth on edge. They may not listen when you try to converse with them, because they are too busy with their nervousness to notice anything else. Their agitation seems never to cease. They ask for relief and for hope—"When will I get better? Do you think I will ever be well again?"

THINKING MAY BE AGITATED TOO.   I wonder if you have ever imagined the tumultuous ideas that occupy the minds of depressed persons who are extremely agitated. They often look and act as if their thoughts torture them. Guilt, futility, anger, panic, resentment, and the awful sense of a hovering fate may riddle these thoughts. The mental distress can mount to such severe proportions that they may become desperate to dislodge it by whatever means comes to hand. (See last section in this chapter, "Rising Tension . . . A Warning Sign.")

What to Do When the Person Is Agitated

Your natural reaction will be to divert him from his agitation. He may be droning on endlessly about the worries that beleaguer him: maybe he should have taken that job offer of fifteen years ago; look how much better off he would be today. Or, why did he do his son so terrible an injustice—why didn't he insist that the boy go to law school? And look how he bungled things by letting his sister marry a man out of her religion. To you, these are all irrelevancies and you may want to argue their pros and cons, suggesting that perhaps the job would have worked out badly, that his son might not have done well as a lawyer, that his sister's choice of a husband was none of his business to start with, and anyhow all his self-recriminations are unwarranted.

I suggest that you not embark on such a fruitless course. In the depression, his guilt feelings are justified and his worries valid—*to him*. His disturbed nervous system is causing this somber view of life, and debating the matter will not change the thought connections in his brain one iota.

On the constructive side, however, there is much you can do to moderate the agitation.

Bring him (or her) into a quiet room with you, soften the lights, and tune down the radio to background music.

Keep visitors away; give comforting but reassuring solitude. Such measures remove excess stimulation which might tend to increase the tension. In short, create an oasis of tranquillity and mental calm.

Address him softly and slowly. Explain that you know of the many vexations that rush through his mind. (If he is extremely agitated he may, at least once, snap at you in anger and gesture you to vanish. Do not be disheartened. This will change.) Make it clear that you know exactly how he feels and that you are equally certain of his eventual recovery. *But add: How much better it would be if he could tell you about it himself.*

Slowly, he will learn to trust you and spill out all his misery and mental pain, if not that day then the next. Once he does, his inner turmoil is relieved and it subsides. You will then find him amenable to your offer of comfort on the next time around. What is more important, he will fall in with your plans to distract him from himself.

Depending on the hour and other circumstances, see if you can arrange some mild pastimes with him—a slow saunter through the park; a shopping trip (short and uncomplicated); a brief visit with a close friend; a movie (especially a matinee in an uncrowded theater). Or even a prosaic activity that works off the steam of agitation—anything from rearranging a kitchen cupboard or cleaning out an attic to rubbing down the car. Do not expect the agitation to leave for good, then and there. It is bound to recur as long as the nervous system is disordered. But when you bring composure you equalize the person's nervous function and roll back the depression, if only fractionally.

I know of a wife who is devoted to her husband way beyond the call of marital duty. One might call him a "captain of industry," but he is subject to moderately severe depressions at intervals. With the help of psychotherapy and drugs, his low moods ultimately clear up. However, when depressed, his most difficult symptom is agitation. In his last episode his wife followed some of the suggestions I have just outlined. She did more, though. Knowing that in this phase he tended to be wound up and to push beyond his energy limits, she began to make some firm "dates" with him outside the office two or three afternoons a week.

At first he grumbled. How could he leave his desk with a crush of work on it? And what of the business contacts he had to see at lunch every day? She refused all excuses, and he agreed "just this once."

The "once" has developed into a part of his routine. Before meeting him, she makes notes of gossipy bits that he might enjoy and combs the newspapers for any items that will catch his interest. Luncheon is drawn out to an hour and a half or two. They stroll a little; on occasion they do some shopping to replenish his wardrobe or they stop in at a museum. She keeps him amused with her anecdotes and involved with *her* (instead of himself only). The interludes are now welcome respites to him. With this adjunctive help in tempering the pressures and the tension to which he is prone, his agitation is held to a minimum through each episode until he is feeling normal again.

Crying and Tearfulness

These two symptoms are common signs of depression. The person who is slowed down will cry gently or go off in a corner and sob to himself. He wants to be left to his own lonely tears.

The agitated person may cry spontaneously, often with an element of hysteria. No consolation you offer will stop the crying. In severe agitation he will wail of his guilt between sobs and reiterate, "I'm no good and never will be," or, "I'd be better off dead. I've failed you, I've failed you!" He may even beg you to kill him and put him out of his misery. And this is not mere attention-gathering. The tearfulness is genuine. It expresses a despairing, unhappy state.

In some depressed conditions, crying will not come easily. The person may say, "I want to cry but I can't. I know that if I could, I would feel better."

How to Deal with the Crying

If you are a soft, sentimental person you probably cannot "stand" to see your sick relative cry. It breaks you up. However, where tears serve as a necessary emotional outlet they can be encouraged. In a grief reaction especially, when the person has suffered a loss, crying comes easily and produces a healthy release for pent-up emotion. Momentarily, the tears wash away the depressed feelings.

However, when an exhausting bout of tearfulness continues on and on with extreme agitation, breast beating, and self-abuse, it is time for you to call a halt. Let me show you how how to terminate almost any flood of tears by the correct use of a psychologic device.

First, sit directly in front of your relative and say, "Go on crying if you want to, but face me. Look into my eyes." It is a simple fact that no one can sustain crying while gazing straight into another's eyes. If the person does what you ask, his tears will stop. Not right away; he may continue to cry and avert his gaze. Take his hands in yours and again coax him to look at you. You may have to repeat the request several times, but at last he will turn and fix his eyes on you, almost hypnotically. The flow of tears then trickles to an end, and the person may begin to talk about the things that give him mental pain.

Every time you shorten such a spell of crying you stem the waste of energy and give the person a chance to preserve his or her stamina in fighting the depression.

Anticipatory Anxiety

Depressed persons function within a narrow margin of emotionality. Their thinking is blocked, and any occurrence alarms them. Everything is fraught with worry about the next event in life. We call this *anticipatory anxiety*. You cannot appeal to the person's "good sense," because within a severe depression he is too regressed and his normal quota of intelligence does not serve him.

To expect him to plan or prepare for activity at a later date is unrealistic. He finds it difficult to think this far. His curtailed and inhibited nervous function blurs his perceptions of tomorrow. Sometimes he cannot project his feelings even to the next hour, so much do his miseries, obsessions, guilts, and mental pain of the moment engross him.

Thus, if a future event is thrust at your relative for consideration, it may jar his nervous system because he cannot cope with the effort to envision it. In his present state, anything *ahead,* however innocuous to you, portends "trouble."

How You Deal with Anticipatory Anxiety

You can often circumvent the person's forebodings by confining him or her to *the present only.*

For example, if you mention that you are planning a vacation for him on his recovery, he will moan, "No, no, I'll never be well enough to enjoy it . . . leave me alone with that kind of talk." Defer this discussion. Wait until he is ready. Or if you announce that a favorite niece is coming to visit next week he may get excited and start to fume. How are you going to entertain her? Maybe she'll expect to be waited on. And he may add belligerently, "I don't like her and I never did" (not so) and continue to work himself into a lather (because in his agitation he may be spoiling for a fight anyway). Mention it just before the visitor is due to arrive. This prevents prior anxiety from accumulating and once she walks in he is in better condition to give her a more gracious welcome.

In another instance someone may raise the subject of a gala family occasion a few weeks hence in the naïve belief that the prospect will cheer the emotional invalid. One depressed patient of mine who was informed that he and the family were going to a wedding commented sourly, "Why do they have to get married? There's enough trouble in the world." Omit any reference to such affairs in advance. The gayer and more festive they sound, the more your relative contrasts them with his own joyless state. When the day arrives he may be rid of his depression and glad to attend. If not, a wedding is no place for him.

Relatives constantly make this error of confronting the depressed person with the future. If you were an invisible witness, you would find it hard to credit the tug of war that they set in motion by pure mischance. They will discuss the matter and harry the patient with it for weeks. They stir up the household as if life or death were at stake. They work the depressed person into a stew without the faintest glimmering of the havoc wrought. If they would just keep quiet until the appropriate time the problem would resolve itself. With a depressed person, stick to the axiom: "Deal only with the present. Don't test tomorrow."

Fear of Being Alone

It is disconcerting to see this condition in persons who were always courageous and venturesome in their undertakings.

Suddenly, such an individual becomes timid about riding in buses, through tunnels, or over bridges, if unaccompanied. Before, he (or she) may have driven to work each morning. Now he falters at taking the car around the corner. Irrational fright clutches him when caught in a crowded store or theater unless a companion is along. Even a change in the weather and a mild rain can induce terrifying fears of lightning, thunder, and of threatened floods and cyclones. Any experience at all will, in the patient's own words, "scare me out of my wits if I'm by myself."

I knew a bustling housewife who handled a large household and had it running on greased wheels. She was wholly capable. But when she became depressed she telephoned her husband constantly to quiet her fears. Or she implored her mother to stay and keep her company. She was afraid to enter the kitchen alone to prepare a meal. Going to the market became a major expedition. In short, if this woman or someone like her were your relative you might recognize her depression when you saw that she was so fearful of being alone that she could not discharge the very responsibilities that she had always assumed, as a matter of course.

What to Do When the Person Is Fearful of Being Alone

This fear means that the individual is in panic.

Here, encouragement alone will not help. Provision must be made *for someone to stay with the patient.* A tight-lipped or bickering relative will not do, no matter how close the family tie; better a neighbor or friend who can be counted on to be amiable and stanch through the person's racking moments of crisis when fear gets the upper hand; who will join companionably in small chores, distract him or her with talk of local events, and give assurance in a kind and easy manner.

The eminent Dr. Horsley Gantt of Johns Hopkins University has demonstrated that a dog conditioned to be fearful and tense will evidence a very high blood pressure and a rapid pulse rate in the throes of anxiety. But let his master come into the room and gentle him and his fears subside immediately. The blood pressure and pulse rate return to normal, as a result of what Dr. Gantt calls "the effect of person."

This is true of the human being too. Nothing can substitute for the effect of person on person when there are fears. Being within telephone distance is not enough. Neither are morning goodbyes with words of devotion and encouragement. The physical, live presence of another is the only help for this condition until the fearridden person is back into emotional control.

Fears of Death

These fears usually stem from the depressed person's morbid ideas about himself and the feeling that he is alone with his suffering. He is afraid that if "they let me" he will act on his impulse to die and kill himself. But here is his conflict: he does not really want to die; he wants to be rid of the ghastly premonitions about his own death, yet he also feels that he must court death as the only relief from the premonitions.

Moreover, in the confusion engendered by his death thoughts, he may become obsessed with fantasies of murder, social violence, and other disasters that he hears about. This magnifies his fear of dying, but it also combines with a fear of causing someone else's death. As the obsessions expand, he grows more positive that he is going to injure or kill a person close and dear to him. Ten to twenty times a day he asks: "Why am I so scared all the time? What's wrong with me? Maybe I'll be arrested for a crime. How will I get better? When will I be rid of this torture? Am I going crazy?"

To you, fright of this kind may seem ludicrous. Where is the foundation in reality for it? Your relative is in sound physical health. Why should he die? And how could he, such a mild, considerate person, possibly hurt someone?

What to Do When the Person Has Fears of Death

These fears are paradoxes, as you may have gathered from the last page or so. However, if all you plan to do is tell the person how nonsensical they are, save your breath. To one who is assailed by death fears, they are never foolish. Their torment is real. Moreover, when you dismiss the subject lightly you turn the person's thoughts inward, and he or she begins to wonder what awful thing you are hiding that may *cause* his death.

Instead, offer the truth. Explain that the depression is an illness and, because of it, his nervous function is out of kilter. Most persons can accept the fact that their nerves may be frayed. Then name the fear for what it is— *an obsession*. Point out that a depressed state with sadness and low spirits might generate obsessions of death in anyone. Remind him of the absence of death thoughts when he was not ill; explain how his ruminations coincided with the appearance of the depression; and assure him that these obsessive thoughts will vanish when the depression is gone.

Once your relative can accept this concept he will gradually move away from the over-all fear of dying and begin to objectify it as the obsession that you have described—a symptom that he can live with for hours at a time in the knowledge that one day, like a cramp or a headache, it will disappear. I have even known patients to develop curiosity about the nature of obsessions and to read and learn about them further.

When your relative relapses (as he or she will), you may go through another stretch of nursing him through the fears. But each time they will lessen. In stressing that his fears of death are obsessive thoughts, you are telling him the truth, and the truth in this case conveys a diagnostic reality to which he can cling. It is the best antidote to hysterical dreads.

Rising Tension with Loss of Hope: A Warning Sign

These symptoms go hand in hand with many fears; the tension often shoots up to hazardous levels. Although more obvious in an agitated depression, they can also appear in the slowed-down type.

The person's appearance and general behavior reflect the tension and loss of hope. His face is gaunt, his mouth drawn; there is profuse sweating. He is restless, stubborn, negativistic, taut, and irritable. He may cry out, "I'm a lost soul. There's no future for me. It's all so useless. Why don't you put me in a box and get it over with?" He is telling you that the depression is now so unbearable that he is approaching the breaking point. He is signifying his suicidal intent.

What to Do About the Rising Tension and Loss of Hope

In Chapter 2, I gave you the first cardinal rule about the risk of suicide—to be with the person *at all times* until the danger passes. This is imperative for someone whose mounting tension has reached a peak.

Usually, the determined suicide will not make the attempt while in the company of someone he knows. He waits until he is alone. (This drive to self-destruction is unlike the neurotic suicidal gesture, which is generally carried out on the spur of *impulsive* behavior and even though others are present. See Chapter 5.)

I recall a husband who hoodwinked his wife into going out to buy him some milk and then went to the roof and jumped off. She had left the house "for a few moments only." In another case, a woman urged her husband to "take a breather" at a neighbor's house for a short time and when he returned she had swallowed a fatal quantity of sleeping pills.

I cite these instances because when I say that someone must stay with the intensely depressed person at all times I really mean *twenty-four hours a day and each of the sixty minutes of every hour.* If the drive to suicide is fiercely malignant, other precautions too must be taken. The patient cannot be alone while bathing or performing any other bathroom function. Certainly he or she must not be allowed to fasten the door even if it means removing the lock temporarily. Keep all sleeping pills and other potentially harmful medications in your custody; and if you live in an apartment building stay especially alert to the possibility of a jump from the window.

Obviously, you and everyone else in the family need sleep and privacy at times; therefore such tight security will entail the help of several family members and possibly a nurse or aide. The person who is fixed on suicide usually does yield his will to another who tries to stop the self-destructive act. But the protector *must be there in the presence of the depressed individual.*

It goes without saying that if the suicidal determination is beyond your control your relative must be hospitalized (see Chapter 16), because no amount of home care will entirely safeguard him in his present state.

HOW DO I KNOW IF MY RELATIVE MEANS IT?

We have no infallible test for the intent of suicide. One must develop an ear for the message that the depressed person tries to get across.

For example, if he or she announces, and perhaps with no theatrics, "I'm going to walk into the river and just let myself go down . . . it's the only way out," do not shrug this off as an "absurd notion" or a bluff of some kind. Such words and their manner denote that the person believes he is undone, beyond remedy, and has a premeditated plan that he will carry out.

However, if he wails disconsolately, "I wish the earth

would open and swallow me up. Why can't something happen to take me out of all this misery," then *at that moment,* the function is passive and retarded. The person is not *planning* anything. He would just like it to occur. His suicide is not an imminent threat, because of his lethargy. Nevertheless, this individual must be watched closely as he improves. Given a bit more energy and not quite enough relief from the mental pain, he might make the fatal move. This is why it is mandatory to consider most depressed persons as potentially self-destructive (whether driven to it by rising tension or provoked to it by an impulse), until they are well along to full recovery.

CHAPTER EIGHT

Slowed-Down Symptoms and What You Do About Them

SINCE SLOWING down is such an important and obvious symptom of some depressions I am devoting a chapter to it. Slowing down is noted in:

1. Expressions of boredom.
2. Complaints of being tired and weak.
3. Sluggishness of thoughts, feelings, and activities.

The Person Seems Overcome by Boredom

Everyone feels bored at times—the elderly, younger adults, adolescents, and children. Should the boredom last a day or two, or even a week, it might be normal under most conditions. For instance, after a vacation at a summer camp with planned activities and a high excitement level, children return home and find "nothing to do." They are out of sorts. They mope and sulk. Their boredom represents a mild depression, which usually disappears once school starts. An adult too, after working on a project over a period of time, experiences a letdown phase when the task is completed with "nothing new ahead." This too is mild depression, which disappears when fresh activity arises.

However, a relative of yours may seem continually bored, and you may conclude that he or she is "spoiled," lazy, or unwilling to be useful. "Why can't he do something about himself?" his family and friends impatiently ask. They do not realize that, while there are plenty of goals for the person to reach for, he or she cannot do so, because ability to mobilize the self to *act* is absent. The so-called boredom, then, signifies a retarded depression, which no one is recognizing.

Complaints of Being Tired and Weak

Your relative may fret because the energy to take what is required of him has dwindled away. If you try to console him by pointing out that he is managing most of his usual tasks, he will reply that he is doing it under great strain, that the least exertion, even to dress, exhausts him, because the tiredness never leaves. And as you take a closer look you see that fatigue *is* ever present, no matter how much rest he gets. There may be other minor complaints, but the symptom of tiredness is foremost.

Slowed-Down Thoughts, Feelings, and Activities

When *thinking* is slowed down you will notice that, if you speak rapidly or normally to the person, he or she will not gather what is said. You must talk deliberately in long-drawn-out syllables (as if using a foreign language). The patient confirms your observation; he tells you that his thoughts are slow in coming, that he cannot think fast enough to perceive what you are saying.

A slow-down in *feelings* may take the form of apathy, or "nothingness." The person indicates that neither pleasure nor pain exists for him. He cannot respond to you, because of a feeling of "numbness." (It may surprise you to know that apathy—that is, the absence of feeling—can be as agonizing as pain itself. Sometimes the person wishes that death would wipe it out.)

Slowed-down *activity* is seen in over-all body movement. The person unwinds slowly from a chair and shuffles across the room. He or she even speaks lethargically. Sometimes a sentence is never completed; it trails off because it seems to require too much effort to finish it. This retarded movement (slowed motor activity) reveals the depressed condition. The internal functions also decelerate. The person digests slowly and complains of biliousness, "gas," and constipation.

When such slowing becomes extreme it borders on *catatonia* (lowered muscle tone). It is an effort for the person to chew, and he lets the food remain in his mouth. He may sit in a chair and stare all day, not changing position, and allowing the bladder to become so full and distended that it causes severe suffering. At this point he may be too retarded even to complain of it.

Should this stage worsen, he or she becomes *totally catatonic*. Catatonia is the lowest level of conscious being in the retarded behavior of depression. The catatonic person will seem reduced almost to stupor. If placed in one position he will stay that way until moved to another. He will not swallow, and saliva drools from his mouth. His gaze is fixed. He does not eat or empty his bladder or bowels. If you talk to him you will receive no answer nor any sign that you were heard. There is consciousness, yes, but so depressed that nothing whatsoever stimulates it.

How You Help the Person Who Is Slowed Down

Whether he or she is bored or chronically fatigued, or whether all the thinking, feeling, and behavior are dragging, use this major stratagem:

*Get the Person Stimulated and Mobilized**

Any kind of slowing requires this approach. The person must be directed *away* from the illness and reanimated *to live with purpose.* You may reply, "I tried doing that but it didn't work." Then perhaps your method was wrong and other approaches were needed. For example, here is one.

Probe for a Spark of Interest

It may be just a gleam in your relative's eye, but follow it up as a detective would a clue. You *are* the detective here.

---

* None of the following methods of helping the slowed-down person applies to catatonia. I cannot say too strongly that once the person has reached this extreme condition he or she *must be hospitalized.* See Chapter 16.

You may have guessed that your relative is tired because of the depressive boredom, and you are not wrong. They are twin symptoms. The boredom tends to be silent. The tiredness and weakness are voiced. But for practical purposes you treat them as one complaint. In short, you must find ways to "recharge" the depressed person.

Do not start by inquiring what interests him or her. The answer will be "nothing." If you ask, "Would you like to go to a movie, bingo game, boxing match, night club, fashion show, et cetera," you will receive a no to each one. Instead, take a more circuitous route.

Open a conversation with him, touching on general topics. It may be a monologue for a while, but do not stop. Bring up the day's news or family affairs. Work into some of the things you have been doing, reading about, or would like to do. Enlarge on a subject a bit, such as the educational system, politics, "kooky" fashions, inflation, travel, science, the stock market. Inevitably, you will hit on something that engages his attention. Watch closely for this reaction, no matter how minute it is. Do not pound. Be offhand. But give him the opportunity to respond. When he does, nudge a little to keep him going. Sooner or later he will start to expound on past enthusiasms—or maybe pet peeves. Whatever they are you have succeeded, because the person is talking and renewing his interest in *something*. You have pressed the right button *to counter his chronic inertia* and push him out of his slow-down.

Another way of provoking the spark of interest is to reel off some incorrect details on any given subject. Absurd as this gambit may seem to you, it works. Try to hit on a topic that your relative is more familiar with than you are. And do not be taken aback when he or she suddenly bursts out, "You don't know what you're talking about," then proceeds to correct and enlighten you. You might comment, "I never knew that," and ask some further questions. The part of the person's function that remains normal will force him to rise to the bait and dredge up the facts contained in his memory storehouse. This widens his narrowed attention span. Stimulation has taken over. From there to an interest in other areas is not too long a step. He may then be mobilized into activity of one kind or another.

For example, I once treated a fifty-year-old truck driver who suffered from a chronic retarded depression. He had lost all interest in his work and family, and would sit for hours staring out of the window. He complained of being tired all the time and getting nothing from life. Different relatives would take him out and try to distract him, but he could not wait to get home and sink back into his chair.

One day I was talking with him, seemingly at random, about vacation plans. His memory was jogged and he began to tell me about the family summer cottage at the lake. A stone wall in the driveway needed repair. Mulling this over he wondered aloud if it would ever be fixed. We drifted into the problems of masonry and when he left he said in mild astonishment: "I really enjoyed the visit today, Doc."

It was still early spring and cold, but I persuaded his brother-in-law to drive him up to the cottage on Sunday. After surveying the wall they began to putter around, then to work on it. My patient decided to drive up again the following day and the next. One morning he called—he could not come in that day. Repairing the wall had become a full-time project. He had also noted that the boat dock, pump house, and tool shed needed fixing and he planned to attend to those too. It was not long before his depression lifted and he returned to his regular work.

Such motivations for living exist in everyone, but they must be pinpointed and utilized to stimulate the person back into normal activity again.

Organize a Routine

Slowing down in activity is most apparent in a reactive depression (grief) due to a loss. When you are dealing with this reaction initially, your empathy for the feelings of sadness will be predominant. After a while though, your main task will be to keep the person from drowning in his or her grief.

I recall a young mother who continued to mourn a five-year-old daughter, the youngest of three children, whom she had lost in an automobile accident. The father's sorrow was just as heavy, but cut short by the urgency to return to work and earn a living. Her friends, neighbors, and relatives showered her with attention. They were *too* kind. Each day they trooped in, determined to shield her from her sorrow. They looked after her children, ran the house, shopped, cooked, and cleaned. And when she took to her bed there was always someone to wait on her. She remained immobilized in the grief.

Their fine intentions were not helping one bit, because over-solicitude creates more harm than good. It stretches out the grief and weakens the person's strengths.

One allows a reasonable interval of mourning, to be sure, but after that the depressed person should not be allowed to abdicate his duties indefinitely. He or she must be returned to them. If this seems hard and unfeeling, please believe that it is the only way to rescue the person from despair.

In the case just cited, a relative followed my suggestions. Intead of allowing her sister to languish in bed she routed her out one day. Then she organized the entire household routine, devised a time schedule for it, and hung it on the kitchen wall. The schedule included each of her sister's daily tasks: when to feed the children, clean house, market at the grocery, launder, prepare dinner, do the mending, even when to read or look at TV. For the first few weeks she was on hand to help. When she left, the patient was able to continue on her own. It was this routinization (following the same principles of an organized hospital program) which drew her back to her obligations and into her previously conditioned habits of work. Finally, as her normal proclivities for an orderly, fulfilled life reappeared, she was freed of the depression.

Did she still miss the child she had lost? Without doubt. But as time wore on, the edge of her loss dulled and her response to her family matured again.

This method of routinization is imperative in reactive depression with slow-down. If you can organize the individual into an effective routine, the doctor and/or nature will do the rest.

Draw the Person into Activity with Encouragement

Perhaps the patient is your mother, afflicted with endogenous depression and slowed down in all areas. Unlike the person in a grief reaction, she cannot be organized out of it. (Those in endogenous depressions do not respond to this technique. They would feel cornered and would defy it). Nor will it do to be perfunctory or imperious.

For example, suppose you casually *ask* your mother, "Would you like to go to a movie with me?" Her answer will probably be silence or, "I don't know." She is too listless in her illness to decide what she wants. Unable to deal with her, you may leave abruptly. Or if you announce that you intend to *take* her to a show because you are sick and tired of sitting around listening to her being sorry for herself, she will no doubt refuse and privately think you a selfish, bossy daughter without an ounce of sympathy or understanding. Instead, it is better to "lure" the patient into activity and mobilize her through encouragement.

Try it this way. Explain to her that you realize how much she has suffered (by putting it in the past you suggest that the depression is now behind her), but in your opinion she is entitled to some pleasure in life after all she's gone through. There are still areas of enjoyment for her, maybe not so many as before, but why not take what they offer? And you would like to share them with her.

She will not refute your words, because secretly she too is tired of facing the same four walls and is waiting for your suggestion. Do not expect the miracle of instant response. But she has food for thought and she will chew on it for a while.

Next day you can take a not-too-subtle action. In her hearing, telephone the movie house: "The main feature goes on at eight P.M.? Thank you." And with a glance at her, "We'll be there for it." Now you have set a time and given her some kind of deadline to shoot for. At this point the situation is fluid and fragile. Handle it with care. Do not press. She knows what you are up to and wants to fall in with it. But one false move and it can be spoiled. You have made headway if she does not protest too hard.

Wait until it is time to leave the house, and without comment bring her coat. Do not be surprised if she starts to apply lipstick, fix her hair (don't rush her) and generally primp a bit. You have brought her out of her shell for the first time in six months.

After that you have many alternatives. Next time you might say, "Come out and help me shop for a new outfit. You know I rely on your taste." Even if you do not, she has no intention of disputing it. She wants to believe you, because it gives her the excitement of being needed. From there on continue in a similar encouraging vein at each opportunity—and watch her become a new person again.

Too often, relatives fail in rallying a slowed-down person because they attempt it through arguments, bullying, or sometimes a noble forbearance. None of these yields results.

The same methods can be applied for a depressed father, aunt, uncle, brother, sister, and so on. Use your imagination. One person may respond when you ask him or her to help "mind the store" or office because you are shorthanded. (Whether you are is not important.) For another, an invitation to wait on a booth at the local bazaar may be the thing. I know of a woman who started returning to normal when a job was obtained for her at the "Lost and Found Department for Children" in a park. Or you could persuade the person into helping put together a new hi-fi set. One patient of mine was drawn into splicing the reels of some home movies. On recovery he became an amateur movie enthusiast and wound up with a new career—making film documentaries.

In accepting your encouragement the person is stimulated into enjoying his own potentials again. Be satisfied if he or she merely goes through the motions at first. But as time passes, he is divested of his symptoms, his energy is revived, and as he recovers, he is roused into new activity.

The person in endogenous depression almost always responds to encouragement, especially if you combine it with kindness and the hidden force of suggestion.

CHAPTER NINE

Delusional Symptoms and What You Do About Them

PECULIAR AND bizarre thoughts often accompany depression, thoughts which are out of keeping with the person's former thinking. They are *delusions*.

What Is Delusional Thinking?

Simply stated, a delusional thought is a fixed, false belief. The person cannot be talked out of it; this is why it is called "fixed." Also, it does not conform with reality and is therefore considered "false."

The delusional thoughts of a depressed person may perplex you. A woman who brought her husband to me summed up her bewilderment in this way. "He says all these funny things that just aren't true, Doctor. I know they're not. And he twists everything *I* say. I think he must be out of his mind."

But even when family members realize that their relative is delusional they sometimes recoil and want to walk away from the problem, because they feel helpless to deal with it. Yet nothing shows more glaringly that the sad person is mentally ill and needs special care than the appearance of delusions. They signify a danger to him and to others and make psychiatric consultation imperative. Only treatment directed at restoring the normal brain process can *erase* delusions.

However, at the same time, the patient will require expert family management. Before I discuss the delusions that are encountered most often in depression and how you handle them, I will specify two general rules for you to follow unfailingly in all delusional states.

Rule One: Do Not Try to Reason with the Person

I have known husbands and wives to spend hour after hour trying to convince the depressed spouse that his or her delusion had not a grain of merit or reality to it. Sincere as such efforts may be, they are a waste of time and devotion.

The delusional person is one whose mentation is impaired because the chemical imbalances of his brain function preclude a normal flow of energy to the circuits. Thus, his behavior is based on warped perceptions of reality. So long as the chemical imbalances remain, the delusional ideas will persist. Striving to alter them by reasoning will just inflame the person's thoughts; it provokes and extends the delusional process, because his disordered thinking apparatus cannot tolerate the strain of rational argument. The crux of the matter is this: when you attempt to force reasoning on him you are, in effect, attacking his delusional orientation and this frightens him. You are then the "enemy" whom he must vanquish at any cost. He becomes obdurate. Thus, in reasoning with him you lose the battle before you begin.

Rule Two: Stop Him or Her from Acting on the Delusion

Never let the delusional person "act out" his unreal thoughts. The behavior of such persons is often very strange when they respond to their perverse ideas. If they keep silent about the thoughts, or just ramble on harmlessly, they will not become embroiled in difficulties. But when they act on them anything can happen. This is where the family must be alert, anticipate the acting-out, show their strength, and assume responsibility.

Paranoid Delusions

Paranoia (par-a-*noy*-a) means distorted thinking. In most cases the twisted thoughts become evident when the person thinks that somebody or something is trying to harm him. Your relative may begin to voice suspicions of everyone. You know that neither you nor anyone else wants to injure or molest him, but you cannot make him believe this.

A typical paranoid delusion occurs when the person says, "The astronauts are sending secret waves to destroy me," or when he or she declares that "the radio announcer is broadcasting coded messages that are telling the whole world filthy lies about me." Another paranoid delusion is exemplified by a man or woman accusing the spouse of infidelity when the charge is clearly absurd. I have seen depressed men and women in their seventies and eighties accuse the spouse (same age) of "carrying on all day and night right under my eyes," with the next-door neighbor (age thirty). Or a delusional college student will declare that his chemistry instructor is tampering with his equipment so that he will fail his course; a truck driver will believe that everyone on the road is plotting to push him into a ditch; or a secretary will tell her boss to stop tapping her home phone to learn her intimate secrets. The delusion of being robbed is also common, and the person who harbors it may refuse to budge from the house, in order to stay home and trap the burglars.

The paranoid person bends the facts out of shape in order to justify his or her position. One woman suffering from the hot flushes and depression associated with change of life complained about the heat in the apartment. She taxed her husband and the superintendent of the building with scheming to aggravate her flushes and to "do away" with her. Her husband shut off all the radiators, but she triumphantly pointed to the wallpipes which remained warm. When she was told that it was impossible to control them she shook her head wisely. "Oh no, I was right. I knew all along you would find some way to turn on the heat to make me suffer."

Paranoia is also expressed when the patient refuses medication because he believes that it is poison and the person administering it wants to kill him. He may refuse food, too, for the same reason. One of my severely depressed patients declined to eat in anyone's home except her own, because she was certain that even her married daughter wanted to "exterminate" her.

How to Help When There Are Paranoid Delusions

In paranoia especially, the end results can be disastrous if the acting-out is not stopped. When the paranoid individual writes obscene, accusatory, or threatening letters to strangers and those in public office, make sure that you intercept them before they are mailed. Or a man's paranoia may instill in him the belief that his wife is out to destroy him. If he is not controlled, he may beat her so severely as to cripple or kill her. In another case a young woman may fancy that every man she sees is making a sexual approach. While riding in a bus she accuses an innocent passenger of assault and demands his arrest. The possibility of such acts must be detected in advance to forestall the publicity, the embarrassment, and the legal mess that ensue. The best way to avoid them, of course, is to seek professional advice once you recognize the delusions and realize that they are symptoms of a disturbed emotional state.

The paranoid person who mistrusts everybody is usually one who has felt cheated of a fair share of affection in life. Conversely, he may also be an individual who has never learned to give of himself. Generally, then, such a person is not exactly the most lovable type in the world. Nevertheless, it is remarkable how an angry and agitated paranoid who is depressed will respond to demonstrations of love and kindness. For example, if the sick person is your relative and you take the trouble to convey that you hold him dear and because of this you want him to be well and free of depressive pain, watch him melt and then struggle to react to you in kind.

So keep a spare smile around for him, exert your charm, and win him over with it. When you see that your endearments reduce the anger and distrust which exhaust his energies, and bring him that much closer to recovery, I am sure you will agree that it is reward enough for expending a small supply of your warmth and affection on him.

Delusions of Guilt and Unworthiness

In several places I have indicated that guilt pervades many kinds of depression; that in one form or another the person's behavior tells you that he believes retribution to be his just due for his misdeeds. However, in delusions the guilt and unworthiness are based in *unreality*. They are fixed, distorted ideas, and their content is inappropriate and false.

I recall a woman of sixty-two, known for her exemplary life, who developed intense guilt in a severe depression when she believed that at age twelve she had stolen some rosary beads from her aunt. (The real culprit was her cousin, but now, in her illness, she had identified the thief as herself.) One young matron, when depressed, wept over the mortal sin of her infidelities (they were all illusory), thus expressing a delusional guilt which sometimes emerges from recollections of masturbation in childhood. Another patient "confessed" that he had falsified his books for years and cheated his partner. The latter testified that the records were accurate and the patient had always leaned over backwards to give a meticulous accounting of their funds. Nevertheless, the patient could speak of nothing but the horrible swindle that he had perpetrated; in his own mind he was criminally guilty and unworthy of living.

THE MOST MORAL FEEL GUILTIEST: You may find it strange that the person who feels most guilty when depressed is one who has always been most straitlaced. In Chapter 5 you encountered this individual whose holier-than-thou-ness makes everyone squirm and whose rigid moral and ethical codes are a byword. If your relative is this kind of person you will be rocked off your feet when he proclaims his guilts.

Let me clarify this for you. In such cases, the depression has undermined the strength of the person's inflexible value judgments. These judgments have acted as his psychologic defenses. Now, in his illness, they are shattered and he laments his condition. "Why did this happen to me?" he cries, unable to condone his loss of emotional control. In addition, the chemical brain imbalances that I mentioned to you earlier in this chapter are inducing aberrations in his thinking. Thus, he ruminates delusionally that since depression is a bad feeling he must have done something bad to deserve it. Before long he invents some flaw in his moral rectitude to explain his illness, and the delusions now expand into a full-blown pattern of guilt.

THE DEMAND FOR PUNISHMENT: A very real danger here is the person's need to atone for his "evildoing" to expiate his sins. He believes that the mental pain is not enough punishment. Maybe he should die. And with this he abases himself and weeps. The following excerpt is verbatim from a patient's record: "I'm no good. I'm not worthy of your respect. I don't deserve all your consideration and kindness. I've let you down and made a botch of everything. You should turn your back on me and not care what happens. You've got to make me pay for my sins, you've got to."

Since family members or friends do not unleash the punishment he demands, the delusions of guilt and the rising tension that follows may drive him toward redemption through suicide. A patient of mine who had unsuccessfully made a suicidal attempt pleaded for injections of "strong stuff—a large overdose" that would kill him. In his delusional guilt he welcomed treatment, hoping that he would die of it because he was not worth inhabiting the world any longer. On recovering, he could not recall this in the least. When he learned of it he smiled, politely incredulous.

How to Help When There Are Delusions of Guilt and Unworthiness

Delusions of guilt can be quieted only if you take a position of absolute authority; that is to say, you tell your relative that he has forgiveness and therefore you forbid him to feel guilty any more. It must be put as categorically as this, because your purpose here, primarily, is to release him from guilt and thereby from the agitation.

Such an approach is especially effective when the person believes that he or she has failed you and is oppressed by shame for it. You cannot be hesitant with your authority, because the depressed person will sense it and discount your ability to absolve him. Thus, it may be necessary to implement your forgiveness by explaining that you have transferred the blame to yourself and are going to shoulder it for him. This expedient also holds good if he thinks that he has failed or harmed someone else or even himself. Since we are dealing with guilt for events *that never occurred,* you are free to use any device that will calm him. He will gladly accept your power to forgive; more than anything at this time he wants your magic words of absolution. Speak them resolutely and note the relief they bring. Even if you get but the shadow of a smile in return, you will know that you have made a dent in his depressive condition.

Delusions of unworthiness, unlike loss of self-esteem (Chapter 7), are also impossible to resolve through reasoning.

In loss of self-esteem the person comprehends reality, can put himself in perspective, and can modify his views. Though depressed, he is fully oriented. He responds to the reasoning process and to logical thinking.

However, delusions of unworthiness are rooted in *unreality* and are fixed by distorted orientation and judgment. Nevertheless, they must be dealt with in order to relieve the pain, bewilderment, and despair that they generate.

For example, a young college professor who was *summa cum laude,* fully qualified, and rated highly by his students and faculty, became depressed and actively delusional. "My whole life is a fiasco," he wept. "I don't amount to a grain of sand. . . . I ought to be dead." He felt unworthy of his appointment and certain that he should never have been entrusted with it; it must have been given him only because of his father's influence. (The latter, a cabdriver who had worked hard to finance his son's education, and with no pretensions to "contacts" in the academic world, was dumbfounded and could not account for the patient's statements.)

In dealing with such delusions your most valuable instrument, apart from psychiatric care, is the *enforcement of reality.* The substance of facts, and facts only, must be emphasized, kept in the foreground, and the person must be steered back to them at all times. This young man was exposed to steady, unrelenting reminders of the work he had put into his career, and of the position he had attained through it, together with assurance that whatever honors he had achieved were rightfully earned. He was confronted with the fellowships he had won, the commendations he had received, the brilliance of his Ph.D. thesis, the offers of other universities, and the book he had published which had brought him so much critical acclaim. In short, he was kept "busy" with this information. No attempt was made to reason him out of the delusional story of his father's influence. Whenever he returned to it, a diversion was created until it was forgotten.

One day, after several weeks of treatment, he expressed surprise on realizing that the person whose many accomplishments he was discussing was himself. Not long after that he reentered the world of reality on a full-time basis.

It is destructive to fall in with a person's delusional ideas of unworthiness merely because it is easier to nod and "agree." This fortifies the abnormal thinking and helps him retreat deeper into unreality. However, mark the distinction here: You do not *argue* with these delusions (remember Rule One) or try to show the person his faulty logic (as in loss of self-esteem). Instead, you focus his or her attention on the record of indisputable fact. The delusions are set aside as irrelevant and replaced by actuality. As the patient begins to improve with psychiatric treatment, the program of reality in which he has been steeped also takes effect and modifies his thinking. The delusions that harass him are finally eliminated.

Delusions of Poverty and Nihilism

These delusions are, in effect, the farthest reaches of unworthiness. The depressed person will believe that he possesses nothing or consists of nothing. He feels canceled out by impoverishment or nonexistence.

In *delusions of poverty* the person is convinced that he is bankrupt and desperately poor. He will say that he owns nothing and feels lucky just to have the clothes on his back. The discrepancy is especially marked if you know that your relative is financially secure. No matter what documents you bring out he will assert that his home does not belong to him and must be someone else's. If you produce bank books and bonds in his name he will be puzzled but still reiterate that they are not his. He will even disclaim his social security income, insist that he is not entitled to it, and that the government has made a mistake.

Nihilism (*ny*-ill-izm) is an extension of the poverty delusion. It may be partial or total in the patient's denial of existence. He or she believes that "everything is dead and gone. It's useless and dried up. The world is empty." He says that he is a corpse, with no stomach, heart, or other internal organs. He will see you and talk with you, but will contend that neither you nor he "is there," and that the surroundings are not there either. To him, everything is vapor and shadows, a complete nullity.

Such delusions rarely contain mental pain, and suicidal thoughts are usually absent. But the conviction of nothingness breeds total regression in the patient.

How to Help When There Are Delusions of Poverty and Nihilism

A *poverty delusion* may drive the person into giving away all of his possessions, since he is certain that they are not his to begin with. Never underestimate the cunning or determination of the delusional person in devising ways and means to gain his ends. He (or she) may talk a lawyer and/or an accountant (who seldom recognize a delusional state) into drawing up papers that will relieve them of all assets and thus permit them to be handed over to others.

It is up to you to break off such a transaction by contacting the lawyer or other parties involved, explaining matters, and stopping the whole dismal farce. In some circumstances it may be necessary to petition the courts to declare your relative incompetent in order to preserve his estate. (See Chapter 18.)

In a *delusion of nihilism* a middle-aged woman I saw could not be budged from the notion that she had no head. Even when she was made to touch or feel it she would say listlessly, "No it's not there. It's gone. Nothing is here. I only feel emptiness." According to her lights, then, since she was extinct, why bother caring for herself in any way?

Here, self-neglect becomes extreme; a relative must take charge and groom and bathe the person as if she were a small, forlorn child. She must be dressed by someone and directed to eat, because her "nothingness" will not ask for food. However, to question the weirdness of her thoughts would be fruitless; to be facetious about them would be needlessly cruel. For the most part they can be ignored. You cannot drive out nihilistic delusions. Only treatment will do that. But protection and nursing care will preserve the patient's body health through the depressive episode, so that when mental stability returns she will be physically well and able to care for herself.

Grandiose Delusions

These symptomatize the high or manic phase of manic-depressive disorders and other endogenous depressions. As I told you in Chapter 3, they may alternate with depression in manic-depressive illness. Grandiose delusions can also indicate delirium in toxic depressive conditions.

Such high moods appear suddenly or develop slowly out of a depression; the person expresses a belief in his own omnipotence and exalted state, declaring himself King, Dictator, Statesman, or God.

How to Help When There Are Grandiose Delusions

Persons with grandiosity are remote from appeals to sober judgment. Nevertheless, they must be prevented from acting rashly on their "wonderful" feelings. Sometimes they charge into wild speculation, organize mammoth parties, contract for large building enterprises, or negotiate the purchase of a fleet of taxis. I have seen these riotous attempts at acting-out in persons of every socioeconomic level. They must be stopped. At the same time, one cannot play games with this condition. Such individuals invariably require commitment to a psychiatric service, and the sooner the better for their health and general welfare.

Religious Delusions

These appear in men and women (mostly the latter) who have felt alone and deserted much of their lives. They have turned zealously to religion as a solace, when belongingness and social or sexual fulfillment passed them by.

Such depressed and delusional persons may plunge into extravagant rituals of penance. Many odd forms of devoutness color their religious delusions, on occasion, that of the "miracle" in which saints appear to the person in a burning bush. Their religious fantasies may not relate to their previous beliefs at all. In the illness, they jumble facts and fancy and they quote the Bible at length (out of context) to prove their sinfulness. Sometimes they roam about and prophesy the Lord's coming vengeance on an iniquitous world.

Religious delusions also show up in young men and women suffering from depressive illness associated with various psychoses. In the elderly person, peculiar or excessive ideas of religion can usually be ascribed to senility.

How to Help When There Are Religious Delusions

When delusional persons, imbued with religious mania, pursue their devotional activities you must keep a tight check on their movements. They may spend interminable hours in some dark recess of a church on their knees, forgetting to eat or to attend to their body wants. If not taken in hand they lose weight, become undernourished and frail, and develop illnesses. Or in accosting strangers with "God's Word" they may encounter the vicious individual who assaults and injures them. Such occurrences can be prevented by making certain that they are not out on the streets alone.

Besides such precautions for their safety, you can administer lavish doses of love and kindness to help make up for the years of loneliness and rejection. This will not change their delusional thoughts, but it will comfort them, will create an inner quiet, and will decrease their need to indulge excessively in ideas of beatitude. For the rest, continued care and sympathetic attention in a companionate environment may be all that are needed to remove their preoccupation with religious fanaticism and to orient them back to reality.

Somatic Delusions

Somatic refers to the *soma*, or body. In depression, it is usually the weak, dependent individual who shows an affinity for somatic delusions. He or she will fix on some organ or body part and believe it to be diseased when it is really normal, or claim that an arm is withering away although it is intact. In another case, the person might think that his nose is being eroded into a smaller version, or that his stomach is shrinking, or that the normal ridge on the gums is cancer of the jaw.

None of these delusional beliefs ever shows any basis in fact except by sheer coincidence.

How to Help When There Are Somatic Delusions

A depressed patient whom I saw had the somatic delusion that she was suffering from a large rectal mass. She frantically tried to rid herself of the nonexistent ailment by taking as many as forty enemas a day, inviting serious body damage. She ignored all reminders that every physical examination had proved negative and that perhaps her thinking was defective. Her self-abuse could not be stopped until the family took direct action by removing the enema equipment and setting up a careful watch to ensure that none was brought in to replace it.

Somatic delusions can reach incredible proportions. I have known more than a few such patients who have insisted on countless examinations with elaborate X-ray and laboratory studies. In some cases one might well ask:

WAS THIS OPERATION NECESSARY?

I remember one woman whose jaw was operated on six

times because she persuaded six different oral surgeons that "a degenerating cyst" was giving her excruciating pain. Numerous others have convinced surgeons that only excision of certain body tissue will eliminate a constant ache that "keeps me in a state of nerves and exhaustion" (depression).

The somatically delusional person can sound very plausible in reporting his or her symptoms. But if he is operated on, the delusion switches to something else, such as "adhesions" (also non-existent) which are "tying my insides in knots."

Repeated medical and surgical checkups that result in "normal findings" will never satisfy the person with somatic delusions or make him recognize that his symptom recital does not hang together. This is why you and your doctor must scotch any contemplated procedure by explaining your relative's mental state to the consultant involved. In short, make sure that no medical or surgical measures are taken, even though in good faith, simply to appease the delusion.

At the same time, psychiatric treatment should be instituted and directed at the primary disorder, the depression itself.

PART TWO

OVERCOMING
DEPRESSION

CHAPTER TEN

Drug Treatment

DRUGS ARE not a recent or a novel development. Over the past centuries, they were given for illness that included symptoms of depression, anxiety, and tension.

More than two thousand years ago Hippocrates prescribed hellebore for the emotionally ill. Before that, the Chinese used ephedrine for nervous disorders. Our medical literature also reports that in many of the older civilizations, opiates, herbs, and other plant and berry extracts were taken for their sedative effects. Interestingly too, the medicine man of primitive cultures used extracts of cocoa leaves, peyote root, and poppy seed for their hallucinogenic effects in counteracting the pain or lethargy of anxiety and depressive states.

Today, most drugs are chemically manufactured synthetics, although some are still extracted from plants and other natural products. However, our current drug armamentarium for treating depression consists largely of compounds and chemicals which were developed in the past thirty years. Most of these were introduced from 1955 on.

I will now familiarize you with the more important ones in general use.

Tranquilizers (Sedatives)

To *sedate* means to soothe or slow any body function. Your doctor may tell you that a drug he is prescribing is a gastric or bowel sedative. He expects it to reduce acid secretions in the stomach or eliminate spasms of the bowel.

Similarly, sedatives are given to lessen excess nervous-system activity and to ease a feeling of tightness or tension in the body, that is, to relax or calm the person.

Tranquilizers, used as sedatives, are among the newer crop of synthetic drugs. Often, they are aimed specifically at reducing the fear, anxiety, or anger that are part of depression. Thus, they are given to augment *antidepressant* medication.

Sleep-Inducing Drugs

The most familiar of these are barbiturates, which became commercially available about the time of World War I. Prior to that, bromides and opiates were the common drafts for sleep. Opiates and other narcotics have quite properly been restricted to medical use by most governments. In recent years, all barbiturates and many new synthetic chemicals have been added to the category of restricted sleeping drugs.

The term *sleeping pill* is sometimes confused with *sedative*. This occurs because most sleep-inducers (medically known as hypnotics) can also be used as sedatives, to ease nervous tension, when the person takes one eighth to one half of the sleeping dose. In reverse, some sedatives (tranquilizers) can be used as sleep-inducers. If you yourself have ever taken a tranquilizer, you probably noticed that it slowed you down and produced some drowsiness.

Stimulant Drugs

These work in an opposite way to tranquilizers by increasing the excitement level of nervous-system activity. Such drugs are meant to promote greater alertness, facilitate easier and quicker responses, sharpen perceptions, and temporarily raise a low or depressed mood. Most stimulants of today are variants of the extracts and synthetic compounds that I mentioned a while back. The most common natural stimulant that you know is *caffein*. It is found in natural form in coffee and tea and as an additive in most "cola" drinks, giving all these beverages the quality of a "pickup."

Specific stimulants or "pep" pills usually contain an

amphetamine. (Although a synthetic, amphetamine bears a close chemical relationship to [1] *ephedrine,* originally from plants; [2] *mescaline,* found in peyote; and [3] *adrenaline,* the body's own powerful stimulant and energizing hormone.) Other synthetic stimulants, not related to caffein or amphetamine, are entirely the products of chemical and biologic research.

Stimulant drugs also serve as appetite killers, that is as *anorexiants.* Those who are overweight take them to suppress the appetite. However, I am inclined to believe that many compulsive eaters who want to control their food intake by using these drugs actually *need the stimulant effect* for a low-grade but *hidden* depression. When this depression is finally relieved, the compulsion to overeat tends to disappear.

On the other hand, when a depressed person has lost weight that he or she should regain, stimulant drugs may be contraindicated, because their anorexiant effect will lessen the desire for food even more. Here the doctor will juggle medication in order to stimulate the patient and yet not curb the appetite.

Stimulants give the depressed or tired person a lift, because they activate chemical reserves in the nervous system to work at a greater pace. The feeling of being energized, even if only for several hours, can be an excellent day-to-day measure for mild depressions and an occasional fatigue state. However, if drug stimulation is continued for a long time, let us say every day for several weeks, it stretches the body reserves too thin, thus creating a potential for nervous collapse and mental exhaustion.

Antidepressant Drugs

We sometimes call antidepressants "psychic energizers" to differentiate them from stimulant drugs. They seem to achieve their purpose by stabilizing the chemical balance of the brain tissue and assisting the passage of nerve impulses through brain circuits which are blocked or inhibited (slowed down). In other words, they help the nervous system to integrate and to transmit its messages throughout the body more efficiently and smoothly.

However, antidepressants, unlike the stimulant drugs, do not activate the nervous system artificially and cause it to use up its reserves. Rather, they are given as a specific in many types of depression, to elevate the person's mood and bring him or her up to a steady emotional level.

While the *concept* of antidepressants is not a new star on the medical horizon, most of the effective compounds and synthetic preparations which have grown out of it have been developed, as noted earlier, since about 1955.

Adjunctive Drugs

In addition to the four major drug categories just described, which are utilized explicitly for depressive illnesses, other drugs may also ease individual symptoms. For example, the doctor may prescribe gastric sedatives and antacids to relieve stomach distress, nausea, and heartburn; or tonics to enliven the appetite. In some cases hormones are used to stabilize glandular metabolism, or antitensives to lower blood pressure. And, of course, we also have aspirin as the good old standby for headache or nonspecific pain.

How Drugs Help

By and large, the antidepressants, of which there are several kinds, do the most good. But here, time and dosage are all-important. For instance, any antidepressant drug requires from one to six weeks (the average is two weeks) before its effect can be fully evaluated. Generally, the doctor will prescribe maximum dosages for the first three weeks to get the best results. He will also want to observe your relative closely; *first,* because he wants to make sure that he or she is not a potential suicide; *second,* to record improvement and adjust the dosage accordingly; and *third,* to make certain that the drugs are not producing side effects (see below). In order to keep track of all this the doctor will want to consult with the patient at regular intervals either in his office or over the telephone.

If the depression is not relieved by the fifth or sixth

week, the drug in all likelihood will not work. Another antidepressant will be substituted; when one variety does not help, another may.

The tranquilizers, stimulants, and sleep-inducers which the doctor may add to the drug schedule will help diminish the excess tension, ruminative thoughts and obsessions, fears, sluggish feelings, insomnia, and other distressing symptoms.

Side Effects of Drugs

No drug will always do exactly and only what is asked of it for everyone. An aspirin may relieve a headache in one case. In another, it can irritate the stomach and induce heartburn; or it can also cause ringing in the ears. The latter two symptoms are side effects.

Antidepressants, tranquilizers, and stimulant drugs, all powerful and complex chemicals, can give rise to quite a few side effects in different people or in the same person at different times. Most of them are not serious. For example, an antidepressant may cause the person to perspire and develop dryness of the mouth, mild constipation, and some blurring of vision. While these side effects can be distinctly annoying, they are not critical.

But what if the person's special sensitivity to the drug produces side effects that signal more than this? Perhaps danger? While the incidence of such sensitivities remains small they can occur. For example, some drugs may raise or lower the blood pressure when combined with alcohol, certain foods, or other medication. Still others can destroy blood corpuscles and leave the person open to infection, liver trouble, or other complications. To be sure, none of this need go to serious proportions if your relative, when placed on a drug program for depression, remains under medical care and observation.

How Many Drugs Should One Know About?

Certainly not all. I have given you general information about some that are used for depression, but this is not the place to identify all of them. Firstly, the preparations on the market and their brands are far too numerous. Secondly, every drug presents a problem in itself, because of the great variations in response, as you learned in the previous sections. Therefore, while I want you to know about drugs for depression and to be able to discuss them with the doctor intelligently, the responsibility and authority for their use and dosage belong in his domain.

Which Is the Best Drug?

No one drug can be hailed as the best, because none *cures* depression. Each may alleviate some of the person's anguish in the illness or partly remove the most oppressive symptoms. But only the drug or combination of them that turns the trick for your relative is the best for him or her. This result will emerge mostly through your doctor's experience plus his individual program of trial and error for each patient.

Let us suppose that your relative cannot tolerate the side effects of a certain antidepressant that is, however, relieving his depression. In that case the doctor may decrease the medication or change it. Or maybe there are no side effects, but the drug is not working. This might indicate that the dosage must be increased. Or perhaps the medication is doing an excellent job for another patient but is doing just so-so for your relative. This could mean that if it is combined with another drug it will be more effective. The variables are so many that naming a "best" drug is like trying to designate a "best" food. The answer is: It all depends.

How Long Must a Drug Be Taken for Depression?

Drugs will not vanquish this illness in the same bull's-eye fashion as that in which antibiotics conquer an infection. On the positive side, they support and maintain satisfactory nervous function while the person heals. Your relative may have to rely on the drug for a year or more if the depression is chronic. In most depressions, however, drug treatment lasts from three to six months. In some instances, after an acute but possibly brief depression (of a few weeks duration), the person's return to his normal self comes about so fast that the doctor will withdraw the drug completely. (You may recall that in Chapter 1, it was noted that some depressions remit spontaneously.)

General Results of Drug Treatment

Experience and evaluation show recovery with antidepressant drugs alone in about thirty-five per cent of patients with acute and moderate endogenous depressions; in about fifty per cent of patients with neurotic depressions; and in about sixty-five per cent of those with reactive depressions. These percentages drop when the depression is severe or long-lasting. The chances of recovery and greater improvement rise appreciably, however, when physical procedures and psychotherapy, where indicated, fortify drug treatment.

CHAPTER ELEVEN

Your Role in Drug Treatment

UNLIKE PHYSICAL illness, depression annuls the person's ability to arrange his or her own medical care or to instruct others in what plans to make. One can rarely count on the depressed individual to obtain help by himself. It requires too many decisions and too much effort. Just picking up the telephone, dialing the number, and talking with a secretary to make an appointment may be far beyond him.

Getting the Person to the Doctor

Someone else must be the pilot and steer the course. You will probably designate yourself.

Once you have called the doctor's office and made the appointment, simply announce to your relative, without needless discussion, that you expect him to be ready for it and that you will keep him company. If there is any protest, point out, with no heat or rancor, that you are not a physician, that you cannot treat the symptoms he complains of, and therefore consultation is indicated. You can add that you are sure the illness is not serious, but that it should be checked on to relieve everyone's doubts. Then drop the subject until it is time to go. In most cases, the person is reconciled to your action and possibly cheered that you have taken over.

The Drug Program

Should the doctor diagnose a depressive disorder in your relative, you can expect that he will also evaluate the intensity of the illness. If the depression seems mild and does not interfere too much with the patient's daily function, the doctor may decide to let time, nature, supportive drugs, and sequential events heal it. In that case he will prescribe stimulants, an occasional tranquilizer, and perhaps a sleeping pill for bedtime.

However, if the depression is more incapacitating—that is, of moderate intensity rather than mild—the keystone of the drug program will probably be antidepressant medication.

What You Watch for with Antidepressants

These drugs must be taken regularly each day. They may be given in maximal doses at the start in order to obtain the earliest possible improvement.

It will be up to you to make sure that your relative takes them as prescribed. Try to keep an eagle eye on him. You will soon learn whether he can be trusted to take them as required, or whether you must keep reminding him of every dose at the proper time.

Concurrently, you should bear in mind the information about side effects that I gave you in Chapter 10. With antidepressants, these may consist of:

Some drowsiness. When this shows up, the patient would be most unwise to drive a car. Tactfully but firmly make certain that he or she does not.

Dryness of the mouth. For some persons this can be an annoying reaction. However, sucking on a lozenge not only relieves the dryness but neutralizes the "funny taste" that occasionally goes with it. Most depressed persons have been bothered by this dryness as a symptom of their illness before taking antidepressants; they are usually accustomed to the condition and therefore tend to accept it.

Mild sweating. This discomfort can be overcome by more frequent bathing and changes of clothing.

Some constipation. Minimal and occasional doses of a mild laxative such as milk of magnesia are all that are needed to help this nuisance reaction.

A slight blurring of the vision. Your relative may complain that his eyes are bad and insist that he needs new glasses. But wait until he is off the drug and see whether the blurring clears up. In all likelihood it will.

When You Can Expect Results from the Antidepressant Drugs

Do not look for prompt relief. As I told you in Chapter 10, a two-week average is needed for any noticeable benefits. This is when you do everything possible to encourage your relative to wait out this trying interval. You will not be alone in your support; the doctor too will be heartening him or her, either on the telephone or in office consultation or both.

Once any substantial headway is made in eliminating the depression, maintenance doses of the drug will be prescribed (usually one-third to one-half the therapeutic dose) for three to twelve months or longer.

Other Drugs That Can Be Taken with Antidepressants

Most tranquilizers, sedatives, and sleeping pills are readily combined with antidepressants. However, stimulants, pep pills, and appetite-reducing pills for dieting *do not mix well* with them. This is why you must always let the doctor know what other medicines your relative is taking. Keep this information at the edge of your mind during an initial consultation and volunteer it should it be overlooked in the rush of all the other details that you and the patient may deem more urgent.

Vitamins can be taken with any prescribed drug and you are safe in giving your relative *plain* aspirin—one or two tablets for headache or pain. But do not offer aspirin *compounds,* because many of them contain the stimulant caffein, which may be incompatible with antidepressants.

You should also be aware that alcoholic drinks do not go well with many antidepressants. The combined reaction may precipitate rapid changes in the blood pressure to produce sudden, intense sleepiness or severe headache.

What You Watch for with Tranquilizers

You may have heard the terms *major* and *minor* in connection with tranquilizers. Such classification is inaccurate and misleading, because all tranquilizers are strong chemicals. The true distinction lies in the dosage. For a milder, or "minor," effect, the doctor prescribes a smaller dose. Where a "major" effect is wanted, as in the use of a tranquilizer to slow down the brain centers and act as a sleeping pill, the larger dose will be given. And while we are on this subject, let me point out that since tranquilizers, like the antidepressants, can produce drowsiness, you will have to intervene here too, should your relative want to drive a car while under their influence. In this case, it is not only that they induce sleepiness. They may also inhibit the person's reflexes and dull his alertness, conditions which make for dangerous driving.

Most tranquilizers mix with other drugs, but *some* do not; so make sure that you learn about such combinations.

Also, another caution about alcohol here: When mixed with it, tranquilizers may have the effect of mild knockout drops. Some of my patients on regular tranquilizer schedules have learned that they can stay on the drug and still accommodate to one or two drinks (no more) in the course of a social evening without bad results. Others find that they handle the liquor better if they "skip the pill" for at least four to six hours before drinking anything alcoholic. Make it your business to keep tabs on this kind of juggling before the patient goes out for an evening. This is too important to lose sight of.

Tranquilizers are not a specific for depressive illness. Their purpose is to help reduce the anxiety and agitation that often accompany the disorder. However, if your relative fights taking them because he or she dislikes the dull or "doped-up" feeling they may produce in his case, then the better choice is to omit the drug and let him put up with his discomforts, tension, and anxiety until you obtain a substitute from the doctor.

Some tranquilizers seem to aggravate depression. If you notice that they make the patient cry more easily, create fogginess, or blunt his or her spirits even more than before, report this to the doctor too.

A further word of warning: Tranquilizers sometimes produce what is called a paradoxical effect. Instead of quieting the patient they may do the exact opposite, that is, create intense restlessness and the "jitters." The person cannot sit still, his skin crawls, and he is unable to find repose anywhere. His body is like a running motor wanting to take off. This reaction is called *akathisia* (ak-a-*theez*-ya). Should it occur, stop the drug and the person will be free of the akathisia within twenty-four hours. A prescription for a different tranquilizer may then be required.

When akathisia appears, its greatest hazard is the patient's response to it. He develops a frenzied need to regain calm. Thus, he keeps taking more and more tranquilizers, but as he does, the akathisia gallops on at an ever-faster pace. If it goes too far, he or she may then have to be hospitalized for a day or two in order to overcome it.

What You Watch for with Stimulants

As I mentioned in Chapter 10, these drugs are sometimes prescribed for mild depressive disturbances or as a quick booster for an occasional fatigue state. In some instances they are given for a retarded (slowed-down) depression if the doctor anticipates that the mood disturbance will end within a few weeks. Their greatest advantage is in the energizing lift that the patient with an endogenous depression obtains when he takes just one stimulant pill on arising, to help him start the day. But this medication should be avoided after four o'clock in the afternoon, otherwise it will interfere with that night's sleep.

Stimulants should never be taken regularly over an extended period. They have several serious drawbacks. *First,* they may "hop up" the person without necessarily improving the depressed feelings. *Second,* he or she comes to rely on them too much; since the effect diminishes as time goes on, larger doses are needed; this then creates a drug habit. *Third,* they distort judgment. This is why anyone entrusted with grave responsibilities should avoid important decisions while under their influence. They may cause irritability and recklessness without the person's realizing that his behavior has become erratic and a threat to himself and others. *Fourth,* they can ultimately engender toxicity and lead to severe mental derangement.

You will know that stimulant drugs are having an adverse effect on your relative when his face flushes, his breathing becomes too rapid, and his appetite falls off markedly. He may also complain of dizzy spells, palpitations, and queasiness of the stomach.

What You Watch for with Sleeping Pills

In depression, especially when agitation and insomnia are predominant symptoms, the immediate concern is to give the patient enough rest and sleep. These must be ensured in order to allow the nervous system to slow down and repair itself. Thus, sleep-inducers are often a "must" for depressive illness.

But do not be surprised if the doctor withdraws them after a few weeks and lets the antidepressant drugs alone sedate the person into more natural sleep; or if he suggests only a tranquilizer at bedtime to guarantee easier release into slumber. This is because sleeping pills, like many other medications, are potentially addictive. You see this addiction when the person shows a feverish and continuing need to use them as a push button to send him into sleep.

However, other factors, unnoticed by you, may be contributing to the insomnia—factors which could be eliminated and perhaps could alter the person's dependence on the sleeping pills. For example, your relative may stay on the brink of wakefulness because the TV is blaring or someone in the house is hammering out a do-it-yourself project. Certainly you can put a stop to such disturbing noises. You might also search out other hindrances to sound sleep. Is the patient's bedroom quiet and dimmed? Does it give him enough privacy? Is the bed comfortable? Can he doze a bit later in the morning without being disturbed? I ask these questions because, when the family relies exclusively on sleeping pills, even those prescribed by the doctor, to "put the person out," they overlook the conditions in the physical environment which are remediable if some thought is given them. Very often when these conditions are corrected the need for the sleeping pill disappears.

Should the Drugs Be Taken with Meals Only?

No, although many persons believe that medicines work better if taken immediately after eating. Doctors tend to prescribe them this way, but not for that reason; rather, as a reminder for a specific time. Some medications, especially those for the stomach distress and indigestion that often accompany depressive illness, should be taken as prescribed, either before or after the meal, for a maximum effect. However, such drugs as antidepressants, sleeping pills, stimulants, and tranquilizers perform better when they are timed to the speed of the drug's absorption into the body system.

For example, suppose you have learned that it requires one hour for a sleeping pill to act on your relative (that is, to absorb) and that he or she should be asleep by eleven P.M. The pill would then be given at ten P.M.

With antidepressants, it is well to know that they are effective only so long as a sufficient concentration of the drug remains in the bloodstream. To keep up the blood level required, the doctor may prescribe a dose for every five hours: the time schedule could be one pill at eight A.M., one at one P.M., and one at six P.M. But what if the patient sleeps until nine A.M.? In this case, the schedule can be shifted to ten A.M., three P.M., and eight P.M., without disturbing the blood level of the drug at all.

What Drug Supervision Should Mean to You

It should imply a new awareness on your part that when drugs are properly used they can help, but when taken erratically, in excess, or contrary to the doctor's instructions, they can hurt. It also requires that you become thoroughly conversant with them. It is a good idea, too, to memorize or write down their names rather than to refer to them as the "yellow," "blue," "pink," or "small," "round," or "oval" pill. Thus, when questions about them arise, especially on the telephone with the doctor, no time is wasted in trying to identify them. You and the doctor will both know, *by name,* which one you are discussing, with no chance of an error.

You may feel that it does not require great brain power to supervise a drug program. Perhaps not, but it does involve a close vigilance, the use of native wit, and the desire to help.

For instance, one day your relative is, in *his* opinion, completely well and sees no reason why he cannot stop the antidepressant drug. However, his or her improved state of health is probably a result of the very medication that he wants to give up; it does not mean that the illness itself has remitted as yet. This is why you should never concur with such a decision on your own. You may be way off the mark, because very often when the medication is discontinued too soon a relapse will occur. If for some reason you cannot check with the doctor immediately, continue to supervise your relative's regular dose, even if it means persuading him or her to take it each time in your presence. This measure may be necessary simply because at this stage he is beginning to balk at it.

The stimulants, tranquilizers, and sedatives have their own rationale. As *adjunctive* medications to antidepressants and other drugs (or to physical treatment and psychotherapy), they are used for their specific effects on *symptoms.* Should there come a time when these symptoms disappear and the patient feels that he can get along without such "crutches," they will be discontinued.

Even with these adjunctive drugs, however, before varying or omitting them consult the doctor. By all means convey your observations, but let him make the change no matter what you think or the patient says.

There is just one major exception to the above—that is, when any drug is producing an effect that is obviously too strong, harmful, or disturbing, as in the examples I mentioned earlier. In such contingencies, if you cannot reach the doctor, then withhold the drug for the time being until you can get in touch with him for further instructions.

CHAPTER TWELVE

Physical Treatment

FROM EARLY history on, through many eras of medical development, man continued to believe that feelings of depression were the curse of an evil force. He sought ways to overcome these feelings; in addition to the drugs that he extracted from plants for their curative powers, he invented other corrective agents. He bored holes in the skull to let the "poisonous vapors" escape, flagellated himself to beat out the "vile spirits," took cleansing baths and water cures, and leeched the body until the "bad blood" was drained off (a practice still existent in some parts of the world). He had two aims: to soothe the tense and nervous feelings of anger, fear, guilt, and depression; and to drive out the mental pain and bring about a return to normal function.

Modern cultures, with their abundance of research studies and scientific data, have produced various methods of physical treatment for man's nervous system, from diathermy to neurosurgery. However, I will review only those which have been investigated and proven effective for *depression* over the past fifty years.

History and Background of Physical Treatment for Depressive Illness

One of the first all-out attempts to treat nervous function chemically was made by Dr. Jakob Klaesi (1922) when he used barbiturates and other chemicals for prolonged sleep—up to one week. The basic idea was to put the nervous system to rest. This method was helpful, especially for patients whose emotional illnesses were characterized by severe agitation.

Then, around 1933, Dr. Ladislas Meduna initiated the

use of intravenously injected stimulant drugs (metrazol) to produce a convulsion, which in turn improved mental function. He noted from his experience *that more than seventy per cent of depressed persons got well with this treatment.*

At about the same time that the above was happening, Dr. Manfred Sakel discovered (1931–1933) that the injection of insulin produced a physiologic coma that also improved brain function, especially in schizophrenia.

These three procedures—prolonged sleep, chemical convulsive treatments, and insulin coma—were subsequently modified and perfected. Still used throughout the world for treating depressions and other mental disturbances, they are all of continuing interest. However, in this text I will concentrate on the outgrowth of Meduna's chemical convulsive method, which was ultimately refined into present-day electric stimulation, specifically for depressive illness. You may have heard of it as electroshock, or simply "shock," treatments.

Electroshock Treatment*

As ill luck would have it, the term "electroshock" became a disquieting misnomer for an excellent and highly beneficial treatment method. More aptly, it should have been called a "stimulation" procedure. However, the word "shock" attained general usage through one of those quirks of language application.

In Italy, during the late 1930's, Doctors Ugo Cerletti and Lucio Bini belived that the beneficial effects obtained with chemical convulsive treatment in depression were due to the *neural discharge* of impulses in the brain rather than to the induced muscular convulsion. After several years of animal research, they demonstrated that an electric current applied to the human being's temples could produce the desired neural discharge with an absence of pain, instantaneously and safely, and with equal or greater effectiveness than the chemical-injection method of Dr. Meduna.

Doctors Cerletti and Bini, in publishing their observa-

* Technically, it was and still is designated as electroconvulsive treatment (ECT) in the United States.

tions on this important subject in 1938, used the common Italian term *l'elettroshock,* meaning "the electric stimulus." In a subsequent publication in 1950, Dr. Cerletti deplored this word and assumed responsibility for its unfortunate use as the name of the treatment. (At the same time he disclaimed any originality in the application of electricity to the body for beneficial purposes, noting that the electric stimulus from the torpedo fish had been used as a therapeutic agent as early as 43 A.D. to relieve headache.)

By then the nomenclatural damage had been done; the term "shock treatments" had invaded the medical lexicon and fastened on the frightened imaginations of many persons, especially the emotionally insecure. Further, psychiatrists were by this time too preoccupied with the beneficial results of the treatment itself; they felt that its advantages far outweighed the quibbling over terminology and did little to overcome the anxiety-producing effect of the name.

For myself, I cannot agree that it was wise to shrug off the problem, and since the very connotation of the term is false I prefer *electric-stimulation treatment,* which says exactly what it is. For easy reference I call it EST. Please remember this abbreviation, because from here on and throughout this book I will speak of it as such.

Most knowledgeable psychiatrists consider this procedure to be the treatment of choice for all severe depressions and many of the moderate ones. Certainly, over the years repeated clinical investigation has proven EST to be the most convenient, reliable, and effective method of overcoming intense or disabling depressions.*

I will now describe its modern techniques.

---

* Unhappily, information about EST has reached the average person through the melodrama of fiction, motion pictures, television, or magazine stories. One television episode that I saw presented EST in a setting of "Gothic" horror. The nurses' eyes bulged, tension blanketed the scene, and even the doctors surrounding the patient seemed aghast at the prospect of administering the treatment. This sensationalism is inexcusable. A writer or research person can easily establish the facts of EST in any psychiatric office or hospital where it is given and learn that in no way does it resemble the preposterous dramatics I have just described. What is worse, among those viewing this scene were probably some who needed the treatment and were alienated from it by the chilling atmosphere portrayed. I would not blame them.

How EST Is Given

Treatments can be administered at any time of the day, provided that the patient has not eaten for four hours or more.

He or she reclines on a comfortable bed. In a doctor's office, ordinary street clothes are worn, but these are loosened. The shoes are removed.

Then a quick-acting barbiturate is injected intravenously; this puts the patient to sleep in about ten seconds. From this point on, the patient feels nothing and remains asleep until after the treatment. (While most persons do not like to contemplate being "put out," many patients tell me that they welcome the pleasant sensation of falling asleep quickly and smoothly, possibly because they experience an instant release from mental pain.)

Following the sleep-inducing injection a second chemical, succinylcholine (*suk*-sin-ill-*ko*-leen) is administered. This drug is a relaxant which eliminates all strong muscular contractions. It takes about twenty to thirty seconds for the muscles to relax sufficiently for purposes of treatment.

Now the patient breathes pure oxygen by positive pressure through a face mask. This ensures full oxygenation of all body tissues. At the same time, an extremely low-amperage electric current, applied to the temples for one second or less, provides the stimulus for the neural discharge that will set the healing process in motion. (See section on Unilateral EST, pages 158–59.)

The patient sleeps throughout this procedure.

The entire treatment is painless except for the pinprick of the first injection. In all it has taken about two minutes.

Now for the initial recovery phase, which extends over ten to fifteen minutes but sometimes less: in the first minutes or so, the anesthetic wears off and the effects of the muscle relaxant lift. Then (in about ten minutes) the after-discharge and deep sleep of the electric stimulation pass into light sleep.

After an additional ten to twenty minutes the patient awakens but feels a bit groggy. Soon the whereabouts and the identities of those in the surroundings are recognized. The patient is then allowed to sit up. Gradually, the fuzzy feeling clears and orientation is regained. *At no time does he or she remember the treatment.*

The entire procedure from start to finish has taken about one hour. The patient can now go home. If the treatment was given in a hospital he returns to his room.

Most Commonly Asked Questions About EST

Usually, when EST is recommended it provokes a searching demand for more information about the procedure. The following questions are typical.

Is There a Shock to the System?

No. But, as I have explained, the word *shock* itself carries an impact. A person (patient or relative) may associate it in his own mind with some kind of "electric chair," a lethal shock from a bolt of lightning, a "third rail," or a faulty electrical outlet. For this reason I repeat that the word was a poor choice and is to be regretted.

Is the Treatment Safe?

An abundance of recorded evidence and validated experience has shown that EST, in accordance with recognized medical standards, is considered to be a safe procedure. This is especially true when it is given by a trained and competent psychiatrist who can evaluate his patient's condition and is prepared to deal with any expected contingency that may arise during the treatment. I, along with many other psychiatrists, prefer to be assisted by an anesthesiologist. In my opinion, this further ensures an uneventful recovery from the treatment.

What Are the Complications to EST?

The most common are occasional headache and nausea in the recovery phase, after some of the treatments. The headache will disappear quickly with aspirin and is rarely bothersome. The nausea can be prevented if the patient takes dramamine or any other "seasick" remedy before treatment. The most annoying complication can be some temporary memory loss following EST.

How Much Memory Loss Occurs?

Most patients become aware of mild lapses in memory after the fourth or fifth treatment. This deficit is noticed when the person forgets casual appointments, the names of persons seen infrequently, and little-used telephone numbers. The forgetfulness then persists for the balance of the treatment program, but once the patient is well it clears up within two or three weeks after the last treatment.

Some patients who do not recover fully from the depression immediately after treatment complain that the memory remains poor and they blame the treatments for it. The complaints seem to come from those whose illness hangs on as a chronic disturbance. However, a great deal of psychologic testing and many clinical studies indicate that it is the continuing anxiety and depression that cause the memory disturbance, not necessarily the treatment. My own experience has shown that virtually all depressed patients have developed memory troubles *prior* to treatment; they have not concentrated or noticed the surroundings for weeks or months before psychiatric consultation. (I discussed this point in Chapter 7. You may want to refer back to it.) Patients who recover totally and on schedule as a result of EST rarely note continuing memory difficulties. Instead, they are aware that with improvement of the depressive mood, their perceptions grow clearer each day.

Older persons, or those with moderate to severe hardening of the arteries of the brain, or those with hidden brain defects associated with other processes, tend to forgetfulness in any event; EST may aggravate this condition temporarily or in rare instances cause confusion. When the depression lifts, the memory usually returns to its previous state. Should confusion persist, it is probable that the EST has exposed a previously existing disorder that requires further investigation.

Are There Afterpains with EST?

As a common reaction, the jaw may ache for a day or so following the first treatment. This is why: If a sensitivity to the succinylcholine (muscle relaxant) appears in the person it will be in the strongest muscle of the body, usually the jaw, although someone with well-developed calf or shoulder muscles may feel the ache in those places instead. However, this is after the initial treatment. It is quickly overcome with two aspirin tablets. As a rule it does not recur with further treatment.

Does EST Hurt the Brain?

I have found no convincing clinical or research evidence to confirm that EST impairs the brain. After extensive use throughout the world for over thirty years it is plain that in a large majority of cases EST *benefits* the person. By means of it he or she becomes rational and well. But if you put it this way—does EST *alter* brain function?— yes. When the brain is stimulated by electricity or chemicals in the dosages required and the duration called for, the treatment clearly modifies brain activity toward improvement. Indeed, it is given *in order to create responses that are part of this modification.*

If there are any permanent side effects on brain tissue as a result of EST, these cannot be demonstrated by any reliable tests. To me it is apparent that electric and chemical application to the brain produce stimulatory effects that help the depressed person return to normal function.

Does EST Cause Fractures?

Rarely, if ever, with modern techniques. Before relaxants were introduced (about 1953) as a routine part of the treatment, EST induced a strong convulsion. Because of it, some patients developed a fracture or a pulled muscle. But with the convulsion virtually eliminated, these complications are almost never seen. In fact, we can now give EST to depressed patients with multiple fractures. Not long ago I treated an elderly woman who had attempted suicide by jumping from a second-story window. She had sustained eighteen bone injuries and dislocations, including a compound fracture of the leg. Not only did she recover from the depression with EST but, because the treatment revived her will to live, she ate and slept well. This was conducive to good tissue regeneration and she enjoyed an excellent and speedy convalescence.

Previous to the use of muscle relaxants this patient might have died, because EST would have been ruled out for her; the depression and resultant poor nutrition would then have interfered with good bone repair; her continued weakness, with a long stay in bed, would inevitably have resulted in a fatal pneumonia.

How Many Treatments Are Needed?

This varies widely. For example, some persons with endogenous depressions make complete recoveries after eight to ten treatments and some with as few as six; or a neurotic depression may require as many as ten to twelve treatments, and others in this category, only three to four. Generally, I do not expect to see significant improvement until five or six treatments have been given. Most patients show their greatest gains between the fifth and tenth treatments. Following what might be estimated as the "last" treatment, it is best for the patient to receive a final prophylactic treatment in order to prevent a setback. Undertreatment leads to relapses in about thirty per cent of cases, whereas the "one more" may prevent the relapse and can do no harm.

How Often Are Treatments Given?

About three times a week. This means that the average person suffering from a moderate to severe depression and receiving eight to ten treatments stands a seventy per cent chance of getting over the illness in about three weeks.

What Is Maintenance EST?

Some persons who suffer from chronic or cyclical types of depression are maintained comparatively free of the illness by receiving one treatment every ten to thirty days for an indefinite period (from six months to five years, or up to ten years or more). This program works especially well for those with a chronic depressive type of manic-depressive disorder, or the recurrent type, wherein normal intervals of function are brief. Maintenance also offers good results in controlling any other chronic depressive illness, whether endogenous or neurotic. I think of maintenance EST as a monthly or bimonthly booster shot to a nervous system that tends to run down. It often stabilizes mental function where all other methods fail.

Can the Person Work While Receiving Treatment?

In some unusual cases, yes. It depends on how much pressure and responsibility the work entails. I generally advise the patient to take time off throughout the course of EST. While he or she may be able to manage a job (including that of housewife) during the treatment period, this imposes an unnecessary burden. Bear in mind that *any* kind of treatment acts as a stress and, since the purpose of this procedure is to help the person regain his full quota of nervous energy, he is entitled to complete repose and freedom from all cares between the treatments.

None of this, however, applies to maintenance EST or any single booster treatment. In these instances, the person need not interrupt his regular schedule of activities except for the time allowed on the day of treatment.

Can Everyone Take EST?

Nearly everyone. Among those rejected for it are persons with an extremely damaged heart or a history of recent coronary attack; those in the throes of an active infection (such as acute bronchitis with fever, or tuberculosis); or individuals who suffer from unusual debility. Treatment is usually withheld from those with extensive brain damage, although in some cases of this sort EST can be given successfully for symptomatic relief of a severe agitated depression.

Women who are depressed and pregnant also can be

given EST. Studies of children born of mothers who received this treatment while pregnant show that the EST had no adverse consequence upon the child. I have never seen a miscarriage or other prenatal or postnatal disturbance caused by the treatment. Indeed, if depression is allowed to flourish in a pregnant mother it may ultimately damage her and indirectly hurt the developing child. In treating a pregnant woman I much prefer EST to drugs. Drugs *may* harm the fetus, particularly in the first three months, whereas there is no evidence that EST will injure either the child or the mother.

When the person is deeply depressed but in good physical condition, EST should not be ruled out because of age either. As a general principle I try to avoid treating youngsters under sixteen with it; yet I have seen splendid results from EST in children and young teen-agers who showed suicide potentials and acute disturbances. The oldest patient I ever treated was a woman of eighty-seven, who made a matter-of-course recovery after six treatments. Patients with diabetes or liver, kidney, and like diseases can all be treated with EST. One gauge of the person's ability to take the treatment is his reaction to an intravenous anesthetic. If the physical condition can tolerate the anesthetic he or she can usually be given EST.

It may be appropriate here to raise a sociologic point. Why does the person at the lower or middle income level seem to recover from depression more easily than those in the more affluent groups?

To begin with, those in the first two categories tend to accept (and look for) EST more readily. In my opinion such persons are keenly aware that they cannot afford a protracted illness and must get back to the job; hence, they are strongly motivated to find the treatment that works fastest, benefits the most, and returns them to a normal state that much more quickly.

On the other hand, the fears and credulities of those in more sheltered economic strata, and particularly of the intellectual who worries about "impairment" of his mental faculties, are often played upon. The mistaken notions of EST which such persons absorb overshadow the fact that the depression is clouding their mental abilities in any case, and that they will not live up to their capacities

until it is cleared up. Thus, when the illness is handled
with equivocal methods in order to appease vague ap-
prehensions, it lingers on and on into chronicity and the
person may be forced to await remission over a painfully
long period of time.

There are the exceptions, of course. Offhand I recall,
among others, a celebrated actress, an eminent industri-
alist, a famous statesman, and a well-known author, all of
whom, without fuss, accepted my diagnosis of depression
and embarked on a course of EST. They recovered quickly and were back at their work in a month to six weeks.
Having recognized the imperative of the treatment, they
benefited from it to the same degree as their less illustrious
fellows.

Unilateral EST Treatment

The standard EST treatment that I described several pages
back calls for the simultaneous application of the electric
impulse to both temples. This is known as *bilateral* treatment because it stimulates both sides of the brain equally.
A modification of this technique calls for *unilateral,* that
is, one-sided, application of the electric impulse. Here,
the non-dominant side of the brain is stimulated. (In a
right-handed or right-dominant person, the right half of
the brain is non-dominant; in a left-handed person the left
half of the brain is non-dominant.)

Many distinct advantages accrue to the patient from
unilateral EST especially when we compare it with the
standard, bilateral technique. In recent years I have used
it extensively. For one, it is considerably less stressful to
the patient; secondly, it does not produce troublesome
post-treatment confusion and thirdly, it prevents most, if
not all, of the memory loss. The results of unilateral treatment are about the same as the results of bilateral treatment, although in some instances of deep and chronic
depression, additional treatments are needed to obtain a
full remission. However, in cases where the depression is
very severe and the patient is determined to kill himself,
or when he or she is overwhelmed by intense fear and
many obsessions, I prefer using bilateral treatment since

the memory loss may then serve a temporary, but beneficial, purpose of blocking out the patient's anxieties for a while.

Other techniques in EST treatment, some of which are still under research, offer the possibility that severe depressions may be eliminated within a few days. One of the most promising of these procedures calls for several treatments to be given in one day or on two or more consecutive days, resulting in a rapid recovery from severe depression. It may be wise to inquire about the availability of such treatment in your community.

Indoklon Treatment

This variation of electric-stimulation treatment was developed about 1960. The technique is identical with that of EST but, instead of applying electricity to produce a neural discharge, Indoklon, a chemical related to one of the ether compounds, is given by inhalation or intravenously to stimulate the brain and nervous system. It produces the same beneficial effect for depression as does the electric impulse. Essentially, it returns to Meduna's chemical convulsive procedure that I mentioned earlier in this chapter, with the convulsion abated.

A choice between EST and Indoklon stimulation treatments becomes one of technical discretion. No essential difference in the clinical results is seen and the same number of treatments are needed with each procedure to produce the desired improvement. Generally, I use Indoklon when a patient, within the distortions of his current emotional illness, develops morbid obsessional fears of "electricity."

To What Extent Is EST Still Used?

To a great extent, despite the current vogue for drug treatment and the ease with which drugs are provided. Indeed, because the advent of drugs has also brought with it many serious complications, we have seen a widespread return to EST, as the safer, more reliable, and effective method for treating disabling depressions. The clinical evidence is conclusive: compared with the thirty-five per cent statistic for recovery with drugs, EST gets seventy to eighty per cent of persons with endogenous depressions well—doing twice as good a job as the drugs. In reactive and neurotic depressions, the over-all improvement rates with EST are about the same as with drug treatment, except in their very severe manifestations, when EST produces a more clear-cut remission in a much shorter period of time.

CHAPTER THIRTEEN

Your Role in Physical Treatment

MOST PATIENTS in moderate and severe depressions will readily agree to the doctor's recommendation for physical treatment—that is, EST. Their reasons are threefold: they have faith in the doctor; there is a pressing need to find relief; they believe that the treatment will help them.

Among the smaller number of patients who demur at EST are some who have been misinformed about it; those who have heard the word "shock," fear its implications, and say no automatically; others who harbor delusions of unworthiness and can no longer conceive of their right to be well again; those whose fears, prejudices, and anxieties cause them to reject any kind of medical procedure; and finally, patients who cannot decide about anything and thus hesitate at EST too.

You Make the Decision

Just as for initial consultation, *you, the relative, must make the decision* for treatment and not leave it to the uncertain depressive who is helpless to take any action at all.

Time and again I have been dismayed to see a depressed person struggling to make up his mind about treatment while the spouse or another family member sat on the sidelines waiting. Just recently I was forced to confront a husband with the bald reminder of his obligations to a wife who was too wretched to help herself. Why couldn't he mitigate her ordeal and himself assume responsibility for getting her into treatment? He was startled, since he had honestly believed that it was "up to her." On reflection he recognized his role in the matter and agreed

161

to take charge. When he saw the relief that spread over his wife's face at this he commented that he could kick himself "for not doing it before."

How You Maintain the Treatment Program

The doctor will specify a time and place for the treatments.

At the beginning be prepared for some disappointment, because once the schedule is set up patients sometimes begin to ruminate about it. They wonder if the treatment will really help. Or they believe that they cannot muster up the energy to dress and be at the doctor's office or the clinic on time (whether early in the morning or later in the day).

Yet you must deal with this problem. Try approaching it in the following ways.

Avoid Arguments with the Patient

Do not discuss the treatments in advance or challenge your relative's second thoughts about them.

You will recall one of our rules in Chapter 7 for managing a depressed person: "Don't test tomorrow." He or she is just not capable of handling anticipation. If you talk about the appointment schedule days ahead of time the patient may then direct a series of arguments at you, contesting the need for the treatment. Before you know it you are arguing back. In your anxiety you fling at him the evidences of his poor emotional health and it ends in a session of blistering questions, angry retorts, and name calling.

Both of you are the worse for it. Skirt away from the subject of treatment. If your relative brings it up, change it as gracefully as possible. Or you might say, "Why discuss it now? Let's see how you feel when we have to go." Thereafter, mention it only once, on the day of the treatment and as close to the appointment time as possible.

SUPPOSE HE SAYS THAT HE'S AFRAID?

Multiple fears arise out of the very nature of depression. With its aura of doom goes a dread of everything. Most of all, the person is afraid that he will never get well and the treatment may be only another false hope. To him it seems easier to stay home, cry, and suffer. Hence, he says, "I *can't* go today. I'm afraid. But if I'm not better tomorrow I promise I'll go then."

What folly to suppose that this solves anything! You may be unable to arrange an appointment for tomorrow, and a week later he will again refuse. "The doctor can't do anything for me. I'm worse now than I ever was. And maybe the treatment will hurt."

You can overcome his fears. One way is to look into *your* thinking, which may be stimulating them.

Examine Your Own Attitude

From the moment that EST is prescribed to the last treatment, the patient's actions will be prompted by you. If you have reservations or misgivings about the treatment, these emotions will be communicated to him, no matter how much you try to hide them. When you waver, so does he. However, if you are convinced of the merits of the treatment and that it will get him better, your feelings will dominate the issue and he will reflect your confidence.

Thus, on the day of treatment if you stand fast, act certain of what you are doing, state your destination, and suggest that you and he will be leaving shortly to keep the appointment, you will find him ready, because he has accepted your authority and trusts it.

Will all of this repeat itself for the next treatment? Possibly. But after the second or third treatment, the grievances subside to a large extent, usually because he or she is beginning to get better.

When You Misinterpret the Resistance

I recall a housewife who "knew" that her depressed husband was both angry at the need for EST and afraid of it. As he waited for treatment the first time, he muttered something to himself about having missed his lunch. He then grabbed for the box of cookies that is always on my secretary's desk. When she removed them and explained that they would be there for him *after* the treatment he glowered at her.

His wife sat out in the waiting room, tense, jumpy, and chewing her nails, until the treatment was over and her husband was brought out to her. She had braced herself for his tirade. He looked around and demanded: "I want my cookie." His wife goggled at him. "Cookie?" she said weakly (as my secretary tells it). "Yes," he barked, "it was promised to me. I'm hungry." After each succeeding treatment his opening remark would always be: "Where's my cookie? I'm hungry. I want it now."

His wife had misjudged his anger and fear. There was none. Simply, the treatment meant no lunch; therefore, he was hostile to the treatment.

Another patient, who had not objected at all to EST, could not be organized to dress and get to the doctor's office on time. By chance I learned that his wife was dedicated to the proposition that "sick or not, people should always look proper." She demanded that he shave first, because no husband of hers was going to leave the house "with the neighbors seeing him look so messy." In his depressed state shaving was the one straw too many. He would not budge. When this came to light his wife was prevailed on to relent and forget the daily shave for the time being. He then came quite willingly. The shaving, not EST, was the big hurdle.

Precautions to Take on the Day of Treatment

Follow the doctor's instructions to the letter. For example, if EST is scheduled for the afternoon the patient can be given a light breakfast before nine A.M., and no food or liquid for at least four hours before treatment time. When treatment is slated for the morning the patient has *no* breakfast. A small amount of water is permitted.

Never deviate from these instructions. There is good

and sufficient reason for them. If the patient eats within the prohibited time he may vomit during treatment and since he is under the influence of an anesthetic he may inhale the regurgitated food and choke on it. True, we have ways of dealing with such a contingency, but why tempt fate for any complication? "No breakfast" or "no food or liquid before treatment" means just that. Do not let your relative sneak even a cup of coffee. And you must really stand guard. This is not the time to be "good-natured" or sympathetic to his or her hunger.

EST is most effective when the schedule is diligently maintained. If treatments are missed, the results are poor or inconclusive. What is more, the course of EST is then prolonged and everyone becomes discouraged.

All the more reason to keep an eye on your relative so that he cannot sabotage the schedule by eating when he should not. He will know that if he does take food at the wrong time no treatment will be given that day. He may thus play a game of sorry mischief, eat when you are not looking, and think he is outwitting you without knowing that he is hurting himself. However, if he follows directions as most patients do, then you need not take special precautions unless you think he will forget that it is the day of treatment and eat by mistake. This sometimes occurs, so be alert to it.

SHOULD I ACCOMPANY MY RELATIVE FOR THE TREATMENT?

It need not necessarily be you each time, but make certain that it is a companion with whom the patient feels secure. Some persons, especially those who are only moderately depressed, can come to the office alone, particularly after the first treatment, unless they are too fearful to cooperate. Most patients experience few after-effects and are sure that they can manage well when they leave, especially if they live close by or can hail a taxi easily. However, I do not usually permit a posttreatment patient to go home unaccompanied. There is always the chance of delayed nausea, dizziness, or a simple attack of anxiety. While none of these is serious, someone should be there. Alone, the patient is liable to panic, whereas a

companion or aide can give immediate assurance which
will overcome the anxiety.

In the Doctor's Office After EST

While your relative is being treated, you will be in the
waiting room or recovery area. Try to refrain from pacing
the floor and building up tension. Such emotionality is
bound to affect the patient when he or she comes out to
join you. Until then, sit quietly, listen to the soft music,
read a magazine, or chat with the others who are also
waiting. At the same time, keep in mind that in the treatment room the patient is being given constant care and
close attention by the doctor and his aides.

When your relative comes out to sit with you for a
while before going home, he may still be a bit foggy and
withdrawn. If you behave properly, all will go well; but if
you grab at him anxiously and keep talking *at* him for
your own reassurance, it will not.

I have seen a husband in the waiting room do just that
to his wife and never let up. In a low undercurrent he
maintained a steady, intense monologue, recounting every
recent symptom to her, explaining why she was coming
for treatment, how many were planned, and why she
would not be "right" without them. All that this defense-
less patient wanted to do was to rest passively for a bit,
then leave and get home to dinner and the children. Her
husband, however, was determined to "make her feel
good!"

Other relatives will fidget and rub the patient's arm or
shoulder compulsively and blurt out the first thought that
comes to mind. "Are you awake yet?" "What's hurting
you?" "Are you getting a headache?" "Why don't you eat
a cookie . . . we're paying for it. No? Okay, I'll eat it."
"Why are you so quiet? Can't you answer me?" "Do you
want to vomit?" "Look at that young fellow who just had
a treatment. He's talking to *his* mother."

Do not undo the good work of the treatment. The
patient reacts badly to this kind of prodding. It jars his
nervous system, even though at the moment he is too
fuzzy to protest. All that he or she needs is for you to be

there, quietly emanating love and serenity and offering a kind word now and then. Obviously, neither the doctor nor office personnel can monitor the relative every moment. But call on your common sense. This is all that is asked.

The Patient's Reactions Following a Treatment

Each person shows a different response. Moreover, the response may vary after each treatment. In general, though, most patients are a bit drowsy for several hours after the first three or four EST's. Others develop both alertness and relaxation from the initial treatments. Some persons, especially those with retarded depressions, suddenly feel a new life and exhilaration coursing through them, something they had not believed would ever happen again. This encourages them and bolsters their willingness for the additional treatments needed. A few patients may seem to feel worse after a treatment and evidence more agitation than before. It may simply mean that the depression was far more intense than suspected. This is not uncommon, so do not lose heart if it happens. The only answer here is to persist with treatment in accordance with the doctor's recommendation.

Questions and Answers About the EST Patient

WHAT SHOULD MY RELATIVE DO AT HOME AFTER EST?

Let him sleep if he likes. He may want to do so for several hours. But if he is wide awake when he reaches home he will do better watching TV, chatting with you or other family members who drop in, reading, going for a walk with someone, working at a hobby or a puzzle, or just sitting and daydreaming. In other words, let him or her set the pace.

There are some limitations. Exclude anything too exciting. I discourage patients from attending sports events, movies, church services, even family gatherings or parties, because the stress of a crowd after EST may overwhelm and possibly panic them.

CAN I LEAVE MY RELATIVE ALONE AFTER A TREATMENT?

It is preferable that you or someone else keep him company for the remainder of the day, not so much because of the treatment, *but because the depression still exists,* even though the person is now smiling and feeling more at ease. In the two- or three-week period of the treatment program the patient's nervous system is in constant flux. The ravages of the depression keep it that way while, at the same time, maximum stimulation is being applied to heal it. As a result there may be occasional confusion. So let me put it this way: He (or she) can be left alone for short periods of time or even for a few hours, on condition that (1) he is fully awake; (2) his depressed mood is abated; (3) he seems to be clearheaded and in reasonably good control.

WHAT SHOULD THE PATIENT EAT AFTER A TREATMENT?

Following the EST he will be more or less hungry (mostly more) and can be offered his usual foods. For example, if treatment was given him in the morning, he had skipped breakfast. Coffee and a bun or toast may then be satisfying enough after the EST. But if a full breakfast is wanted, serve it of course. When the treatment is given late in the afternoon and lunch is missed, the usual dinner can be served.

It is well for the person to eat. To take nourishment immediately after treatment replenishes the blood sugar level to normal and eliminates the tension caused by hunger. (This is the main reason for the cookies in my office.) However, do not force food on the patient who continues to have a poor appetite. Wait for an hour or so after the treatment, then offer it again, and with a bit of coaxing he or she may accept it. It is also a good idea to tempt the person with enriched drinks of enticing flavors such as malteds, eggnogs, or liquid protein food. Be patient though. With continued EST your relative will start to eat spontaneously within a few days, this in itself denoting improvement.

CAN I GIVE MY RELATIVE VITAMINS?

By all means. Vitamins supplement the diet and can be taken regularly, especially when nourishment has been poor during the depression. They are perfectly safe with EST.

WILL THE PATIENT BE TAKING PRESCRIBED DRUGS WITH EST?

Yes. Both antidepressants and the adjunctive drugs that I spoke of in Chapter 10 are combined with EST. However, certain tranquilizers and marketed compounds which are used to control blood pressure can be dangerous with EST. One of these is *reserpine*. Therefore, as in drug treatment, it is essential at all times that the doctor know which drugs your relative is taking, *including those prescribed by another physician*, before EST is administered. You should also inform the doctor of any sensitivities or allergies to particular drugs, antibiotics, or other substances that you or your relative are aware of.

I recall one patient who was sensitive to aspirin. Since it is usual to give a patient one or two tablets for the occasional headache that may appear after a treatment she might have received it and in her woozy condition at that moment not remembered to reject it. I had questioned her about sensitivities before the treatment and at the last moment, her mother, who had accompanied her, recalled this one. It was a lucky afterthought; the patient would have suffered an intense stomach upset had she taken the aspirin.

IS IT HARMFUL TO LET THE PATIENT BATHE THROUGHOUT EST?

A very emphatic no. It is *beneficial*—for all concerned. In Chapter 7, I stressed the importance of your helping the patient maintain a high level of personal hygiene, thus enabling him or her to retain a sense of normal living. EST in no way contradicts this recommendation.

CAN I BRING MY RELATIVE FOR EST
WHEN SHE IS MENSTRUATING?

Of course. But take note that it is not unusual for the
treatment to cause her to miss a period. This is nothing
to worry about. A month later she will be back to a
normal cycle. On the other hand, a young woman whose
menstrual periods have been irregular or absent for four
or five months (possibly because of the depressive effect
on her system) will find her menses returning to normal
once the EST clears up the depression.

SHOULD I LET MY RELATIVE DRIVE A CAR
WHILE RECEIVING TREATMENT?

I brought up this point earlier in connection with drugs.
Again the answer is no—absolutely no driving after EST.
Above all, the patient should never remotely consider
driving himself home from the doctor's office or clinic.
Let me underline several related facts: No matter how
good a driver the patient is, depression distorts his judgment and behind the wheel his mistakes could be disastrous. Added to this, the action of an anesthetic and EST
on the neural circuits, even though corrective, may at
this time decrease the accuracy and speed of his reflexes.
Until he is well, then, and his nervous system is back to
normal equilibrium, keep him away from handling an
automobile.

SHOULD I HAVE COMPANY FOR MY RELATIVE
WHILE HE IS BEING TREATED?

I would say no. During the two or three weeks of treatment, the reinvigoration that EST provides may be as
much of a stress as he or she can take. It will be time
enough to expose your relative to social excitement once
the treatments are finished. Keep visitors down to the
immediate family and, even then, only those who are good
medicine for him.

While we are on this subject I will call your attention

to one other pertinent fact. It may never have occurred to you that most ill persons (whether the illness is emotional or physical) are embarrassed at letting others, even the most cherished of friends, see them at their worst. They want to be screened off from them. This is even more important when it comes to those well-meaning but inquisitive souls who love to pry into every detail of the illness and then enjoy a good clucking session over it. Keep such visitors off the premises. They usually leave commotion behind them when they depart.

How Soon Can One Expect Improvement from EST?

Relatives usually see a change for the better after a week or two (three to five treatments) and once the stimulative action of the EST has been built up. This buildup must be continual, which is why treatments should not be missed. In each person the speed of the cumulative effect varies. If the depression is stubborn and intense, more of a buildup toward a turning point will be required before you see a favorable change.

Occasionally the patient will admit that he does feel a shade better after the first three to five treatments, but the admission will be grudging because he fears that he may be wrong and desperately hopes that he is not. It will take six or seven treatments before he or she feels secure enough to comment freely on the difference in well-being.

Sometimes a person may go along showing no clear-cut progress at all for nine or ten treatments. Then, with the next treatment or two, the patient may suddenly reach a nodal point of change and be well. In other words, some persons show a progressive and gradual upswing beginning with the third, fourth, or fifth treatment (in rare instances, the first), and some exhibit absolutely no change until the last or next to last, which may be the eighth, tenth, or twelfth treatment.

No depression falls into an exact slot of predictability. In unusual cases, the depression may require more than twelve treatments and perhaps as many as sixteen or eighteen. In my experience the general average is about eight

or nine for an acute endogenous depressive episode. But
have a care. Note that I said the "average." Do not grab
at this figure and decide that it fits *your* relative to the
exact number and then be let down when it does not.
Family members tend to do this; or they latch on to the
minimum number that the doctor mentions and close their
ears to the rest. In your relative's case it may take more
treatments or less. Only the final outcome counts.

When Can the Patient Return to Work?

The simplest answer would be, "When he or she is
well." But this rarely satisfies the impatient individual who
still retains vestiges of the depression, requires more treatment, but insists that he must get back to his job because
he is the only one who can do it.

Try not to succumb to his urgency. You risk losing all
the hard-won gains of the treatment if you do. You must
hold him back until the doctor is certain that he can
manage his work and his emotions reasonably well. If
he returns to the job prematurely all of its stresses and
strains will descend full force and prove intolerable. Total
convalescence will not have been achieved and relapse
may occur.

If he or she is just the opposite kind of person, one
who needs a bit of pushing, start terminating the convalescence sooner. In either case, however, you should work
out this delicate bit of maneuvering with the doctor, who
will know "how much" and "when."

Let us say, then, that the average person who obtains a
good result with EST returns to work about two weeks
after the last treatment. But, as I just warned you in a
different context, "average" may be a misleading statistic,
because the variations are many. Some of my patients
have continued to work right through their depressions
and treatments (without my approval), and others did not
return to the job until six months after I had considered
them fit for duty.

As a rule of thumb I would say that the patient can be
encouraged to resume his usual tasks when, in his opinion,
he feels that he is totally well and normal again.

CHAPTER FOURTEEN

Psychotherapy

THE WORD *psychotherapy* has come into such popular usage that I am sure you are acquainted with it. No doubt you have heard it spoken of as "talk" treatment—that is, a way of delving into the patient's problems through a close discussion of them. It is this, but it is much more. Before explaining the use of psychotherapy in depressive illness let me define it for you.

What Is Psychotherapy?

In a general way, psychotherapy is a process through which a person learns (1) how to examine his values, needs, judgments, and behavior (and those of the persons and the society around him); (2) how to understand them in order to resolve anxieties, doubts and conflicts; and (3) how to act on the understanding for the purpose of adapting more successfully in life.

Summed up, the psychotherapeutic method for attaining these results consists of techniques used by one individual to influence the thinking, feeling, and behavior of another. For example, a young man may be nervous and mildly depressed about the way he is handling his job, but he is shaky about taking it up with his boss. He is afraid that he may sound weak, antagonistic, or silly, and then fluff the whole thing. While mulling about it, he fumes at his own cowardice.

Finally, he talks over the situation with a friend or relative whose judgment he trusts. This may be you. You then advise him as to what to do and how to do it. He acts on your counsel, opens the subject with his employer, presents the ideas you have helped him develop, and all works out well. If we break down this episode into its parts we see that several things took place:

First, your relative cast you in the role of therapist (someone to help him) and you accepted that role.

Second, since he respected your good sense and you were prepared to help, a rapport (mutual trust and goodwill) was established.

Third, this rapport became the basis for an interaction between the two of you toward a specific purpose.

Fourth, as you listened with empathy and understanding, you encouraged him to communicate his anxiety to you, to ventilate it, and to assess the pros and cons of the problem.

Fifth, you gave him direction and guidance, coupled with emotional support, all of which helped him to mobilize his resources.

Thus, you proffered a psychologic hand to assist him in organizing his thinking, making decisions, and taking an action that would reinforce his security. As a result, he felt more cheerful and gained the necessary strength to face up to the coming interview. One might call this interchange a condensed episode of psychotherapy which technically included release, support, and direction.

However, most times "friendly advice" such as this does not turn out so well, because it tends to be *subjective.* The friend or relative who is called on urges and imposes *his* convictions and values on the other. In effect, he or she says, "Listen to me and see how I would do it. It has worked in my case and perhaps it will work for you." But this is like taking your friend's antidepressant pills. If you are fortunate they may help. The chances are that they will not. Friendly advice is bound to be hit-or-miss and may or may not serve the troubled person's needs.

On the other hand, professional psychotherapy must be *objective* at all times. Neither dogmatism nor personal bias should play any part in it. The primary considerations are the patient's needs and the forces that can influence him or her to overcome the depression. For this, an expertise and flexibility with many techniques, far beyond the competence of the amateur, are required.

HOW PSYCHOTHERAPY IS GIVEN FOR DEPRESSION

The patient is seen once or twice a week for about thirty to forty-five minutes each session. Telephone contact and, at times, written communication are also used with him or her on occasion.

In the following pages, some short résumés of the more common psychotherapeutic devices applied for depression are described. Some or all may be used in combination at different times by the therapist.

Emotional Support

When the person is utterly dejected, with anxiety and fright paramount, emotional support ranks high as a therapeutic agent. In depression, the normalcy of others shrivels the spirit of the person, but when he or she receives acceptance from the therapist, this is a morale boost that expands his sense of dignity again.

Such support is a main requisite to recovery, because it also embodies encouragement with vitalizing assurance. These give the depressed person the fortitude to overcome his fears and, for example, to venture again into a crowded store, to conquer a tremulous voice in replying to an important question, to mingle with others (if only marginally), and even to keep abreast of the work load. He or she no longer tastes the humiliation of feeling deficient and inferior.

Very often the person experiences a lessening of his emotional burden as soon as an appointment for psychotherapy is made. There is immediate comfort in the awareness that someone "who knows what it's all about" will sustain him through his periods of despair. His anxiety recedes as he realizes that he will not be struggling with it alone.

Indeed, throughout the therapeutic relationship, the patient gains the feeling of being fortified simply from knowing that *his* therapist is available if needed; and that in their sessions together every fleeting expression of the therapist's face and inflection of his voice denote an interest in *his* welfare. Other patients find relaxation in the certainty that they can pick up the telephone for a heartening word from the doctor should any pricklings of fear arise; just knowing that they can telephone is balm to their nervous systems even if they do not make the call. One patient of mine took advantage of modern technology and made tape-recordings of several of our consultations. In moments of despondency she played them back for the support they gave her.

Emotional support is rooted in the doctor-patient relationship. When this rapport is good, support can do wonders. This is also the cornerstone of all other psychotherapeutic procedures that are used to infuse the person with courage, create new optimisms, and establish better social and work interests.

Release

When psychiatrists speak of psychologic release they use the term *catharsis*. One may also think of it as a form of confession. However, no matter what it is called, when release is achieved and your relative finds the right person to unburden himself to, the weight of his emotional load is reduced considerably.

You may not realize that the depressed person lives with a harsh predicament; he "locks it all in" (especially his guilts), but at the same time he wants to get his miseries out of his system. As a rule, family members have no inkling of this. However, let us suppose that some kindhearted relative does perceive the repressed anguish and expresses a vague sympathy; inadvertently this starts the person talking about the worries that mill around in his mind. Soon, however, he seems to be just rambling on and the relative finds it tiresome and shows it. When the depressed person recognizes that he is being shut up he again withdraws, this time deeper into himself.

In treatment, however, the therapist is aware of these inner constraints. His immediate aim then is to get the patient to open up and, so to speak, let loose. That is what the therapist is there for—to learn about the person's confusions and guilts; and more than that, to direct the discharged material into constructive channels.

For example, I see many parents of adolescents these days who react with mild depression and guilt when their children drop out of school, take drugs, and are sexually promiscuous. From many different sources these parents have been given an odious self-image. They have come to believe that they alone are to blame for their children's shortcomings and lack of purpose; they do not comprehend the cultural elements involved. Their most desperate need then is to "talk out the guilt."

One mother, whose daughter was exhibiting rebellious behavior, had no more than greeted me and sat down when she burst into tears. She began to revile herself, sobbing out her remorse for returning to work years before, when all the societal mores of motherhood had decreed that she remain at home to care for her baby. "I was never really a proper mother, was I?" she cried "That's why she's gone wrong."

However, once the guilt was expressed and her emotionality spent she was better able to take stock of the quandary she was in, to answer the questions she herself was raising, and to recapitulate the circumstances that had existed years back. With growing vividness she began to recall her husband's financial straits at that time, the additional income needed to support a baby and two young parents barely out of their teens. In subsequent sessions, other recollections returned: the cautious provisions she had made for the child's care in her absence, the hours she and her husband had devoted to the youngster, the intimacy, laughter, and comradeship with which they had warmed their home.

Her guilt ebbed as she recognized the economic forces and the naked survival needs which had excluded any choice other than a return to work. In short, psychotherapeutic release now gave her the opportunity to place events in their true proportions and within the framework of past conditions. This in turn freed her from despondency and allowed a logical discussion of ways in which she could work toward the goal of salvaging her daughter.

The symptoms of another woman I knew who was suffering from a mild to moderate involutional melancholia included recurring guilt thoughts about her father. He had died some months ago, and for several years this woman had been required to give him morphine injections for the pain of an irreversible illness. Now, in her depression, she was certain that by some "criminal" lapse she had administered a lethal overdose on the day of his death. Never daring to mention it to anyone, she had nurtured this conviction for some time, positive that she was her father's murderer.

However, having at last put it into words, her self-condemnation subsided. She was led into retracing her father's illness, the gradual decline in his health, and the terminal phase when only increasing amounts of morphine could ease his pain until the end came. With greater calm and clarity she acknowledged that each increase in dosage had been ordered by the doctor. She could even repeat the detailed instructions he had given her and recall her precise preparations for the injection, the doctor's words of trust in her, and his commendations for her help.

To complete her recollections she called her father's doctor one day from my office. Having checked through his records, he confirmed each point that she raised down to the dosage for the last injection. Finally, with the knowledge that her "fatal error" was nonexistent, she obtained release from her tensions. Her response to treatment was immediate and the depression left her shortly afterward.

When a person can give free rein to damaging thoughts and emotions within the sanctuary of the therapist's office and receive empathy and indulgence, he or she undergoes a process of renewal. I have seen many persons "reborn" with the relief of exposing their most galling and abrasive secrets—a man whose self-disgust at his constant desire to hurt his wife was "killing" him; another person whose shame at repudiating a religious background was causing depression; the many whose ego-needs to hide family and business conflicts sear their entire beings; a woman whose pent-up guilt for hating her son's mediocrity and boorishness was creating melancholia because "I'm an unnatural mother, Doctor . . . he's my son and I don't like him. But it's wrong of me."

Such confession is good not only for the soul but for

the body too, because guilts, fears, and obsessions can poison the human organism as surely as any toxic substance. Once the person is rid of these poisons his mind clears. He shakes off his depression and faces his problems more objectively.

Directive Therapy

For the depressed person who cannot make decisions or take action, directive therapy must go into operation right away.

With older or partly senile patients who are unable to organize their own care and activity the entire day may have to be planned in detail. Their freedom from depression will depend on the extent to which they are kept busy, routinized, and entertained. However, take note that the activity itself puts the mind and body to work; it stimulates blood circulation, muscles, brain cells, and so on, all of which impel the person into further activity on his own initiative. Directives toward this end, with a resultant energizing force, often induce an improvement that cannot be duplicated by drugs or any other form of treatment.

Directive therapy also succeeds in a mild or moderate depression when the patient is immobilized only temporarily. First, he (or she) must be shown how to estimate the dimensions of the stress that oppress him, then be told how to circumvent or overcome the stress.

Such instructions are given in plain language and are shorn of intricacies—for example, what to say and what not to say to a fellow worker who delights in baiting the depressed person; how to respond to a difficult schoolteacher or parent without arousing conflict; what elementary rules of conduct to follow for achieving a harmonious social evening; how to pace out one's tasks, hour by hour, in order to maintain an even run of affairs despite the drag of despondency. The patient is thus given a storehouse of directives to draw upon, as the occasion may arise within his milieu. Later, with greater resilience after the depression wanes, he will adopt these directives as principles of conduct and make them his own.

For directive therapy, the doctor needs much more than his psychologic skills. He must also have at his fingertips a fund of knowledge in many areas, since the depressed person's drive is too blunted at this time to enable him to acquire it for himself. This information will include the names of the best job agencies for the individual to contact; the correct way to fill out an application or to organize a *curriculum vitae;* whom to engage to arrange a daughter's wedding when it is beyond the patient's own depressed capacity; where to take a cooking course in order to lure a husband from "mother's cooking"; a good vacation spot for a single woman who is lonely and blue; and where she might get clothes and makeup counseling to enhance her charm. And if the doctor does not have all the answers he should know who does.

For example, a young Negro man living in a ghetto area became chronically depressed. His mother, a cleaning-woman, had managed to sustain him through high school. After school hours and since graduation he had obtained a job as a delivery boy for a grocery store, but he could not mobilize himself to improve his work level. Because of his depression, his doctor referred him for psychiatric consultation.

Through directive therapy he was supported and encouraged into pursuing an intensive job-hunting campaign aimed at specific work targets; and since insomnia and sleep reversal (awake at night, asleep all day) were main symptoms of his depression he was instructed to look for a nighttime position. Although he was cynical about his chances, he found employment as a trainee in the data-processing field because he had requested night hours, for which applicants were in short supply. Later he worked himself into a higher position and salary as a valued employee, minus, incidentally, the insomnia and depression.

By setting up such an action or goal, one that falls within the person's potentials, the therapist prevents him from getting bogged down in deciphering his own motivations, desires, or doubts. The patient's depressed mood would keep him at a stalemate, but here he can put his trust in the therapist's judgment. Good direction can help the person move forward to produce. This cuts down the rigors of the depressive moods.

Suggestion

In psychiatry, suggestion is the art of implanting workable ideas into the patient's thinking. This may be done obliquely, and it works best with those who can react to their own constructive abilities once the suggestion is made. Such persons, when well, are the kind we recognize and admire as positive and assertive individuals. Therefore they do not respond well to directives; rather, they resent them and stiffen with resistance. But when they believe that a course of action is intrinsically their own idea they will proceed with it.

Suggestion helps in many areas of the person's life: it can instill in him graciousness and good manners for dealing successfully with others; it can challenge him to self-disciplines in work habits; it can intimate ways and means of transforming disadvantages into assets. It is especially good for insinuating new and valid goals into the consciousness of a person who is depressed.

In one case, a patient of mine who had retired from the presidency of a large corporation was so affected by his new inactivity that he sank into a reactive depression. Dazed and hurt, he felt that life had deserted him and only dreary empty years lay ahead. As we explored his feeling tones he recognized that he was grieving over a "loss" (his work). But it was not his prestige or ability to make money that he missed. "It's just that I don't feel useful any more." He agreed that he had many executive talents and energies, but where was he to take them? It was a young man's world. All the experience and wisdom he had acquired through the years amounted to zero if no one wanted them. "That's why I like to come here to chat with you, Doctor. It isn't that I feel sick—just depressed. But being here takes my mind off myself. And you act as if I'm interesting. The pills help too."

He began to muse aloud about the way his ambition had petered out since his retirement. For instance, a while back, before leaving his company, he had bought a large tract of land, an excellent piece of real estate in his community. At the time he had considered building a golf club on it. Now he didn't care what happened to it. There was no meaning in it any more.

One day before he arrived at my office, I placed a newspaper clipping on my desk where he would see it. We talked of his problem for a while before he spotted the news item. He read it several times—a story of a summer camp being developed in the Middle West for low-income families and their children. He continued to study it with an absent air then asked leave to keep it.

The next time I saw him he showed some enthusiasm for the first time in weeks. A gleam lit up his eyes as he explained that he had been thinking about the land he had bought. Why couldn't he build a place like the one out West in that news story? There were plenty of golf clubs, but how many people had access to a camp like that? He could go out there, study it from top to bottom, maybe improve on it. "With all I know about developing a project from the ground up, I can't miss on this." He actually did proceed with it, and within a year he brought the camp into being. He became its managing director and not long afterward it was going full force. When I saw him last he said, "Wasn't it lucky I thought of the camp in your office that day, Doctor? It was the best idea that ever came to me. I've never had so much fun. I feel ten years younger." And he looked it.

In another case, the mild depression of a young matron who came to see me had been triggered off by a mother-in-law, a retired schoolteacher, whose veiled innuendoes and quick barbs were interfering with the marriage. What it boiled down to was a clash between two headstrong women violently opposed to each other. (The bewildered young husband had retired from the fray and declared neutrality.) My patient's refrain was: "She treats me like a third-grade student. Whether I'm sewing curtains or changing the baby's diaper, she always criticizes. She sticks her nose into everything I do."

Her depression improved a little, and at that stage I suggested that perhaps she could persuade her mother-in-law into some activity that would deflect attention away from herself. Like what? Well, how about getting her mother-in-law involved in a hobby like painting? My patient could buy her some paints, an easel, brushes, and other equipment as a peace offering and see what came of it. "You mean she might get so busy with it that she'll lay off me?" "Something like that." She agreed to try it, but plainly showed her scorn for the proposal.

However, having made the purchases, the young woman could not tolerate the idea of offering a gift of appeasement (not entirely unpredictable). Instead, she began to dabble with the paints herself; with some encouragement, she worked into charcoal sketches and finally went on to sculpture. Before long this absorbed her so totally that both her mother-in-law and the depression were shut out. She gave more and more of herself to her art work, and today some of her pieces are displayed by the local bank and utility company. Her mother-in-law takes all the credit!

Thus, suggestions are first-rate therapy for the person who can be maneuvered subtly into paths of new accomplishment. They permit the depressed person to feel that he or she set up the goal and made the decision independently; and that the therapist simply gave his blessing to it.

Explanatory Therapy

When the person's thinking is so dulled and choked off that he cannot focus on any one thing and his memory betrays him from one moment to the next, he begins to doubt his sanity. It is then that clear explanations, coordinated with other treatment, can be used to allay his agitation and guide him back into "thinking straight."

In *endogenous depressions* patients are confused and muddled. They are terrified of their condition and beg to know "what hit me." In such cases, explaining the relationship of upsets in the delicate balance of chemical brain substances and nervous function to depressive illness can offer much relief from fear of the unknown. Very often curiosity supplants the anxious feelings and agitation. In the patient's eagerness to understand what happens to his physiology as improvement takes place, he becomes so absorbed in the answers that the fears no longer ride his back.

In a *grief reaction* that culminates in depression the

person may well be aware that it is a loss which has provoked his or her illness but nevertheless be alarmed by his symptoms. Here the first explanation will deal with the normalcy of the grief and how long it may be expected to last. Then the patient is told what has happened to him with the stress of loss. He is shown that the human being leans on his dependencies for survival, and therefore a major deprivation will pull the props from under him. Life will then seem insupportable and so crushing a burden that the psychic fatigue of depression overwhelms him, with a temporary inability to go on.

However, in comprehending the loss reaction, the person can then assess his or her *remaining worths and strengths;* and once he puts these strengths to work again, he subordinates the loss and gradually rises above the depressed mood.

In a *neurotic depression* the person usually does not understand that his adaptive reserve has been exhausted and that consequently he feels unable to face up to tasks and relationships. But when the adaptive process is explained in terms of stimulus and response and in terms of the individual's reaction and counterreaction to conflicts in living, the mystery of the symptoms is removed, and with it, much of their intensity.

Although patients do not always grasp every technical detail, their fears are lessened by the knowledge that explanations *do* exist. Patients want to hear such explanations, because these indicate that the illness is not an enigma, peculiar to them alone; rather, that it can be dealt with and cleared up just as any other illness can.

Precise explanations, then, not only provide information but also restore confidence by renewing the one essential that every depressed person needs—hope.

Behavior Therapy

Direct reeducation for more successful living is a conditioning process. We call this "behavior therapy." It can educate the chronically depressed person to perform with more incentive and greater optimism. It is useful also for patients with mild-to-moderate degrees of reactive and neurotic depressions and as a combined or follow-up procedure for any person who has adjusted poorly to life situations before, during, or after a depressive illness.

Behavior therapy applies learning techniques and the principles of conditioning to teach the person how to modify maladaptive personality attitudes, traits, and behavior. For example, it trains him how to relax and avert fears, panic, and anger explosions within the depression. It also trains him how to express his innermost feelings and thus dissipate his depression. The longer-range goal of this treatment method is to overcome neurotic patterns so that they will never again terminate in nervous collapse and depressive illness.

The obsessive-compulsive who is depressed offers especially fertile conditions for improvement with behavior therapy. Such persons are "remade" when they learn how to be more resilient in order to accommodate to life's twists and turns. These victims of the compulsive need to check on each of their actions over and over again often respond to the conditioning process more quickly and effectively than to any other psychotherapeutic technique. Thus, they are taught to train themselves to walk with greater ease and more frequency on the right side of the street, when their compulsion screams to keep to the left; to refrain from going to the back door a dozen times to see if it is locked; to stop counting all the items in a bundle of groceries repetitively; or to cut off at the start any other compulsive act in order to carry out an obsession.

Behavior therapy breaks up rigid patterns and helps the person to establish new ways of life much as certain exercises make creaking bones and tight muscles supple and pliant for unaccustomed physical activity. It steers him or her away from the exhaustion of adaptive reserve that leads to depression.

Environmental Manipulation

This procedure is used to find or establish a milieu in which the patient can live and adjust without further wasting his strengths or testing his regressed function.

One might say that it simply means changing his physical and social environment. But the results are by no means simple, because they ultimately modify all aspects of his personality function and developmental patterns. The purpose of manipulating the surroundings is to reduce stresses that take a heavy toll of the individual and pound at his resources beyond endurance.

For example, the therapist may persuade a family not to harry the depressed person into withdrawal. This can mean that he or she is provided with a quiet room, one separated from the mainstream of family noise and the turbulence which provoke him to nervous excitement. Or, in a more extended goal, especially in neurotic or chronic depressions, the patient may be prodded into a new and less demanding job; into switching over to a college where the competition is not so stiff; or into moving to a locale which does not involve the frenetic commuting that empties his or her vitality supply.

One environmental change that may be required as a life-saving measure is to hospitalize an acutely depressed person in order to protect him from his agitated or suicidal thoughts. Here one is manipulating to avoid self-destruction.

Trip Therapy

This kind of environmental shift is a tactic that can be used for mild depressions caused by excess fatigue or a recent depressing event. In such cases, the distraction of a change of scene alone will constitute the treatment. This applies particularly to the neurotically depressed individual who needs to regress to carefree vacation patterns. Such escape offers some healing. Certainly it is vastly preferable to an imminently explosive situation that may thrust him or her into acute depression.*

---

* Here I will add the negative side of Trip Therapy. Once the person is in an acute stage of depressive illness, going away on a trip contains little worth. Actually, vacationing at this time may hurt him by intensifying his awareness that he cannot enjoy the sunshine, the sports, and the dancing as everyone else does. Moreover, he will still not find sleep, savor food, or develop an iota of cheerfulness. He merely takes his depression with him to the vacation resort and continues to be miserable. In such a state, active treatment, not rest, is required to repair the nervous system.

Group Therapy

All the psychologic procedures that I have described in this chapter can be enlisted with benefit in a group setting involving four to ten patients.

Group therapy is advantageous to the chronically depressed neurotic person. Apart from its lower cost, it forces the patient to see himself in relation to others. He can then recognize and assess both his weaknesses and his strengths among his peers. He also finds many of his needs answered quickly: he discovers that he is not alone in his illness, that the group will support him emotionally, encourage his efforts to improve himself, and admire his restraint in not succumbing to self-pity.

He grows in stature too, because he learns to give to the others through their most trying moments. This helps him remodel his own tendencies to linger in despair. He sees that "they're just as bad off as I am . . . if they can make the grade and pull out of it, so can I." Group therapy may be combined with any type of individual treatment for the depressed person. However, a word of warning: Moderately to severely depressed persons should avoid encounter, sensitivity, or T-groups, marathon group meetings, and similar highly charged programs. The individual in a debilitated emotional state needs support. His lowered threshold cannot tolerate many of the current group therapies which are faddist, unproven, and potentially destructive. The depressed person should not participate in such treatment except on the recommendation of a psychiatrist.

Family Therapy

Here only the members of one family constitute a group and are treated as such. An even newer concept is that of Multiple Conjoint Family Therapy, wherein several patients with their families meet together.

Family procedures are recommended when a key member suffers from chronic depression and his or her illness tears apart the emotional fabric of the others, creating turmoil and a resultant tangle of hostilities. For such situations, family therapy can be the answer. In this procedure, the patient *plus* a large and important segment of his environment are being treated and maneuvered at the same time; and it is hoped that out of this group work a satisfactory *rapprochement* among all family members will be achieved, with each one educated to exert fewer pressures on the depressed patient himself.

Other Psychotherapeutic Procedures

There are several other major psychotherapeutic techniques which I have not brought up here, but which you have probably heard about. They are described below.

Interpretative Psychotherapy

This highly intellectual and complex method explores the many symbols in communication and their role in mental function.

The purpose of this procedure is to give the person *insight* into his motivations—that is, to have him understand, for example, the meaning of his self-image and his behavior in terms of such symbols as the car he buys or the address at which he chooses to live; the significance contained in the threat to his survival when an epithet is hurled at him; and what his likes, dislikes, and attention-seeking signify under the surface. The emphasis is on the hidden *why's* of the person's thinking, feeling, and behavior as they are interpreted from his dreams and conscious speech. It is assumed that benefits will ensue from the therapy if he or she learns to interpret the symbols and then change the patterns of living accordingly.

However, I use this procedure only for the treatment of certain personality disorders *other* than depression. When combined with drugs and explanatory therapy it occasionally helps in mild cases of reactive and neurotic depression but it contains little or no value for patients with endogenous or other kinds of acute or severe depressive illnesses.

Psychoanalysis

Psychoanalysis is the classical method of interpretative therapy (i.e., free association; the patient usually lies on a couch and talks at random). It is founded on Freudian theory, which interprets the person's unconscious and instinctual libidinous drives and his psychosexual development, how these forces create fixations at immature levels of personality function, and why they embroil him in conflict and other difficulties.

However, most of my Freudian and neo-Freudian colleagues agree that psychoanalysis is too prolonged and intensive a procedure for the treatment of depressive disorders, especially those which are acute or show severe agitation. The responsible spokesmen for the psychoanalytic schools today feel that the tempo of social and medical change has been stepped up so greatly that psychoanalysis, as a treatment form, needs extensive modification in both theory and practice in order to provide briefer methods of psychotherapy for dealing with depressive illness.

Those psychoanalysts who work in clinics and have seen the rapid improvement of the person's depression when brief psychotherapy is applied express enthusiasm for this method and a greater satisfaction with its results.

CHAPTER FIFTEEN

Your Role in Psychotherapy

WHEN THIS method of treatment for your relative is suggested, your first question may be: "Which kind of psychotherapy is best for depression?"

There are so many theoretic approaches to psychotherapy, each propounding different concepts, that if you are confused by them it is understandable. However, let us start with this premise: *in the treatment of depression,* no one procedure in psychotherapy should be considered "best" or be used to the abandonment of all others. Rather the gauge should be: *first,* whether the method of psychotherapy contains the means of dealing effectively with the ever-present danger of a suicidal intent that always lurks in depressive illness; *second,* whether it can give the patient quick relief for his symptoms; *third,* whether it will eliminate his hopelessness and thus enable him to stand on his own feet as soon as possible in order to fulfill his potentials, achieve his goals, and interrelate successfully with others. And as I just mentioned at the end of Chapter 14, there is general concurrence among psychoanalysts and nonpsychoanalysts alike that for depression the abbreviated forms of psychotherapy are best for meeting these conditions.

The important questions for you to raise, then, are these: has the doctor the training and scope of knowledge to diagnose the illness and release the patient from his depressive inhibitions and the thoughts of self-destruction that preoccupy him? Does he possess the basic humanity and intuition to create a rapport that will sustain the patient through his blackest moments? Can he reeducate the person to better value judgments for facing life without conflict and despair? Are his experience and authority broad enough to free the individual's drive by changing his background if need be, in order to help remove his melancholia? And can he relieve the despondency by inducing and directing him or her into making good decisions and acting upon them?

At this point, perhaps, there is a further question: How do you, as a lay person, make this appraisal? One way is to undertake intelligent queries (see Chapter 18) about the psychiatrist or other therapist that the patient may want to consult. Another can be your own (or the patient's) evaluation of the therapist in an initial interview with him. From these inquiries you can learn whether the doctor is circumscribed by training or preference to a particular theory or method or whether his outlook embraces every aspect of psychotherapy and societal awareness that will meet the patient's needs, in clearing up his depression.

WILL PSYCHOTHERAPY ALONE HELP DEPRESSION?

Provided that the emotional upset is mild and not complicated by endogenous factors, psychotherapy may succeed in mobilizing your relative and reestablishing healthy ego function. But keep in mind that if the depression persists or intensifies, drugs or other treatment will be needed to augment the therapeutic program. In severe cases with a suicide potential, psychotherapy alone will not overcome the depression, although it may stave off the suicidal *gesture* and keep the person alive and going until other treatment can be instituted.

Also, you should note that the goals of treatment may change within the psychotherapeutic process. For instance, when the illness is acute but minor, an intensive but relatively short series of treatment sessions may be quite enough. On the other hand, if the treatment uncovers disabling and tenacious personality traits which are stumbling blocks to a full and rapid recovery, the goal will be modified, because the depression and personality are intertwined; they must, then, be treated as one. In such cases therapy may take longer, so be prepared for this development if it arises.

Accompanying the Patient for Psychotherapy

It may be worthwhile to accompany your relative to the psychotherapeutic sessions at first. Depression is a private and lonely kind of illness and whenever you can brace the person's stamina it is an act of mercy; in effect, you are telling him that you want to share his emotional burdens without intruding. Your physical presence at this time gives him a sense of being sheltered and loved.

Nevertheless, do not be surprised if a time arrives when the doctor tells you that to come with the patient is no longer desirable. You can be gladdened by this, because it probably means that he is testing your relative's capacity to stand alone once more and rely on himself. Therefore, when the doctor proposes, not only that the patient should now keep his appointments alone but that you might encourage him to do so, listen well and cooperate. You are then reinforcing the treatment.

WILL THE DOCTOR WANT ME TO REPORT MY OBSERVATIONS ABOUT THE PATIENT?

From time to time, yes, though let us be clear on this. He can utilize a *factual* résumé of the patient's activities at different periods but not your *opinions*. Report only what your relative said or how he or she behaved, slept, socialized, and so on. Do not attempt to interpret any of this or to reel off a list of comments that are, in fact, a summary of your own worries. Let the doctor evaluate the information for himself.

You will not realize how much you can impart within a short time until you try. If you marshal your ideas in advance, your account will offer everything that is necessary. You can also give it to the doctor's secretary or, in a clinic, to the social worker. Another way is to have the patient deliver a note from you to the doctor containing the essence of your observations, written with an economy of words.

At the other extreme, do not be so telegraphic that you wrap it all up in a few terse phrases. For instance, one day when I noted that a depressed patient of mine seemed to be improving I called her husband and asked if she was eating well. He said: "Hardly at all. Like a bird." Now that was a conclusion that told me nothing. Subsequently, I learned that she was having orange juice, hot cereal, buttered toast, jam, and tea for breakfast. Her other two meals were equally hearty, but her husband considered this intake minute since, as I later discovered, his own eating habits verged on gluttony. (Do you recall what I said about the relative being subjective? This is a glaring example.)

Checking with the Doctor

You should call the doctor about your relative's progress when necessary. Indeed, it seems to me that any wise physician would want to keep the next-of-kin informed regularly as to whether the patient is on the mend. If you have been reading this book carefully I need hardly repeat that when a relative is in a depression everyone in the family is touched by its shadow. Certainly you are entitled to know "what is happening" to the patient's health, and if you have not heard from the doctor a telephone call to him now and then would not be amiss.

Still, this is not carte blanche to overdo it. If you do, you make a nuisance of yourself, no matter how much you apologize to him (which also takes up the doctor's time). Depression is not a high fever that may drop to normal an hour later. Healing your relative's depression is a somewhat slower process. When you find yourself calling before and after every therapeutic interview, think about it and you will see that you have become so enmeshed emotionally in your relative's illness that you are asking the doctor to treat *your* anxieties.

Making Your Own Appointment

Some doctors consider psychotherapy a supraprivate affair and refuse to see a relative under any circumstance. I doubt that such refusal is ever warranted in the psychotherapy of a *depressed* person unless the latter absolutely demands it.

You may want to consult the same doctor who is treating your relative because, as I suggested above, the latter's anxieties have become yours and you need the opportunity to voice them. By all means, see your relative's doctor, although here too you may have heard that "it is not done." Perhaps some therapists feel this way, but most are objective enough to handle two or more family members involved in one illness. For the rare time when it might cause friction (if, let us say, the patient is overwhelmingly "possessive" about *his* doctor) you will be informed of this and referred to a colleague.

Offering Your Own Brand of Psychotherapy

A thought may sometimes run through your mind: "Can I put myself in the doctor's shoes and make the patient do what I believe is best?"

After thinking that one over, you had better discuss it with the doctor. I will not deny that your intentions are of the highest order; but your ideas may be so unsound when you fancy yourself as the therapist that you are likely, so to speak, to fall flat on your face with undesired results.

Many relatives have raised this question in disguised ways. Intolerant of the patient's depression, they toy with the idea of giving him or her therapy by administering (in their own words) "a swift, hard kick in the pants." Another family member may unwittingly compete with the relative's depression (for attention) and would like to let the patient know that his illness "is just too much and knocks the stuffing out of me." This conception of therapy is really a demand that the person please get well in a hurry (thus intensifying the patient's guilt) "before I have a nervous breakdown too."

Or, if the relative is a disciplinarian, he may decide that the best psychotherapy is to barge in with brutal frankness (according to his value judgments) to whip the patient into health. "Now listen to me. I want you to cut out this crap and get yourself back to normal. Start acting like everybody else. You can do it. And make it as of right now, pronto!" Relatives should not attempt such approaches. Rarely, if ever, do they help a depressed person.

Some try to interpose their psychotherapy through the doctor. One may be more tactful perhaps and worm his own suggestions into a general conversation. Others are not in the least abashed to instruct him on how to handle the patient or suggest specific medications that they "know" are very good "because they helped my aunt."

One father said to me: "Why don't you just tell Mary to go out on dates more? That's what she needs to cheer her up. She's too shut in. All that stuff about being blue is just the bunk. I know her through and through." Now let us imagine that I did tell Mary that. It might bring a sad fleeting smile to her downcast face and she would nod. "My father must have called you." Mary had been listening to him say similar things for several years before I saw her. But what he did not even guess was that for some time Mary was thinking hard of the peace it would bring her if she could die. In treatment it was my task just to keep her interested enough to stay alive. Going out on dates was for a future not yet in sight. When this was explained to her father he again denied that she was depressed and brushed her suicidal thoughts aside as "nonsense."

Thus, be sure you know the facts, regard them seriously, and see whither you are heading before you interject your own beliefs.

Taking Your Cue from the Doctor

In contrast to the foregoing, you really help when you assist the treatment program *in accordance* with the doctor's procedures.

For example, should the patient need more emotional support than the doctor can provide in his once- or twice-a-week therapeutic sessions, he may ask you to supplement it and then tell you how. Or suppose the depression is a reactive one, due to a loss. He may ask that you spend more time with your relative; or he may explain how you should communicate your awareness of the patient's deep hurt at his or her loss. Relatives sometimes *feel* empathetic but hesitate to speak, afraid that they may say the wrong words. However, you may not realize how much consolation a depressed person derives from verbalized expressions of empathy, groping and inadequate as you think they are.

The doctor may also ask for your help in carrying out his directives to the patient. Once, a young mother in a neurotic depression shamefacedly confessed to me that when she went on a spree of window-shopping it lifted her low mood and for a while sparked a gaiety and interest in herself which had fled. There was one hitch: She was still too frightened to go out alone again and yet too embarrassed to ask for company on these little expeditions, fearing that she would be condemned as frivolous and more interested in clothes than in her home and child.

When I contacted the husband I marveled at this young man's insight. No questions, no doubts. He grasped the need instantly and quickly arranged for a baby sitter and a companion for his wife. After her excursions she would return home, refreshed by the fun of the day and ready to tackle some responsibilities. Without the collaboration of her husband this simple but important therapeutic diversion could not have been carried out.

I also recall a young man who was highly dubious of working in league with the doctor. His father was a sixty-eight-year-old widower who clung to a shoe-repair shop which no longer earned a profit but gave him "a place to go" every day. The father's two brothers, who had bought a small bungalow in Florida and retired there, were after him to join them, but a low-grade depression made him unable to rally himself for the move.

I discussed him with his son. The latter was not convinced that his father was depressed. "I think you're wrong. Dad has never known anything but work. Sure he's close to his brothers but I know it would kill him to give up the shop." I suggested that it might kill him *not* to and persuaded him to take his father to Florida for a visit, then return and negotiate the winding-up of his father's affairs. With open misgivings he went through with it, mainly because his uncles, with whom I had spoken, were backing me up.

Some months later I had lunch with the patient in Florida. For the first ten minutes he sputtered his vexation at me and "the way you had me shanghaied." But as he talked a glint came into his eyes and he could no longer restrain his pleased chuckle at my "highhandedness." This man is in his seventies today and enjoys many activities in his retirement with his brothers. Had his son not worked with me, the father might well have continued to suffer from a chronic depression in a climate that was sapping both his physical and his mental health.

Therefore, while it is true that in most cases psychotherapy is a one-to-one relationship, there are cases wherein the family must be involved. The doctor may call on you to help educate the patient into a new perspective of his illness (as in explanatory and directive therapy); to assist in overcoming the fear of crossing bridges and going through tunnels (as in behavior therapy); to bear with the person without inhibiting him when he has to "let off steam" (as in release therapy); or to help in any other area. This is the brand of psychotherapy that is your contribution.

When Your Relative Becomes Secretive

Patients in psychotherapy often do grow reticent with the family. Different reasons may dictate it. It can be merely that the person is talking things out so profoundly with the doctor that it is too wearying to plow through them again with you. Or sometimes the airing of inner problems creates such a deep thoughtfulness that it preoccupies the patient and insulates him from all else.

In another case he may be so appalled by what he is revealing to the doctor at long last that secrecy is the only course. For example, a woman I know was despondent because she could no longer deal with her husband's abusive and hypercritical temperament. A sweet and dependent person, she was helpless against his harangues. Yet she loved him because in many areas he was considerate, generous, and devoted. Caught in this dilemma, she exhausted her ability to adapt to him and his outbursts at her expense. She became depressed.

In psychotherapy she ventilated her conflict and the rebellious thoughts she had nursed through the years. But once the guard was off her tongue she worried that she might slip up and disclose these thoughts to her husband. She met the predicament with a tight-lipped silence about her sessions with the doctor. It was not until therapy gave her the courage to cope with her marital problem that she again became the warm and cheerful person she had been before.

During the period of psychotherapy, her husband went through an agony of waiting, sure that he had lost her. But in standing by he learned more patience and tolerance than he had ever known before, and he began to appreciate his wife. A better relationship, built on a more cordial foundation of respect and courtesy, emerged, and what he had thought a bitter trial proved to be an opportunity to redeem himself.

There are also times when the patient's lessened communication means that he is waiting for the doctor to disclose to you what he himself is not brave enough to say. It is quite usual for a patient to "speak" to his family through the therapist, especially in depressive illness where feelings of unworthiness may possess the patient. Such people often feel excluded from family life through no fault of the relatives. Simply, the person is too humble to ask for acceptance or affection, but he yearns for them nevertheless. The therapist, in his third-party role, can indicate these needs to the family, who then learn to dispel the patient's loneliness and feelings of rejection.

When your relative becomes secretive while in psychotherapy it often means that he or she is discussing with the doctor some highly charged emotional material which may or may not include you. And when you are shut out it is a shock. As the spouse or parent you may be stunned at having the door closed in your face. But try to avoid the harmful attitudes that I have seen. Do not react with indignation; do not withdraw, or become irritable or sulky, or perhaps bear with it but at the same time visibly grit your teeth. Instead, put yourself in your relative's position for a moment. Review your own personal and intimate thoughts which have bothered you at different times —of hidden angers, guilts, hurts, despair, fears, and mistakes, and judge whether you would want to disclose them lightly and entrust them to anyone but a doctor. If you are honest, your reply will be "No."

Therefore, in this difficult period, respect the privacy that your depressed relative needs. And while you are doing so, try to be gallant about it. In the long run you will be thankful that you did not tamper with this delicate situation at the time.

What to Do If You Are Dissatisfied with the Doctor's Treatment

If you believe that more could be done for your relative's depression or that another therapist's personality or treatment program might be better, take your ideas and doubts directly to the doctor. Any therapist knows that differences in rapport arise; and that confidence and trust, not only from the patient but from the family as well, are fundamental to successful treatment. For myself, I would not care to treat someone whose family were not with me. They would end, whether consciously or not, by undercutting the progress I made. If you have uncertainties of any sort, bring them into the open. The therapist may well be able to erase them for you with answers as forthright as your questions. If you are still not sure, request that he arrange for consultation with someone else. Any reputable doctor will be ready to oblige.

CHAPTER SIXTEEN

Psychiatric Hospitalization

YOUR DEPRESSED relative may be so ill that the doctor will want to hospitalize him—that is, he will recommend *psychiatric* hospitalization in an accredited and approved service.

I am aware that you may become frightened at this (as some do) and perhaps start to plead that you "haven't the heart to lock him up," that you know a psychiatric facility is an "institution," "a booby hatch," or a "snake pit," and you are sure that once there, no one ever leaves again.

However, you may not realize that in reacting this way you are responding in part to a bias whose origin lies in the ignorance of the past, when the mentally ill were punished as wrongdoers, then stigmatized for the punishment they received. But today it is known that your relative's depression is not a moral affair any more than appendicitis is, and if the doctor believes that treatment should be given in a psychiatric hospital your better course is to be governed by what he says.

Nevertheless, your fears are not entirely groundless—but for other reasons. You are correct if you feel that there are things wrong with some psychiatric hospitals, especially the state, county, and municipal facilities. There are. Many are overcrowded and do not have an adequate staff (see Chapter 18), and as a result, patient care suffers. Treatment and over-all supervision are often geared to a limited hospital budget and not to the patient's needs. On the active ward, the chances are that the patient will be treated intensively, yes. But on the chronic wards, and especially where the illness is of long standing, treatment tends to be drawn out and there is not enough concentration on the patient to get him well and functioning as early as possible. In other words, the patient who gives promise of a quick and good recovery receives more immediate attention. The chronic patient is treated on the principle that "improvement will take more time." These are the factual reasons for anxiety.

Your prejudices, however, are another matter. To explain: I am sure that you have been a visitor at a general hospital more than once. As you walked along the corridor you smelled the reek of disinfectants, you saw stretcher cases lined up in the hallways, you caught a glimpse of someone with his leg in traction, and you heard the moaning of postoperative patients in pain. None of this was pleasant, but in a way you *expected* it. One may almost say that it was familiar to you because it concerned the *physical* aspect of patient care to which you have been conditioned; you could understand and accept it.

In a psychiatric hospital, however, should you hear a groan it seems eerie and clutches at your vitals. It is mysteriously *mental*. All that you have ever heard of "lunacy" and deteriorated minds suddenly returns to chill you. In short, when you visit such a facility you bring your prejudices and imagination into play. A patient in an agitated depression may cry out in anguish; instantly this conjures up visions of abuse, neglect, and everything you have unconsciously absorbed from stories of brutal treatment of the mentally ill in the bedlams of the eighteenth and nineteenth centuries.

But try to realize how wrong this picture is. Regardless of your subjective reaction, keep in mind that many laws, strict licensing, and regular supervision by state officials protect the patient in any psychiatric hospital, and that humane attitudes are the guiding principle for the care of all mentally ill persons. The psychiatric facility is a *treatment center* built, not to imprison the patient, but to serve and heal him, and finally to return him home improved and better equipped to manage his life.

So remember this. While only a small percentage of depressed persons needs hospitalization (considering the ease of outpatient care today), when the hospital *is* required, the need for that person at that time is one hundred per cent. It is just as much a point of crisis for him as the emergency of an abdominal operation would be. It cannot be taken care of in an office or on the kitchen table at home.

Therefore, if you ignore the doctor's judgment, refuse psychiatric hospitalization, and, let us say, press him to admit your relative to a neurologic service instead, your choice will give you cold comfort. The neurologic service will provide excellent facilities for a paralyzed patient or for one with a brain tumor, but not for someone who is depressed. And if you want to play the game further and ask that he or she be sent to a medical service, you will get just that—oxygen tents, cardiac stimulators, laboratories, and other equipment for medical, but not psychiatric, care. Moreover, most families do not realize that if the hospital personnel of the medical service find a patient too "troublesome" or disturbed to handle, they will transfer him to a psychiatric facility anyhow. You are back where you started. Rather than go through all this unnecessary wear and tear, you should be asking the doctor the following question.

What Are the Advantages of Hospitalization?

He may counter with two questions: If you needed surgery would you not prefer a surgical facility rather than a medical one? If a woman requires obstetric care will she not seek an obstetric facility rather than a medical or surgical service?

Psychiatric care demands the same specialization. For example, psychiatric facilities differ from others in many respects, including the architecture and services. Among their distinguishing features are lounging rooms for daytime living and socializing, because psychiatric patients are not bedridden (except with a concomitant physical illness). There are dining halls (meals are not served in patients' rooms) with tables set for two to four persons. Large areas for recreational and other activities, for group psychotherapy, and for physical treatments are built into the structure. The décor and furnishings of a patient's room more nearly resemble those of a studio room or a home setting. The lighting arrangements are gracious and soothing and meant for the patient's comfort.

Many special features have also been devised in order to observe and monitor the patient and to prevent him from hurting himself or carrying out a suicide attempt. These features were all integrated into the hospital plans when the facility was built or reconstructed.

Although the above description of some of the physical plants may seem idealized to you, it accurately portrays all of the *new* and *rehabilitated* psychiatric units which have been brought into being since about 1950. Nevertheless, I want to insert the other side of the picture.

It is shameful that in our opulent society of today, a number of state, county, and municipal facilities are shabby and dilapidated, and require essential repairs. This is just as true of some *private* psychiatric hospitals. While the latter usually provide enough personnel, they may offer surroundings just as dismal as those of a state or other public facility. A friend of mine recently visited someone in an expensive private hospital which prides itself on its social exclusiveness. He was appalled. The décor in this place is dark and mid-Victorian, the furniture old, the atmosphere gloomy and musty. It is no wonder that this is now his impression of all psychiatric facilities (although I may add that many medical and surgical hospitals still exist with the same unpleasant *ambiance*).

My friend felt that the appearance of the place was in itself enough to depress the patient. Certainly it depressed him, the visitor. And he may well have been justified. Color and design are known to affect a depressed person psychologically, for good or ill. This is why appealing decorative and furnishing schemes are now carefully devised by experts and incorporated into the newer places. For example, three of the four buildings in a state hospital with which I am familiar were newly constructed (since World War II) and the fourth building will soon be under way. All are attractive and modern. More hospitals like this are being built, other hospitals are being rehabilitated, and new psychiatric wings are being established in general hospitals (see discussion in Chapter 18).

However, at present we must deal with what we have, despite the shortcomings. When hospitalization is required for the depressed person, only a psychiatric facility, regardless of its appearance or imperfect services, will answer the patient's needs and fulfill the doctor's purpose.

Four main reasons dictate that you accept his decision.

The Hospital Provides Comprehensive Diagnostic and Consultation Services

In the majority of cases a depressive illness and its nature can be readily diagnosed and treated on an outpatient basis—but suppose it cannot. What if the patient who is depressed is also afflicted with uncontrolled diabetes, heart or circulation deficits, blood-pressure irregularities, glandular deficiencies, or an active infection? Or suppose he or she is an alcoholic, takes certain drugs addictively, or presents medical emergencies along with the depression? Medical treatment must then be combined with psychiatric care in a hospital that supplies *all* services to the patient equally.

The Hospital Provides Special Observation and Nursing

Trained staff members offer nursing that is far superior to any obtainable at home for a desperately depressed person. How much care will a deeply melancholic woman get from a husband who must work? From children who go to school? From relatives who live at a distance? And what physician will want to rely on family reports about the reactions of so ill a person when he can get professional supervision and precise evaluations from a trained aide or nurse?

In earlier chapters you learned that EST, Indoklon, and drugs or modifications or combinations of these procedures can be given as outpatient treatment. But you also read that each one requires certain kinds of management. If no one at home can provide the care that I described, then what? The only alternative to ensure that your relative gets the needed treatment is a psychiatric hospital. If you insist on home care you may, in effect, restrain the doctor from offering the best treatment that can do the most good in the shortest time for your relative.

For example, the quantity of drugs that he must prescribe in order to conquer a given kind of depression may create too great a risk for office and home treatment. It may require the use of skilled personnel who can spot early warning signs of an adverse drug response.

Let us say that the patient is receiving antidepressant (or tranquilizing) drugs in maximum dosages and complains of a sore throat. To a resident physician or a nurse this could mean that the drug is destroying the white blood cells, a condition which might prove extremely serious. The resident or nurse would call the attending or senior staff doctor and arrange for immediate laboratory tests to confirm their observations. At the same time, standby transfusion equipment would be set up. I doubt whether anyone at home would realize that when the sore throat appeared he was dealing with an emergency.

The Hospital Provides Protective Care

If your relative shows active suicidal tendencies or severe agitation and perhaps destructiveness, a psychiatric service may safeguard him or her far better than you can at home. True, his movements in the hospital are restricted. The doors may be secured to prevent his running outside in a panic of agitation or hysteria. The windows are screened to stop him from a sudden leap. He or she will also be watched unobtrusively from specially placed vantage points to anticipate any self-injury. In some rooms the beds may be only a foot high so that he cannot in a distraught moment throw himself to the floor or fall off accidentally. These safety features are built in to protect the person who might harm himself.

Yes, I know that in Chapter 7, I told you that if someone in the family can really look after the patient and control his behavior twenty-four hours a day all will be well. But I also pointed out that handling a severely agitated person or one who is determined to commit suicide requires more than one relative's attendance. Two or more persons may be needed to supervise the patient with an explosive emotionality. Not only that, someone highly efficient must familiarize himself with all the possibilities. For example, can this person arrange to clear out the medicine chests? Hide scissors, knives and razors?

Have the windows bolted? Take off the latches from closets and bathroom doors?

In the management of deep depression, these are some of the things that round-the-clock care entails. In many cases, only a hospital can offer such precautions.

Another kind of protection is found in the hospital—a reduction of stress on the depressed person. Within such a facility he is spared the bitter contrast of his regressed mood with the normal personalities of his environment. He is no longer caught in the social need to mask his sense of unworthiness and failure, to be forced to respond to relationships which may serve to intensify his depression.

The Hospital Provides Relief for the Family

Apart from medical considerations, hospitalizing your relative may be your wisest choice, because the trepidations of the family, which in turn spill over to the depressed person, are thus eased. To invest in hospital care, then, may also be emotionally and psychologically advisable.

One further advantage is to be had. There is no loss of time or income as in home care, when someone must stay with the patient and nurse him or her through the illness. Thus, hospitalization may represent an economic gain because it keeps the family going as an intact unit of production for income purposes.

WHAT HAPPENS AT THE HOSPITAL?

Admission to a psychiatric facility is little different from admission to a medical or surgical one. If you are the legal and interested next-of-kin you should be there to assume responsibility for your relative's affairs during his hospital stay and to satisfy legal, medical, and financial requirements.

Information That You Give at the Admitting Office

Those in charge will want the patient's full name, address, telephone number, and place and date of birth; also, the vital statistics of marital status, citizenship, name and place of employer, parents, and other next-of-kin.

They will also ask to see the identifying cards of any hospital insurance that the patient carries, such as Blue Cross, Major Medical, Medicare, and so on. (If the patient is not covered by insurance most private hospitals will require some payment in advance, usually for two weeks.)

The Medical History

Even when the person enters a hospital where he is attended by his own physician the resident staff physician must get enough information from you to make an initial diagnosis. Do not be jolted if he queries you about the mental health of all family members, including yourself. He may ask you about nervous breakdowns in the parents and even the grandparents. I urge you not to hide what you may consider skeletons in the closet. It will not help the patient if you withhold anything from the history. Be assured that your confidence will be kept.

You will also be questioned closely as to how and when your relative became depressed, the kinds of changes in his or her behavior, the circumstances surrounding the onset of the illness, and whether there was a previous depression. The doctor will want to know specifically what brought your relative to the hospital: Was there talk of suicide? Was he destructive? Delusional? Hallucinatory? Withdrawn? Give all of this accurately and fully and add anything else that you may consider relevant.

Cooperate with the Resident Physician

This is important. Your private doctor may see your relative a few minutes to an hour a day, but the resident attends eight to twelve hours daily. If you intimate that "my doctor knows all about the case and you needn't bother," the resident may do just that—not bother. Later, when you call him for information about your relative you will regret this. His report to you will of necessity be sparse because you did not want him involved and now he is not as familiar with the case as he would like to be.

Also, you might need a copy of the hospital record at some time for whatever reason. When you do not co-operate it will contain such statements as, "Information not obtained" or "Relatives refused to supply further information." Such a record is useless for future reference. Therefore, give the resident the benefit of courtesy, frankness, and a full account.

Certain Papers Must Be Signed

First, there is the request for admission. Although some hospitals today have introduced the "informal admission," most state laws still require either a voluntary commitment signature from the patient (usually for fifteen days) or a certificate of admission signed by one, sometimes two, physicians, if the patient will not admit himself voluntarily. Physicians' certificates must also be signed by the patient's next-of-kin. (See Chapter 18 for a more extensive discussion of admission procedures.)

Second, the patient or a responsible relative will be asked to sign an agreement to pay the bills and to abide by all hospital rules and regulations.

Third, a signed consent for any specific treatment such as EST will be requested.

There may be other papers too, including assignment of insurance to the hospital for payment of bills.

None of this is complicated if you are prepared in advance. If not, it can overwhelm you when the clerk in the admitting office produces "all those papers." However, as part of the complex legal and social system in which we live today we can only accept this "paper explosion" as equably as possible and make the best of it.

After Admission

Your relative will be taken by a nurse to his (or her) assigned room. An aide will help him unpack, check his belongings, and get him settled. She will take all valuable papers, jewelry, and money in excess of petty cash (the latter is usually two dollars) for safe deposit in the hospital vault or, as I generally advise, give them to you to take home.

While on this subject (it comes up all the time), I want to add that no matter how attached a patient is to a significant document (for example, citizenship papers) or a special ornament (a jeweled wedding ring) or how much he or she wants to hold on to it, do not sympathize with this desire. The chance of loss is too great. Prudence is the better course, because a hospital is no place for valuable personal belongings. Here you should not indulge your relative's sentimentalities.

The Patient Is Examined

Shortly after arrival on the floor he or she is interviewed, usually by the doctor to whom you gave the history. The purpose of this examination, which may last for an hour or more, is to assess the patient's mental status. Within twenty-four hours (or immediately, if the person's condition demands it) he will be given a complete physical examination, including some routine laboratory tests. His heart condition and blood pressure will be recorded along with observations of his physical and mental condition. If needed, there will be consultation with other specialists. (Except in an emergency situation, the family are notified and their approval requested should specialty consultation be required.)

The Patient Is Introduced to His New Environment

Your relative is assigned to a group in accordance with his or her age, the intensity of the illness, and the ability to participate in adjunctive hospital programs (which I will describe below). Introductions are made to the nurses, aides, other personnel, and the patients in his group. His attention is directed to the bulletin board, which lists the day and evening programs, meal times, rest periods, and activity schedules. He is also told about the availability of various personnel services (see Chapter 17). His table in the dining room is pointed out, but eating arrangements are flexible; later he may choose other companions to dine with.

The Treatment Program

Depending on the orders written by the attending or staff physician, the patient will be given physical treatments (EST), drugs, psychotherapy, group therapy, or any combination of these. His other routines will be modified to fit in with his treatment schedule. In addition to the psychiatric treatment he will receive medical care for any chronic or acute illness, other than the depression itself. (See section on comprehensive services, earlier in this chapter.)

Adjunctive Treatment

He may also become engaged in the following therapeutic procedures which fall into the broad categories of OT (occupational therapy) and RT (recreational therapy). Remember these terms, because in reporting to you the staff will refer to them by their abbreviations. These activities are directed and supervised by trained professionals who have taken their degrees in this work.

THE THERAPEUTIC COMMUNITY. Actually, this is another form of group therapy, but in this case it is related to the immediate social setting. It is community work on a small scale, and it imposes a need on the patient to join in the democratic management of all floor activities. It is fine stimulation for the withdrawn and depressed person; once it captures his interest, it precipitates him into the excitement of involvement with others; this in turn impels him to participate in his own improvement.

ACTIVITIES THERAPY. The hospital is equipped with materials for painting, sculpture, ceramics, leather work, sewing, and other arts and crafts. Pianos and guitars are standard equipment. The occupational therapist offers instruction and help in any of these pursuits.

There is also a dayroom for lounging and television; reading nooks stocked with books and magazines; a game room (checkers, chess, cards, shuffleboard, billiards, and so on); and music rooms for listening to tapes and records.

SOCIAL ACTIVITIES. Dances, movies, bingo nights, and similar diversions are part of the weekly schedule in almost every psychiatric hospital. Entertainment is often a regular feature; professional talent may be present among the patients or it is engaged by the hospital administration. There are always parties at the various holidays, with decorations by patients and staff.

OUTSIDE PROGRAMS. To help energize the patients' interests, the RT therapist may organize sightseeing tours, trips to museums, matinee or evening performances of live theatre, telecasts, concerts, and sports or other special events. In most psychiatric hospitals, patients are allowed out on pass to visit with family or to go on some excursion for an afternoon.

The Social Worker Is There to Help You

Most psychiatric hospitals include this excellent professional worker on their staffs. She (or he) will be happy to assist you with any problem created by the hospitalization. She can also answer many questions about the posthospitalization period and get in touch with different agency personnel who will help you with anything from baby sitting to the patient's employment on discharge.

The social worker really excels at her job and will prove a great source of comfort to you. You need never feel embarrassed about appealing to her. She is an important arm of the hospital and is also the most likely one to help wheedle any special privileges for you or your relative when unusual circumstances arise. If she cannot do it, no one can.

CHAPTER SEVENTEEN

Your Role in Psychiatric Hospitalization

Two MAIN anxieties immediately trouble the family when psychiatric hospitalization comes up. One is:

WILL MY RELATIVE RESENT BEING HOSPITALIZED?

Probably not. It may set your mind at rest to know that depressed patients, no matter how resistant in advance, adjust well to the hospital environment once they are there. For one, they feel relieved that someone has taken over for them. Second, hospitalization drives the point home that they are ill and that their only "out" is to get well. Because of this, especially with severe depression, they tend to accept treatment more readily than as an outpatient.

I have yet to meet the person who bore a grudge for being hospitalized (even when committed) after benefiting from it. True, he (or she) may not consider the episode to be the most delightful of his life. But that is so of any other hospitalization, medical or surgical. Moreover, after he leaves and especially when he recovers and learns how badly he required it, he may surprise you with expressions of gratitude. Recently one man said to me, a little sheepishly, "I guess I gave you a hard time when I was sick, Doc. I remember talking about being put away. Maybe it was a good thing you were tough with me. I must have needed it."

No, he or she will not hold it against you, because life is very sweet to the person who has been snatched from the brink of losing it or was living in a state of total despair. The rare patient who remains sour about hospitalization is usually one who did not respond fully to

212

treatment; his resentment is at not getting well. Even then, when all the symptoms have disappeared with follow-up treatment, he tends to drop the subject and forget it.

The family's second anxiety is:

WON'T ALL THOSE MENTAL CASES THERE UPSET MY RELATIVE EVEN MORE?

No, but families worry about this too. They say, "My relative is just depressed, but he's rational. Those other patients are very nervous and peculiar."

However, family members do not realize that their disturbed and depressed relative is unlikely to note any contrast between himself and other patients. You may say, "Oh but I know just how he feels at seeing those inmates." The fact is that you really do not know. Granted, you could have foretold his responses to new situations when he was well; but you cannot when he is depressed. Do not try to judge his sensibilities by yours. *You* are not depressed. He is and he will probably react with indifference to the condition of the other patients (as they do to his), because he is so immersed in his own mental distress.

Finally, cast your mind back to when he or she was living with the family, getting more intractable all the time, and still going downhill. That nice homey atmosphere that you think he would prefer was not relieving the illness one bit and may have been aggravating it.

Which Relatives Can Help?

It is always gratifying to see how some family members rally round when one of them gets depressed. However, others are so alarmed and confounded by the illness that they promptly divorce themselves from it. These two types stand out and, without giving you a psychologic explanation as to why some persons always avoid responsibility at a time of crisis, I believe that you should at least know these people when you see them.

Maneuvering Out of It

When the doctor asks, "Who is the responsible relative?" the answer from one may be, "Not me; I'm the wrong person to butt into a thing like this." Or a wife will retort, "Get his sister, she's the one who's so close to him."

Another remarks, "I'm worried and want to help, but . . ." You can be sure that this is the relative who professes tremendous concern and will chatter about it tediously but, when pinned down, will show a great talent for doing nothing.

The jocular relative says, "We're *all* neurotics in our family, Doc; count me out." This individual, no matter what, is going to stay jocular, even as he backs away from being of help.

There is also the opinionated one who says, "*I* don't think that hospitalization is needed and I'm not going to permit it." But when the patient gets worse this person does a fadeout. Use one simple test here. Ask, "Will you take the blame if your decision is wrong?" You can safely bet that he or she will hedge and beg off.

Other Ways of Ducking Out

A mother may just dissolve in tears and say nothing.

A father finds it convenient to work late.

A brother learns that he must go on a business trip.

A sister is tied up with her children, all of whom seem to have the sniffles at the same time.

And so each of these persons indicates that he or she is too weak, too ignorant, too frightened, too selfish, or too busy to help. When you recognize them, cut your losses, eliminate the arguments, and enlist only those who are to be relied on.

Those You Can Turn To

Collateral relatives (aunts, uncles, cousins, nephews and nieces), even friends, are often in a position to help and will gladly do so if you do not make the mistake of hiding your troubles. Indeed, this is just the time when you may discover in them generous and loyal qualities that you never dreamed of.

Thus, the likable nineteen-year-old-nephew adept in handling grownups may be the perfect companion to take your relative out on pass to a ball game. An aunt of a lovely, warm disposition can act as a tonic, encourage the patient, and push him into a good mood when she visits. A cousin may freely volunteer to take the patient out to dine. Another may not feel the least inconvenienced at bringing clothes to your relative and running any needed errands. And, mind you, all of this without grumbling. So do not overlook these sources whom you can count on.

How to Get the Patient to the Hospital

This problem is often raised by relatives with the added plaint, "He doesn't want to go."

If nothing else works then I say, "Take him." However, when handled correctly, most patients will yield of their own accord, although your first attempts may be met with vehement refusals. There is reason for this. In a severe depression, the patient can speak in negatives only; rarely will he say what he does want to do. Everything displeases him and he rejects most of it, whether it is food, getting dressed, visiting, reading, even moving his bowels. Why not the hospital too? Of course he will not consent to go right off, any more than he will accede to your breakfast-time request that he eat his eggs, which he used to love before he became ill. As he sees it right now, the hospital is the newest stress to arise and the one to rant against.

But if you are perceptive you will know that underneath the bluster and fuss he is timorous and vacillating. Therefore, do not ask what he wants to do. He needs to be told, and he is waiting for this. Just as in outpatient EST (see Chapter 13), if you are fainthearted he will know. Equally, when you are certain that hospitalization is best and you will not settle for less, he is reassured. It is easy to "sell" an idea if you promote it with genuine conviction.

Pick the Right Time

The person is not continually restive. During some
hours of the day mental pain assaults him or her more
than at others. (See Chart, Chapter 6.) For example, if
the depression is severely neurotic, do not broach the
subject of hospitalization in the morning, when the patient
is at his most hopeful for a possible "good" day (which
will probably not materialize). Wait until evening, when
he is at lowest ebb; he may then accept it, because he is
desperate for relief.

When it is endogenous depression that afflicts your relative, he or she will feel better and more optimistic toward
evening. At that time the suffering tends to lift a bit.
Therefore, propose hospitalization in the morning, soon
after he awakens, because then he is feeling his worst and
will reach toward anything to ease his mental pain.

Accent the Advantages of Hospitalization

Discussing its benefits with him point by point may
bring his consent, especially if you couple your reasons
for hospitalization with honest assurances of a favorable
response to treatment. (Be guided by the doctor's prognosis for this.)

Also, use your relative's symptoms to build up your
inducements. For example, suppose he blames himself for
disrupting the household with his illness. Suggest that by
going to the hospital for treatment he will diminish the
pressure at home: Johnny can get his schoolwork done
and not have to park himself at the library; Mary will be
free to have her friends in; others in the family can go to
the theatre as planned or return to work. No one will be
housebound, and he will be seeing each of you on visiting
days.

When the depressed person is also delusional and
agitated, utilize the distorted ideas or behavior to gain
your ends. For example, a woman in a menopausal depression was positive that the neighbors were spying on
her. When her daughter said that the hospital would be a

refuge from their prying eyes the patient jumped at it and could not wait to get there.

In another case, a man of wealth became severely depressed, with delusions of poverty, and begged to go to the poorhouse. He turned down hospitalization adamantly on the grounds that he had no money for it. His wife told him that she would take him to a facility where he would not have to pay any bills (she stayed within the letter of the truth; *she* paid the bills) and he went willingly.

Innumerable other situations can be used by relatives for the same purpose. Ordinary intelligence and some inspiration of the moment should be called on when you want to protect a person's health or life.

However, I will interject one unequivocal "Don't."

Don't Make Bargains with the Patient

Never take the easy way out and "make a deal" with the emotional invalid. It will backfire.

Recently, a man I knew called me urgently to see his twenty-year-old daughter, who was in an acute neurotic depression. She had made a suicidal gesture, threatening to cut herself. The girl was out of control, the family overwrought. I recommended hospitalization, and the patient yelled, "Mother, you said that if I would talk to the doctor I wouldn't have to do what he says. And you promised you wouldn't let him put me in a hospital."

I suggested that one blunder had already been made in dangerous promises. We could not afford another. The confused parents finally mustered the courage to tell their daughter that she must follow instructions. I explained to the patient that she was so ill that she needed protection from her impulses to destroy herself and, however much she objected, I would still call an ambulance for her. The screaming stopped and her resistance collapsed. "But no one told me I had to go for real," she sobbed on the way out.

In another case, bargaining with the sick individual cost a life.

An acutely depressed woman with paranoidal delusions was certain that her husband was trying to "make an end" to her. (The poor man cherished his wife and was frantic at her condition.) At the doctor's mention of hospitalization she shrieked, "You're not going to put me away." Her husband, wanting to show that he was not plotting against her, took the telephone off the hook as proof that he would not talk to the doctor about her again. A worried relative then called him on a neighbor's telephone. He went to answer it and the patient, delusionally sure that he had left to plan her "imprisonment," jumped from the window.

Information About the Hospital Services

Right after your relative's admission, dozens of questions will race through your mind. For instance, the patient's needs may start to worry you. What about his diet, clothes, laundry, personal hygiene, daily enema (hmm-m . . . we-ell), small belongings, and so on? Won't he or she want cigarettes, electric shaver or hair dryer, a transistor radio for listening to the news, certain favorite magazines, and all the other little conveniences of home? You may also wonder about the two bed pillows he uses, whether he can call his mother every day, and if he will obtain other privileges that "mean so much to him."

But the hospital is way ahead of you. They have already admitted thousands of patients and they know all the questions that you want answered. Make sure, then, that before you leave you have the admitting clerk give you their brochure. It will tell you about the following:

Visiting hours.
Where, when, and how to inquire about your relative's progress.
Personal laundry service.
Magazines, cigarettes, candy, and newspapers.
Barber or beautician services.
Religious ministrations.
Protection of personal property.
Special diet arrangements.
Educational and entertainment programs for patients and visitors.
Flowers and other gifts.

Rules about smoking.
Eating facilities for visitors.
The services of a notary public.
Parking facilities.

Information about a host of other things that may not have occurred to you is also contained in the brochure. Any answers that it does not supply can be obtained from the social worker, staff doctor, or floor nurse. But study the brochure first.

Visiting in the Hospital

There is a skill to being a hospital visitor. Let me tell you about it.

Keep Your Visit Short

Even though you are permitted a two- or three-hour visiting period this does not mean that you must stick it out to the end. A short and congenial get-together can leave the patient in excellent spirits and give you a happy afterglow too. Dragging it out fatigues both of you.

For instance, if there is anything a patient dislikes it is to see a visitor who is watching the clock and hoping that the nurse will come to shoo him away. The patient feels your restiveness and knows you would like to bolt. It offends him, especially if he too has had enough but is too polite to say so. Be advised by your intuition, then, and make sure it is awake. If it tells you that the visit has been squeezed dry, speak up and say, "I think you've had enough of me today. Let's save some talk for the next time." With this palatable excuse that satisfies both of you, leave.

How Not to Visit

When you greet your relative your first thought should be: What is best for him? You are not there to express your anxieties, turn on a sacrificial martyrdom, or start crying about the illness. If you think you might do this, better stay away. Or if you are by nature a morose person you will depress the patient more. Here too your absence is the better choice.

Do not hustle the patient through all the stock visitors' questions, nod inattentively without waiting for his reply, then ignore his seething silence. "They treating you okay?" (What does this jackass think is okay?) "Do you want to come home yet?" (He knows I can't.) "Are you eating well?" (Who cares about food?) "Enjoying it here?" (Sure, great fun.) "They keeping you busy?" (They don't let me alone.) "Moving your bowels?" (What's it to you?)

By the time you have pushed through this routine the patient is wondering why you bothered to come and how he can tell you to leave and not come back. Remember, your relative is depressed, not stupid. He or she knows that you are just going through a lukewarm show of interest and wishes that you would at least have the sense to disguise it.

Your Identity and Decorum When Visiting

You will be a good visitor if you act according to your own role and personality. Be yourself—pleasant, relaxed, affectionate, sincere, and smiling.

Some foolish persons who visit a depressed patient believe that they are called on to amuse him by telling funny stories, prancing around, and generally being silly. I have seen this. So do not play the clown. Conduct yourself with propriety and try not to step out of character. Your relative has enough to do overcoming his depression without coping with your idiosyncrasies and wondering who should be the patient, he or you.

The hospitalized person wants to cling to the identities that are dear and familiar to him. It heartens him to see that you are not thrown by his illness, that you and the rest of the world are the same and will continue to be. This is his rock of security, because it gives promise that he too will soon be well enough to rejoin you in the family circle.

Do Not Get Involved with Other Patients

You may intend to be kind and accommodating but resist those generous impulses when another patient requests a favor of you. There are too many pitfalls. One visitor unwittingly delivered narcotics when his relative's roommate asked him to "pick up a package for me, as my family can't visit here." Truth to tell, the family was *persona non grata* at the hospital, because different members of it had attempted to smuggle in heroin for their relative. Do not become an innocent tool for such patients. Your relative too may ask someone to bring him contraband and you would hope that this person would be wise enough to refuse.

In another case a visitor loaned his relative's transistor radio to a patient. The latter then refused to give it up, insisting that he had understood it to be an outright gift. Need I describe the uproar that ensued, upsetting all the patients nearby, including the visitor's own relative?

One more thing. A hospital is a rumor mill. I suggest that you not gossip with other visitors. What you say to them may bounce back to the patient in distorted form and arouse a storm of agitation that may take hours to quiet.

What to Tell the Patient or Withhold About Matters at Home

Relate only the pleasant things. Why pass on disturbing news about which he can do nothing? Should you mention that cousin Charlie is sick? "After all he's so close to Charlie," you may rationalize. But what good will it do either him or his cousin to let him know about the illness? If he starts to fret because Charlie is not visiting, use the "little white lie." His cousin is on vacation and will see him when he returns.

Should he ask about events at home of which he has prior knowledge, guard the tone of your voice and your choice of words in discussing them. It will be useless to admonish him "not to worry." Willy-nilly, the depressed person does worry, especially because he is confined and cannot help. But if you do not refer to the calamitous aspects, and instead speak of the efforts being made to set things right, he will take hope from what you say. For example, if there was a fire in the house and he is anxious about it, do not reveal that the insurance company is disputing the claim (as they always seem to). Tell him that it looks as if the adjustments will all be settled soon.

Emphasize the events that will hold his attention, such as the amusing antics of a new grandchild in the family or the details of a graduation he missed and how handsome and poised the young man was. Give all the details at some length so that he can muse over them, fondle them in his mind, and continue to enjoy them after you have left.

Dealing with the Patient's Complaints About the Hospital

When he tells you that the food is so vile that he cannot touch it and the service is "lousy," check with the doctor and the nurses before you confront them with accusations of neglect. Agreed that hospital food is not great culinary art. However, it is carefully prepared, wholesome, more than adequate, and well served. Any depressed patient with a poor appetite is bound to be picky about food. But think back. Isn't it true that he also refused to eat at home and condemned the food there as the "worst cooking" he had ever been offered? As to the service, you are probably not aware that among many other attentions, the aides spend quite a bit of time coaxing your relative to eat (which he will not admit to you) and manage to get a lot of nourishment into him.

Thus, when his complaints lessen, do not suppose that he was right all along and the meals and services have been upgraded for his benefit. Instead, it indicates that he is much improved and now looks forward to his meals. I have seen patients volunteer to help set the tables in order to hurry the moments to mealtime because their appetites were now so brisk. When they are well and about to leave they invariably grant that the food was not so bad after all and that everyone in the hospital was considerate and kind.

Always Encourage the Patient

Remember that your relative spends many hours casti-
gating himself for his depression and reaffirming his
hopelessness. Therefore, if he grouses about the hospital,
listen studiously. Let him know that you are interested.
But, once he has given vent to these feelings, remind him
that his way of reacting to everything at this time is a
symptom of his depression. Assure him that his complaints are reasonable and consistent with his illness, but
that as he improves he will tolerate the hospital better,
and this tolerance in turn will help him recover and get
home that much sooner.

If in some way you can humor his or her smaller needs,
do so. But should the hospital routine preclude this, deflect the gripe sessions into other channels. Dwelling on
the complaints and dissatisfactions magnifies them. Search
for nicer things to discuss. For instance, he may be sput-
tering about the noise in the corridor at ten P.M., which
he fixes as his bedtime. But you have learned that in the
past two days he has been playing the piano, an interest
he lost when he became depressed. Express your delight
at this and tell him it is a sign that he is returning to his
normal self. You need not embroider on the theme. A
natural conversational manner conveys more sincerity.
Your relative may scoff at your encouragement, but he
will be pleased by it too, and it will show in the brighter
tone of his spirits. He may even offer to play something
for you on the piano then and there.

Fortify the Patient to Cooperate with Treatment

Hospital patients may resent their therapy and constantly disparage its effectiveness. If they are receiving
psychotherapy they may rage that the doctor does not see
them often or long enough; that they do not like his mannerisms; or that he forces them to discuss things that are
unpleasant. If they are on drugs they claim that the
medications give them nervous stomach, make them dopey
or drowsy, or cause headache. If it is EST, they may

object to missing their breakfast or complain that they feel "knocked out" and mixed up for the rest of the day.

Now none of this is necessarily untrue, but do not let your relative's report rattle you. Instead, do some research. Speak to the doctors and find out the *degree* of its truth in relation to the benefits that have ensued. You will probably discover that the patient is showing a gradual recovery from the illness and that his complaints are the expected negativism of the depression and the side effects of the drugs or EST.

Once you are armed with this information, try to inveigle your relative into talking of these benefits rather than let him go on grouching and working himself into a stew. With a little coaxing he will concede that he sleeps much better: he used to awaken at five A.M. and pace the floor; now the nurses must arouse him for breakfast at eight o'clock in the morning. He will also admit that during the day he has many more easy hours, in which he reads, plays Ping-Pong, converses with other patients, shows greater animation, and finds himself interested in his surroundings and activities.

You are now in a position to correlate the gradual diminution of the symptoms that brought him there with the treatment that he is receiving. He himself may express surprise at the cause-and-effect relationship of the therapy with his improvement. Once you have allowed this to sink in, continue to strengthen his resolve to cooperate with all the restorative measures that are getting him well, pointing to the abatement of his symptoms as your proof.

Pledge Only What You Can Fulfill

It is unfair to promise that you will visit the following day or week or even to say that you'll "try," if you know that you cannot make good on it. It is better to explain that you will not be there and why. Letting the patient deal with the reality is often more considerate than having him or her build up to an event that will not take place.

Also, never even hint at the possibility that you will attempt to change the hospital rules to suit him. In his self-centered state at this time he hangs on every word as a *promise*. If he wants to move to another room or wing of the building, tell the truth—that there is probably a good reason for the room he has and to try to bear with it. You should, of course, take it up with the doctor or social worker, who may agree that the request is valid and act on it. But perhaps it is not, so do not tell your relative what you did. The next thing you know, he or she will be asking you to pull strings for privileges that are out of the question such as being excused from occupational or recreational therapy; going out on pass alone; or making unlimited telephone calls.

When the patient attempts this sort of thing, we say—in psychiatric language—that he or she is "trying to manipulate the environment." This is a bad development, especially in a hospital setting, where the crux of hospitalization is for the environment to manipulate the patient into getting well. Be careful not to hinder this program by making thoughtless promises or implying that you can use your influence to suit his caprices.

When Your Relative Schemes to Leave the Hospital

Some depressed persons, moved by delusional thoughts, guilts, and other mental distress, push to return home. At a certain stage they may resent the pressure to get well. They feel that the hospital program and the supervision of the staff personnel rein them in. They believe that at home they would be free to express their depressed moods and not have to make the effort to get well.

It is important for you to detect immediately the person's intrigues to leave the hospital.

In the first line of approach, usually resorted to by the patient in a neurotic depression, he or she will complain bitterly of mistreatment, imply a knowledge of sinister happenings in the hospital, and fly into a hysterical outburst. The purpose is to shock and unnerve you, arouse your pity and loyalty, and soften you into agreeing that hospitalization was one huge mistake. Therefore, as with other complaints, check with the nurses and doctors before waxing indignant, because later you will learn that your relative has been testing you; that once he has shot his bolt and knows that the flare-up will not work, he relaxes and settles down shortly after you leave.

But if he maneuvers you into taking him out, you will soon realize at home that his symptoms have come back in full force and that he is worse than ever. You must now extricate yourself from a new problem. You hate to admit that the wool was pulled over your eyes, but somehow you must get him back to the hospital. This time it is more difficult. Because you have capitulated to him once, he now figures that if he creates enough turmoil about returning he can force you to capitulate again.

The second approach is used by the person in an endogenous depression. I saw a woman completely deceived by her hospitalized father who was anticipating her visit. Making a supreme effort the patient pulled himself together in what psychiatrists call "a flight into health." When the daughter arrived her father had *no* complaints. To the contrary, he declared that everything was just fine, that he was totally recovered, and that he wanted to return to work. He chatted cozily about the family and even managed some flickering smiles.

The doctor was mystified when told by the daughter that her father was being removed. Only the night before, this patient had been talking wildly of killing himself and was stopped in time. Thus, it is wiser to believe the doctor, contradictory as the situation may seem to you. Your relative is manipulating and if he or she fools you into believing in his spurious state of health you may have him home only to lose him to suicide within twenty-four hours. That was the purpose of tricking you in the first place.

If you refuse to take him home he will, of course, revert to a depressed condition. But do not feel remorseful and conclude that this is because you turned him down. He was still sick when you visited, but this was masked by his all-out pretense at being well.

Assuming Responsibility for the Patient's Affairs

Everyone, even the acutely depressed person, whether at home or in a hospital, is considered *legally* competent to manage his or her own affairs unless declared incompetent by a proper court of law. However, when your depressed relative is hospitalized you may have to act on his behalf.

The law says that he is competent, yes, but the reality of his illness and dependent status compels the need for your intervention.

For example, you may have to make certain that his job is held open for him or that his business is kept going despite his current feelings of being unworthy and inadequate to handle them. You must warn the hospital staff that at home he was trying to telephone to resign his job or that he was writing letters to various associates, offering to sell his business at a fraction of its worth—a job or business that he will want when he has recovered.

If urgent questions about his economic affairs arise, bring them to the doctor's or the social worker's attention. They will not make the decision, but they can advise you about the patient's judgment at this time and the extent to which you can rely on it.

In some cases, where there are estates and other complicated financial structures that involve bank loans, property transactions, or other specifically legal matters, you may have to consult your attorney and the hospital administrator. The latter is usually familiar with both the legal and medical problems that a hospitalized patient presents and can give you some expert guidance.

How to Obtain Progress Reports

If you have engaged a private psychiatrist, address your inquiries to him, of course. If the telephone is unsatisfactory or there are many things to discuss (including your own confusion and worries), make an appointment to see the doctor for a personal visit at his office or in the hospital. (You may be charged for this consultation if he has set aside the time specifically for you.)

Another way to learn about the patient's progress is to telephone the staff doctor or see him at the hour he assigns for these reports. Every well-managed hospital stipulates a specific time for consultation with the resident staff physician. Look for this in the hospital brochure you were given. Remember that if you call at *your* convenience you are probably interrupting him while he is rendering patient care. That patient could be your relative.

Then there is written communication as in outpatient therapy. If you have a question (and it may be as simple as "How is my uncle getting along?"), you can write it out and drop it off for the doctor at the reception desk, telling him that you will call at his next telephone period. Or you may request that he call you when he is free. It is likely that he will do this; in the meantime he has been given an opportunity to check on your relative and to offer you an up-to-the-minute report. Or he may have his secretary call and report to you.

I advise you not to contact him from a telephone booth with the plea that you cannot talk privately at home or in your office. I know that you are wrapped up in your relative's problems and are thinking only of that. Nevertheless, if the doctor cannot take the call just then you are wasting time. (This also applies to long-distance calls; they are neither more nor less urgent than others.) Bear in mind that the doctor too will want to talk privately about your relative (whether the latter is an out- or an inpatient), and if you catch him when he is with someone else you force him to expose the confidential treatment of your relative's case; or he must speak guardedly and you miss the real flavor of what he would like to say but cannot under the circumstances.

Therefore, be sensible. Call from a phone where he can reach you; and keep your line free so that he will not get a continuous busy signal.

Another thing: accumulate all your questions at one time rather than telephone whenever an alarming thought or recollection of a friend's advice pops into your head (or a new idea for treatment contained in a magazine article that you have just read).

One family member only should be designated to ask for these reports. (The same is true in outpatient care.) It is exasperating when wife, mother, sister, and son all inquire separately about a man's progress. Doctors and nurses bend every effort to cooperate with the family, but they are so heavily burdened nowadays (more than you realize) that it is unfair to swamp them with multiple inquiries from different relatives about the same patient. The liaison person should be the relative who is managing the case, and all family members should clear through him or her. Not only is this more efficient but it offers a secondary gain. It may well reestablish communication in a family which has been torn by dissension about the care of the depressed relative.

Preparing for Discharge

If the patient falls into the category of "recovered" or "much improved," the transition from hospital to home is easy. In that event, after a short convalescent period, the patient will return to his usual activities. However, if he has shown only a little or moderate improvement or has settled into a chronic depression, he might be better off if he is transferred to a facility geared to his current condition. To be sure, when the family offers personal devotion and a warm welcome, the home environment at this stage speeds up a full return to health. But, if the relatives are simply going "to put up with him," his feelings of unworthiness and other symptoms of depression will reappear. In this case it is better to let him or her enter an extended care facility (see Chapter 18) and adjust to it for a while.

When the time for discharge from the hospital arrives, encourage your relative into further improvement. Also, prepare him for continued observation and treatment with the doctor. The latter may want to see him for follow-up care, which might consist of psychotherapy, drugs and, possibly, maintenance EST, or all of these, on an outpatient basis. Since one out of five patients relapses in the first three months after hospital discharge without such follow-up, plan on it for at least that length of time. And if it is unnecessary, so much the better for everyone concerned.

Should the Depressive Episode Be Discussed with the Patient?

Only as much as he wants to discuss it, once he is home. No more. This means that you should be neither garrulous nor evasive about it. Answer your relative's questions factually and without unnecessary emotion.

Above all, avoid any semblance of "rubbing it in" or expressing the "horror" of it. Your relative may recall that he was delusional or had attempted suicide and be deeply thankful that he was delivered from either condition in time. Do not reveal how it frightened or shocked you. This will force him into defensiveness. If you suffered while he was ill, do not say so. He suffered more, and his apologies will not remove the episode.

Most normal persons prefer to forget any illness and proceed to enjoy life. Some, who tend to neuroticism perhaps, may feel a need to relive their past suffering. But steer away from this. To keep rehashing the symptoms of the depression will not help your relative psychologically. It reawakens anxieties and bores everyone else to tears. Your safer bet is to soft-pedal such talk—with tact, yes, but with finality.

Can the Patient Go on Vacation Now?

In Chapter 14, I discussed trip therapy and pointed out that the time to take a depressed person on vacation is when the illness is mild and possibly transient (not when it is acute and fulminating). However, let me add here that going away is also indicated for the convalescent period, especially if the illness has been severe.

The worst is over now, but the individual is not yet at his best again. True, he may be straining at the leash to attack his tasks and responsibilities and yet be unable to quite make the grade. A vacation *with planned activities*, not just rest, fills the bill at this time. It removes him from the environment in which he became ill (and to which he may still be sensitized) and gives him a chance to orient himself to health again, but in a setting that also offers recreation.

After this pleasurable interlude, those of you who have pitched in to help restore your relative to health can sit back, relax, and be congratulated on a good result.

CHAPTER EIGHTEEN

The Who and
Where of Treatment

WHEN FACED with depressive illness, you have two initial problems: *Who* can treat your relative? *Where* do you take him or her for treatment?

In trying to meet the first problem you will discover that *in addition to your family doctor* there are several categories of therapists who may treat depressive illness. I will discuss them in a moment.

When you inquire into the "where" problem you learn that various kinds of outpatient facilities and hospitals exist, each with special provisions for the treatment of depression. We will take up this subject in the next section.

WHO GIVES TREATMENT FOR DEPRESSION?

There are psychiatrists, psychoanalysts, psychologists, lay therapists, and so on, each of whom may profess to treat this illness.

The Psychiatrist

A psychiatrist is a physician. He holds an M.D. degree (Doctor of Medicine) and is licensed by his state to practice medicine. In specializing as a psychiatrist he has been trained to diagnose and treat every kind of nervous, mental, and emotional disorder. Quite a few psychiatrists work with every method of psychiatric treatment and are called General Psychiatrists. Of all physicians, they are the best-equipped to diagnose and treat depressive illness. Their basic approach is to tailor the treatment to the special needs of the patient's physical and mental condition, rather than force these needs to conform with a predetermined mode of treatment. At the same time, enough flexibility is maintained to maneuver the patient into any other treatment that is required, depending on whatever changes take place in the illness on the way to recovery.

Is It Difficult to Get an Appointment with a Psychiatrist?

No. Your best bet, of course, is to ask your family doctor about it, because he can refer you to a psychiatrist whose work and qualifications he knows and thus answer all your questions about him.

However, almost every county medical society has a roster of psychiatrists who will make emergency and regular appointments. Or you can call your local hospital and ask for the name of the chief attending psychiatrist on the staff. Should his current schedule be filled, he will gladly recommend an associate.

The Psychoanalyst

Here we have two main classifications. The first is a *medical* psychoanalyst. He is a physician (M.D.) who in his psychiatric training has specialized in Freudian or neo-Freudian theories of practice. His major treatment procedure is psychoanalysis, and he works closely within its principles of psychodynamics. He may or may not prescribe drugs or physical treatments, depending on how meticulously he adheres to the Freudian orientation.

The second worker in this category is the *non*medical psychoanalyst. He may be a clinical psychologist (holding a Ph.D. degree; see below) or any other individual (with or without a degree) who has been treated with psychoanalysis and has trained in it.

The Psychologist

This professional person holds an academic title, often a Ph.D. (Doctor of Philosophy), but not a medical degree.

He or she has studied the basic theories of psychologic function and their correlations with human behavior. Some psychologists specialize in testing, that is, *psychodiagnostic studies* of the person's mental state and personality function. Others are engaged in research or they put their talents to use in social problems or those connected with industry.

There is also the clinical psychologist whom I mentioned above, who applies himself to individual and group psychoanalysis. However, in fulfilling the needs of your depressed relative it is only fair for you to know that according to most state medical practices acts, psychologists are not licensed to diagnose or treat mental illness and are not permitted to prescribe drugs, give physical treatments, or use other medical procedures. Nevertheless, many clinical psychologists can provide effective psychotherapy for depressive illness when it is not significantly serious and if they work under the supervision of a psychiatrist or within a hospital or clinic practice.

Lay Therapists

Like clinical psychologists, such persons are not permitted to prescribe drugs or give medical treatment. A lay therapist may be a minister, social worker, psychiatric nurse, or other graduate student, whose work consists of psychoanalysis, psychotherapy, or counseling. In order to employ these techniques, lay therapists may exceed their limited competence by making diagnoses and prescribing psychologic treatment, which they then apply to the patient. Lay therapists hold neither an M.D. nor a Ph.D. degree. However, many render their services in clinic or hospital settings.

WHERE YOU OBTAIN TREATMENT FOR DEPRESSION

The choice in any treatment plan for depressive illness lies between outpatient care (doctor's office or clinic) and inpatient care (the hospital).

Outpatient Facilities

Most persons with depression are treated today on an outpatient basis, because the effective procedures for overcoming or controlling this illness can be administered in an office, especially one that is properly equipped, or in a clinic setting.

Private Psychiatric Care in an Office

Should you consult a private psychiatrist who confines his practice to psychoanalysis and the extended forms of psychotherapy, but who prefers to screen out the acutely depressed patient, the chances are that he will refer you to the general psychiatrist whom I mentioned earlier in this chapter.

Since in depression it is essential for the patient's total well-being to be improved in the very process of reaching for the recovery goal, a comprehensive use of every kind of therapeutic instrument will be needed. Such a program may call for drugs and psychotherapy; EST and psychotherapy; and in some cases, drugs plus psychotherapy plus EST, all of which are available to the office patient.

Private office treatment offers another advantage. If in the course of treatment your relative must be hospitalized temporarily, he or she can return to office care with the same doctor after hospital discharge. As with other medical services, one feels more secure with someone whose knowledge of the case extends from the onset of the depression to total recovery.

The Community Mental Health Center

The closest approximation to private psychiatric care is a mental health center. Find out whether one exists in your community. The concept of such centers, while not new, was given a boost in 1963, when Congress appropriated funds to build and staff them. However, not every community has established such a center. Those which have sprung up are outgrowths and expansions of a general hospital's psychiatric service.

To do a thorough job, a mental health center should offer the following:

Emergency care.
Outpatient clinic care.
Social service.
Day and night hospital programs.
Inpatient hospital care.

Hence, the ideal center provides complete diagnostic and treatment programs and uses every kind of treatment method. This creates a smooth transition from one type of service to another, depending on the patient's requirements and his or her progress.

Day and Night Hospitals for Outpatients

Psychiatrists have long known that some patients with depression and other mental disorders may be "too sick" to be at home but "not sick enough" to be hospitalized. In trying to get around this dilemma, they have experimented with passes; they allow the patient to leave the hospital during the day to visit with family or friends or to undertake some work. In reverse, they permit certain patients to go home for the evening, "sleep over," and return to the hospital the next day for care and treatment. With experience, it has been learned that this procedure resolves the problem of "too sick but not sick enough." Thus, regular programs of part-time hospitalization have been made feasible.

Patients on day hospital care may be given EST, drugs and/or psychotherapy and be drawn into activity programs. Night hospital patients usually receive drugs and individual or group psychotherapy.

Psychiatric Clinics

These facilities are included in a general hospital service or a community mental health center. Or they may be operated as separate services by welfare agencies, churches, charitable organizations, specialty hospitals, and pri-

vate groups staffed by psychiatrists, psychologists, and
social workers. Many schools and most colleges maintain
psychiatric clinics for their student populations. Diagnostic evaluations, emergency care, and social service are the
main work of the clinics. Individual and group psychotherapy constitute the usual treatment methods, because
most clinics are staffed predominantly by psychologists
and social workers, who, as I pointed out, cannot prescribe drugs or physical treatment.

However, if a clinic retains on its staff several psychiatrists who treat patients, it is likely that in addition to
psychotherapy, drug treatment will be prescribed. Should
the clinic function as part of a university and medical
school complex, EST and other physical treatments may
also be available. Patients discharged from inpatient care
are usually kept on the outpatient rolls of the hospital
clinics.

The Aftercare Clinic

These clinics are specifically designated for follow-up
care of patients discharged from state mental hospitals.
Aftercare clinics may be serviced by the doctors on the
state hospital staff. In most instances, very little psychotherapy is given; rather, drug treatment is emphasized.
The purpose of the clinic is to ensure that the discharged
patient who did not completely recover continues to take
his or her medication.

The Walk-in Clinic

This kind of center was originated for psychiatric care
during the 1950's and has since grown popular. The
"walk-in" is operated as an emergency service that is
open twenty-four hours a day, seven days a week. A psychiatrist is always on duty for immediate consultation. A
depressed person, deep in despair, can simply enter without an appointment and be seen right away. These facilities
were developed in answer to the complaints that "every
psychiatrist is booked for appointments weeks in advance"
and "all clinics have a ten-week waiting list."

After consultation with a walk-in patient the psychiatrist will refer him or her to someone on the clinic staff, to another agency, or to one of many psychiatrists on the referral list, for further treatment. It is gratifying to note that most walk-in patients are relieved of their more acutely oppressive symptoms, at least temporarily, by such emergency consultation.

The Suicide Prevention Center

This is another newcomer in the field of emergency care for the depressed person. Originally introduced in Los Angeles, such centers now dot the country and are found in New York, San Francisco, Boston, and other cities. To be precise, however, numerous psychiatric clinics, hospitals, and many private psychiatrists act as *unofficial* suicide prevention centers by their accessibility for emergency consultation.

The essence of a suicide prevention center is to offer *immediate* service by telephone (less commonly, in person). The would-be suicide wants someone to stop his or her fatal action. He tries to communicate his intention but, as I pointed out in Chapter 2, if no one receives his message he may destroy himself. However, if he can get the ear of someone, *anyone,* he may often be talked out of it and live. Given the opportunity, he will "spill his guts" over the telephone. More than this, though, his cry for help is received by a person trained to understand and answer it effectually.

The person at the center will listen as long as the caller wants to talk; moreover, he will coax, persuade, and wheedle him or her into staying on the line until he extracts a name, address, and telephone number. Sensitive almost to the caller's every heartbeat, he will grasp the appropriate moment to encourage the person and make positive suggestions that succeed in at least postponing the desperate deed. In effect, the person answering the telephone at the suicide prevention center reinstates hope and with this "buys time," because tomorrow or even an hour later the depressed individual may feel just enough better to want to live.

Some centers are organized to make referrals for the continued care of anyone calling for help.

The Anonymous Organizations

Many depressed persons are also alcoholics, neurotics or psychotics, drug takers, compulsive gamblers or eaters, and so on—conditions that may be primary or simply complications to the depressive illness. Your relative may be one of those who is attending sessions at Alcoholics Anonymous (AA), Weight Watchers, Neurotics Anonymous, Synanon and Drug Addicts Anonymous, Gamblers Anonymous, and like organizations. These excellent groups extend significant help, not only in an emergency but also for continuing emotional support in chronic situations. However, should the degree of depression exceed their resources to assist their clients, they refer the latter to physicians and psychiatrists who have indicated a willingness to accept such patients.

The Community Service Center

In most communities there is a welfare agency designed to help emotionally ill persons (among others) with social, economic, and similar problems. In large communities, many other agencies and clubs also offer their services, such as arranging for home care of children and other dependents while the depressed patient is being treated. Golden Age clubs support activity centers and offer many diversions with companionship for the retired person who may be mildly depressed. Some unions and fraternal orders operate low-cost camps and organize outings, trips, parties, folk dances, art and music groups, and similar programs, as well as clinic services. It might be well to familiarize yourself with such places in your area.

Also, many philanthropists have endowed their communities with large funds to memorialize their interest in mental health and its extensions. Thus, make sure that you are not overlooking a helping hand; search out the benefits of these foundations and see whether they have something to offer your relative.

Inpatient Facilities

Before describing these hospitals and psychiatric centers, let me first acquaint you with the appropriate admission procedures and the laws that govern the hospitalization of depressed persons and others who are emotionally ill.

In recent years, much progress has been made in eradicating the detrimental concepts of "commitment" and "institutionalization." In their stead we now have Voluntary and Involuntary hospitalization.

Methods of Admission for Inpatient Treatment

A description of the more advanced admission procedures and those used most frequently follows. However, since the laws of the various states are not uniform, and since each facility accepts patients only in certain categories, you must check the regulations governing the hospitals in your community.

INFORMAL ADMISSION: Here, the patient admits himself to a psychiatric service exactly as he would to a medical or surgical service. He can request his discharge and leave at will. This type of admission is now legal in several states. It is used chiefly when the patient enters the psychiatric service of a general hospital.

VOLUNTARY ADMISSION: In this procedure, the patient signs a *written application* at the hospital for admission at his or her own request or on the advice of a physician. (Formerly, this was called a voluntary commitment.) The person agrees to remain in the hospital for three to twenty days. Most voluntary admissions extend for fifteen days. Discharge must be requested in writing by the patient, usually three to ten days in advance. However, a discharge order can be written at any time by the attending doctor. Most patients stay on until they are well and are sent home by their physician.

INVOLUNTARY ADMISSION (HOSPITALIZING THE PATIENT AGAINST HIS WILL): When the person can be persuaded to cooperate, obviously, no problem exists. However, the situation is trying when he strenuously objects. In Chapter

17 it was suggested that you persuade him to go of his own accord when possible. But should this not work, you may be forced to take him over his protests. You can do this personally and provide your own transportation or call upon the local hospital's ambulance service. In other instances, much as it may dismay you, it becomes necessary to request police assistance, especially if the person is deeply depressed, suicidal, delusional, disoriented, manic, or destructive, and urgently requires custodial care or treatment. In most communities the police will help escort the patient to the hospital if the physician provides them with a note clearly stating the critical need for immediate psychiatric hospitalization. In some states, hospitalizing the patient in this way is still called *medical certification* or *involuntary commitment*.

Most states require a petition by the legal next-of-kin (or any responsible relative or a public health officer) for involuntary admission. Further, one or two physicians not related to the patient by blood or marriage must concur in the diagnosis of the patient's condition and certify that hospitalization is needed. Some states provide for involuntary admission only by court order, after two physicians have testified that the person may be a danger to himself or others.

Thus, you can quite properly force hospitalization on the patient if need be, in conformity with the laws of your particular state. Involuntary admissions to psychiatric hospitals may be for fifteen to 180 days and, if the person's condition warrants it, can usually be extended beyond that.

Can the Patient Sign Himself Out?

Not if he or she is admitted without his consent as on the two-physician involuntary admission or by judicial decree.

Legally, the patient may ask for and obtain a writ of *habeas corpus* for an immediate hearing before a judge. However, such writs are rarely resorted to. If a patient who is still ill seeks release and the family demands it, it is usual for the director of the service to issue a discharge or to delegate this authority to the staff psychiatrist or the physician who is attending the patient. However, the hospital director will insist that both the patient and the relative sign a paper stating that the patient has been removed or has left *against medical advice* (A.M.A.).

Types of Psychiatric Hospitals

So many kinds of hospitals and psychiatric services have sprung up of late that their special policies may bewilder you. For example, some are general hospitals that take voluntary admissions only. Others are special hospitals that admit both voluntary and involuntary patients. The following section defines the various types and the services that they render, answering your question, "Which hospital would be best for my depressed relative?"

Private Psychiatric Hospitals

There are about 12,000 private psychiatric beds in the United States operated by nonprofit groups, religious institutions, charitable societies, social service agencies, or community organizations. Other private hospitals are proprietary; they operate for profit and provide about 8,000 more beds. Private mental hospitals generally offer highly efficient and intensive care and treatment for short-term illnesses. Some are also geared to treat chronically ill patients on a long-term basis. Others include medical and surgical services as adjuncts to their psychiatric facilities.

Private specialty hospitals admit both voluntary and involuntary patients. All are licensed facilities. They use every type of treatment, although the emphasis varies. Some accent intensive psychotherapy and others strongly favor EST, especially for depression. The standards of treatment in private psychiatric hospitals are generally a good bit higher than those in most other psychiatric facilities. As one might expect, they are also better staffed than, for example, government facilities; they tend to attract the cream of the crop in personnel, because they are operated and staffed by administrators responsible to the local community.

Psychiatric Divisions of General Hospitals

This new type of service has expanded rapidly throughout the United States. Before 1955, very few general hospitals contained psychiatric beds. I predict that by 1975 virtually all general hospitals will feature a psychiatric service. The general hospital accepts informal and voluntary patients in the main, although some include involuntary psychiatric admissions. Treatment for depression is oriented to the acutely disturbed patient who will benefit from intensive care (EST, drugs, psychotherapy, family therapy), with the result that a fairly accurate limit of one to two months can be set for the hospital stay. (The average patient with a depressive illness requires three weeks of hospitalization in this type of facility.) These services rarely provide for long-term patients or those with chronic depressive disorders.

Many general hospitals concentrate on a comprehensive program of care which combines inpatient psychiatric treatment with an outpatient clinic. A few also have day and night hospital programs and in some cases, a community mental health center.

The Difference Between Reception and Treatment Centers

Because of the legal machinery which constricted psychiatric admissions in the past, it was practical to designate certain local hospitals as "reception" or receiving centers. Patients were brought there for observation and subsequently committed or transferred to a state hospital for treatment. In some short illnesses, the patient might remain at the reception hospital for direct care. Usually a municipal facility in a large city or a county hospital would serve as the reception center. Today, with a rise in voluntary admissions (see below), reception centers are rapidly losing their reason for being. Quite a few patients now apply directly for admission to a treatment hospital within their own community.

State Hospitals

About 450,000 state psychiatric hospital beds exist in the United States. Nearly thirty per cent of admissions to these hospitals are of voluntary patients. Of the involuntary patients, many are still being admitted initially to local reception centers and then transferred to state hospitals. But as the legal and social barriers are demolished, patients are going directly to state hopitals and bypassing the reception centers.

Most methods of psychiatric treatment as well as medical and surgical care are administered at state hospitals. For depression, drugs, EST, and psychotherapy are all used. However, because of perennial overcrowding, a shortage of personnel, and limited finances, the use of drugs as the least expensive form of treatment and requiring the smallest number of trained personnel overshadows other methods. Wherever enough skilled personnel are employed, the depressed person will probably be given EST. For the most part, psychotherapy is limited to group procedures; occupational, recreational, and other activity therapies also play their roles as adjuncts to all treatment programs.

State hospitals accept patients suffering from acute disorders which are expected to improve quickly with treatment as well as long-term patients with chronic illnesses requiring custodial care. Many persons assume that to be state-hospitalized means extended "institutionalization." However, since 1958, greater emphasis on active treatment has markedly stepped up the improvement rate, so that patients can now be discharged in a shorter time. Those who respond only partially to treatment but are well enough to be tended at home are followed up in the aftercare clinics.

County and Municipal Hospitals

The psychiatric divisions of these centers are identical in purpose with those of the general hospitals which I have already discussed; some are supported by county funds, others by city taxes.

As a rule, county and municipal hospitals are equipped not only with psychiatric facilities, but with all types of medical, surgical, and obstetric care. Their psychiatric departments accept voluntary and involuntary admissions and usually serve as both reception and treatment facilities. If your depressed relative is judged to be a short-term patient who will respond readily to treatment, he or she will stay on the active treatment service. Disturbed patients who are expected to require long-term care are certified and transferred to state or federal facilities.

At times, short-term patients are also transferred to the local state hospital. But if this happens, do not let it alarm you and give you the idea that a bad prognosis is indicated. It is undoubtedly because the reception center is crowded at the time. Unfortunately, county and municipal hospitals tend to be overpopulated and understaffed, but whenever possible the depressed person who is already there is treated intensively.

Veterans Administration Hospitals

The VA facilities are general hospitals. Most of them have a psychiatric service as well as medical, surgical, and specialty services. They are located in many communities throughout the United States. Admission procedures for psychiatric care are the same as for medical or surgical care.

Dr. John J. Blasko, Director of the Psychiatry, Neurology and Psychology Services of the Veterans Administration, prepared the following statement for this book:

The Veterans Administration, as of June 30, 1965, had 58,746 psychiatric beds in general and specialized hospitals. Almost all psychiatric patients are accepted on a voluntary basis (without commitment). Emergency services are available at all facilities for the individual who cannot be transported elsewhere without danger to self or others. Admissions are governed by a priority system.

First: Veterans needing hospitalization because of injuries or diseases incurred or aggravated in line of duty in active service have top priority for treatment of the service-incurred or service-aggravated disability.

Second: Veterans who were discharged or retired for disability incurred or aggravated in line of duty or who are receiving compensation, or would be eligible to receive compensation except for receipt of retirement pay, who need treatment for some ailment not connected with their service, will be admitted as beds are available.

Third: Veterans with service in any war, the Korean Conflict or since, or awarded the medal of honor in peacetime service, who were not discharged or retired for disability and who apply for treatment of a non-service-connected disability may be admitted if all three of the following conditions are met: (1) hospitalization is deemed necessary, (2) they state under oath that they are financially unable to defray the costs of the necessary hospital charges elsewhere and, (3) if beds are available.

Eligibility is based on active service in the Armed Forces of the United States with discharge under conditions other than dishonorable. Both men and women are eligible, although some hospitals do not have facilities for caring for women.

Application for hospitalization may be made at any VA office, as well as at the hospital. There are no charges for treatment, but a veteran will generally require about $40.00 a month for clothing and incidentals while in the hospital. These items are furnished, as necessary, to indigent patients without cost. Follow-up care, using VA and community resources, is an important part of the hospital treatment program.

Extended Care Facilities

With the advent of Medicare and Medicaid it became clear that general and specialty hospitals could not service every patient requesting hospitalization. It was equally clear that many patients, for example those with chronic endogenous depressions, could be treated in nursing homes or, as they are now being called, extended care facilities. These patients receive drugs, psychotherapy, occupational and other activity therapies, and of course, adjunctive medical treatment as well.

Admission to such facilities is completely informal and usually follows discharge from a psychiatric hospital service.

Medical Insurance Programs for Depressive Illness

What is the cost of psychiatric treatment? Probably a good bit less than the extravagant reports of it that you have heard, particularly if you have insurance.

I suggest that right now you sit down and read all the health or hospital insurance policies that you own. These may include your Major Medical policies, Blue Cross and Blue Shield, and any union or company policies that cover your relative or family. If you do not have their brochures, inquire at your place of employment or ask the personnel director or union steward to get the information you want; or call or write the insurance companies directly.

Specifically, you should ask whether the insurance pays for all or part of:

Diagnostic consultation, both in an office and a hospital.

Office visits to the psychiatrist.

Any EST treatments, whether given in a doctor's office or in a hospital.

The services of the anesthesiologist (an M.D.) who assists the psychiatrist with EST.

Treatment for *any* nervous or mental disorder, regardless of previous illnesses.

Hospitalization in a *specialty* psychiatric hospital. (Some insurance companies limit their obligations by specifying payment only if the person has psychiatric treatment in a *general* hospital.)

You should also be acquainted with the limitations that are placed on the coverage. For example, will you be reimbursed for the *full* cost of the hospital room or for only part of it? And will you be paid for thirty, sixty, ninety, or more days of hospitalization?

Most persons carry some disability insurance (also

called health insurance) that provides a fixed sum of money per day or week of total disability. Such money can be used to pay for treatment and/or hospital costs. In addition, many workers receive disability and sick pay through their employers' insurance if they must stop work for a while.

Other policies make payment for specific expenses such as prescription drugs, EST, nursing, transportation, and so on. I have known families who avoided psychiatric care because they thought it too expensive, never realizing that the benefits of the policies they had been carrying for years might well account for the largest part of the required expenditures.

Psychiatric care is also a lot cheaper than the cost to the family if your relative is *not* treated. Whenever I analyze the drop in income that the family sustains, not only when the sick person is the principal wage earner, but also when others in the family must miss work to care for the depressed patient, I find that the difference in loss and gain can be staggering. This is something you should calculate soberly when the question of the cost of treatment arises.

Still, over and above the monetary symbol, each person's illness carries another value: How *do* we measure the cost of a depression that leads to interminable anguish and to the shattering of the family's intactness? How does one assess the loss of a family member by suicide?

Surely, not by a mere dollars-and-cents evaluation: Rather, by recognizing that man is nature's optimum achievement; that his inventions have never yet duplicated his own remarkably organized physical structure, his highly complex chemistry, the delicate checks and balances of his function, or the fine intricacies of his brain which give him that extra something that makes him human; and that this creation must be cherished above all else. Yet ignorance and heedlessness may allow him to snuff out this life or let him drag on in the mental pain of a "living death."

We all mourn the waste of human resources when precious lives are lost to accident and the perils of war. But depression is one cause of suffering and death that I be-

lieve can be thwarted, once it is seen that, like other illnesses, it yields readily to the power of healing. The depressed person can be saved. He must be saved, because
no life or right to health should go by default.

INDEX

BOOKS THAT HELP TO SOLVE YOUR PROBLEMS

FORCES AT WORK

AUTHORS

Mary Atwater
The University of Georgia

Prentice Baptiste
University of Houston

Lucy Daniel
Spindale Schools; Rutherfordton, NC

Jay Hackett
University of Northern Colorado

Richard Moyer
University of Michigan, Dearborn

Carol Takemoto
Los Angeles Unified School District

Nancy Wilson
Sacramento Unified School District

Volcanic forces in action

Macmillan/McGraw-Hill
School Publishing Company
New York   Chicago   Columbus

MACMILLAN / McGRAW-HILL

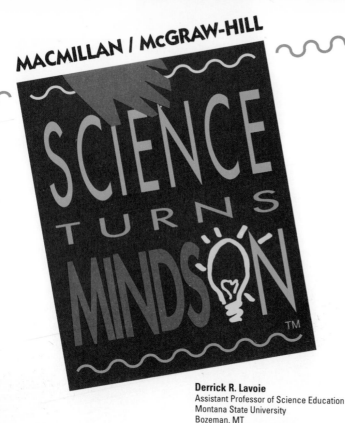

SCIENCE TURNS MINDS ON™

Suzanne O'Connell
Assistant Professor
Wesleyan University
Middletown, CT

Sidney E. White
Professor of Geology
The Ohio State University
Columbus, OH

Environmental Education:
Cheryl Charles, Ph.D.
Executive Director
Project Wild
Boulder, CO

Gifted:
Dr. James A. Curry
Associate Professor, Graduate Faculty
College of Education, University of Southern Maine
Gorham, ME

Global Education:
M. Eugene Gilliom
Professor of Social Studies and Global Education
The Ohio State University
Columbus, OH

Life Science:
Wyatt W. Anderson
Professor of Genetics
University of Georgia
Athens, GA

Orin G. Gelderloos
Professor of Biology and Professor of Environmental Studies
University of Michigan—Dearborn
Dearborn, MI

Donald C. Lisowy
Education Specialist
New York, NY

Dr. E.K. Merrill
Assistant Professor
University of Wisconsin Center—Rock County
Madison, WI

Literature:
Dr. Donna E. Norton
Texas A&M University
College Station, TX

Derrick R. Lavoie
Assistant Professor of Science Education
Montana State University
Bozeman, MT

CONSULTANTS

Assessment:
Mary Hamm
Associate Professor
Department of Elementary Education
San Francisco State University
San Francisco, CA

Cognitive Development:
Pat Guild, Ed.D.
Director, Graduate Programs in Education and
Learning Styles Consultant
Antioch University
Seattle, WA

Kathi Hand, M.A.Ed.
Middle School Teacher and Learning Styles Consultant
Assumption School
Seattle, WA

Cooperative Learning:
Marcia Batcheller Harter
Director, Curriculum and Staff Development
Assistant Superintendent, Educational Services
Monterey County Office of Education
Salinas, CA

Earth Science:
David G. Futch
Associate Professor of Biology
San Diego State University
San Diego, CA

Dr. Shadia Rifai Habbal
Harvard-Smithsonian Center for Astrophysics
Cambridge, MA

Dr. Tom Murphree
Department of Meteorology, Naval Postgraduate School
Monterey, CA

Macmillan/McGraw-Hill School Division
10 Union Square East
New York, New York 10003
Printed in the United States of America

ISBN 0-02-274275-1 / 6

1 2 3 4 5 6 7 8 9 RRW 99 98 97 96 95 94 93 92

Mathematics:
Dr. Richard Lodholz
Parkway School
St. Louis, MO

Middle School Specialist:
Daniel Rodriguez
Principal
Pomona, CA

Misconceptions:
Dr. Charles W. Anderson
Michigan State University
East Lansing, MI

Dr. Edward L. Smith
Michigan State University
East Lansing, MI

Multicultural:
Bernard L. Charles
Senior Vice President
Quality Education for Minorities Network
Washington, DC

Paul B. Janeczko
Poet
Hebron, MA

James R. Murphy
Math Teacher
La Guardia High School
New York, NY

Clifford E. Trafzer
Professor and Chair, Ethnic Studies
University of California, Riverside
Riverside, CA

Physical Science:
Gretchen M. Gillis
Geologist
Maxus Exploration Company
Dallas, TX

Henry C. McBay
Professor of Chemistry
Morehouse College and Clark Atlanta University
Atlanta, GA

Wendell H. Potter
Associate Professor of Physics
Department of Physics
University of California, Davis
Davis, CA

Claudia K. Viehland
Educational Consultant, Chemist
Sigma Chemical Company
St. Louis, MO

Reading:
Charles Temple, Ph.D.
Associate Professor of Education
Hobart and William Smith Colleges
Geneva, NY

Safety:
Janice Sutkus
Program Manager: Education
National Safety Council
Chicago, IL

Science Technology and Society (STS):
William C. Kyle, Jr.
Director, School Mathematics and Science Center
Purdue University
West Lafayette, IN

Social Studies:
Jean Craven
District Coordinator of Curriculum Development
Albuquerque Public Schools
Albuquerque, NM

Special Needs:
Paulette J. Thomas, Ph.D.
Professor of Special Education
University of New Orleans
New Orleans, LA

Students Acquiring English:
Mario Ruiz
Pomona, CA

STUDENT ACTIVITY TESTERS

Alveria Henderson
Kate McGlumphy
Katherine Petzinger
John Wirtz
Sarah Wittenbrink
Andrew Duffy
Chris Higgins
Sean Pruitt
Joanna Huber
John Petzinger

FIELD TEST TEACHERS

Kathy Bowles
Landmark Middle School
Jacksonville, FL

Myra Dietz
#46 School
Rochester, NY

John Gridley
H.L. Harshman Junior High School #101
Indianapolis, IN

Annette Porter
Schenk Middle School
Madison, WI

Connie Boone
Fletcher Middle School
Jacksonville, FL

Theresa Smith
Bates Middle School
Annapolis, MD

Debbie Stamler
Margaret Tierney
Sennett Middle School
Madison, WI

CONTRIBUTING WRITER

Jay Gartrell

ACKNOWLEDGEMENTS

MOVING HEAVY THINGS by Jan Adkins.
Copyright © 1980 by Jan Adkins. Reprinted by
permission of Houghton Mifflin Company and
Curtis Brown LTD. All rights reserved.

Reprinted with permission of
Bradbury Press, an Affiliate of Macmillan,
Inc. from *BURTON'S ZOOM ZOOM VA-ROOM
MACHINE* by Dorothy F. Haas. Text, Copyright
© 1990 by Dorothy F. Haas.

FORCES AT WORK

Activities!

EXPLORE

TRY THIS

Features

Links

Literature **L**ink

Social **S**tudies **L**ink

Health **L**ink

Language **A**rts **L**ink

Music/**A**rt **L**ink

GLOBAL PERSPECTIVE

CAREERS

SCIENCE TECHNOLOGY and Society

Focus on Technology

Departments

FORCES AT WORK

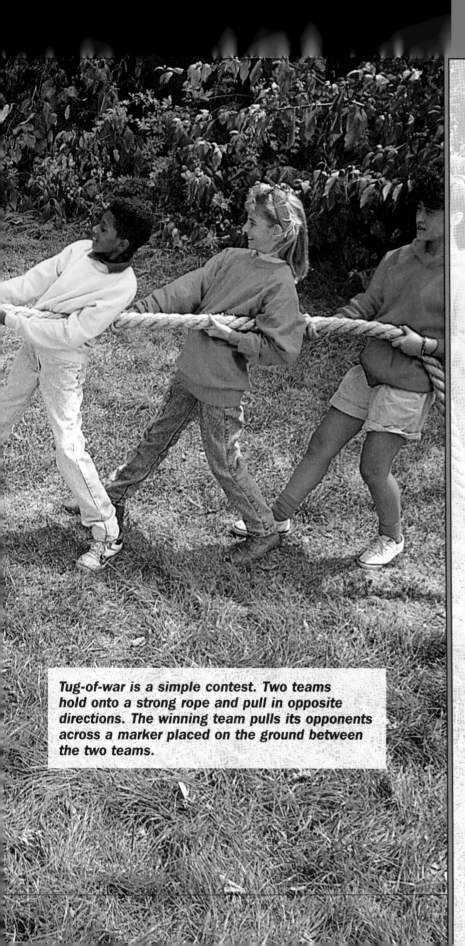

Tug-of-war is a simple contest. Two teams hold onto a strong rope and pull in opposite directions. The winning team pulls its opponents across a marker placed on the ground between the two teams.

You've been chosen captain of a tug-of-war team. Whom do you want on your team? What determines the winner in a game of tug-of-war? What kinds of interactions between the members of each team and between the two teams are occurring? What kinds of changes in position are occurring because of these interactions?

You'll probably want to choose big, strong people for your team. But size and strength alone don't guarantee victory. The people on a tug-of-war squad all have to pull at the same time and in the same direction. Would having several very quick people on your team near the front of the rope help to get the other team moving in your direction?

When choosing a team, you may also want to consider what kind of shoes the people are wearing. Members of the soccer team who are wearing cleated shoes may be good team members, even if there are bigger people available. If the grass is slippery, soccer cleats will dig into the ground and give team members who wear them better traction.

I f scientists were trying to predict the winners of a tug-of-war match, they would probably want to know the same kinds of things about the team members. A scientist might ask, "How much pulling force can each team produce? Which team has the greatest total mass? Which team can react the quickest? Are all the members of a team pulling in exactly the same direction?"

The total force applied to an object (that is, how fast and for how long the pushes or pulls are applied) and the mass of that object are factors that affect the motion of all matter on Earth. Whether you're observing the motions of a dead leaf carried by the wind or an ocean liner leaving a dock, all matter on Earth interacts with forces according to the same rules.

Forces affect all matter on Earth. In this unit, you'll learn how to identify and measure a force, how forces affect matter, and how matter behaves when forces are balanced (cancel each other out) and when they're not balanced. You'll learn to answer questions such as, "What started this object moving?" and "Why did it stop?"

In science classes, you're often asked to observe, hypothesize, collect and analyze data, and draw conclusions. When you do these things, you're using some of the same steps scientists use when they're doing research and experimenting. What are some steps scientists use and what do they mean?

1. State a problem. Many times you observe (gather information using your senses) and then ask a question about what you observe.

2. Form a hypothesis (hī poth´ ə sis). A hypothesis is a statement of what you think the answer to your question might be.

3. Design an experiment. In order for a statement to be a hypothesis, it must be able to be tested. When you design an experiment, you decide what materials and procedure you'll use to see if your hypothesis can be proved.

4. Record and analyze data. Any observations you make, including all measurements, must be

▲ *Tug-of-war between three children and a large boulder*

Tug-of-war between three children and an adult ▼

You'll be asked to use many of these steps as you work through the activities in science this year. Use some of these steps and try to predict the winners in some of the strange tug-of-war contests pictured on these pages.

Minds On! Work with two other people and use your *Activity Log* page 1 to practice using a scientific method process.

Look at the photo of the children having a tug-of-war contest with a boulder. State a problem question, such as "Will the children be able to pull the boulder across the line marker?" Next, write a hypothesis about what you think will happen. Then, decide how you could set up an experiment to test the hypothesis. What materials would you need, and what steps would you use? What observations would you make, and what data would need to be recorded? What conclusions do you think might be reached? ●

If you're aware of this process of science, you'll probably find yourself using some of the steps in everyday situations.

written down carefully and examined to aid you in drawing a conclusion.
5. Draw conclusions. Once the data have all been gathered, they must be interpreted and compared with the hypothesis. Were they supported or not supported?

Usually it's not enough to have only one investigation to form a conclusion about a hypothesis. A scientist may repeat an experiment many times and may have other scientists repeat the same experiment before the results can be accepted.

Science in Literature

In the following books, you can read how forces affect the way you interact with everything around you. The forces might be tiny—have you ever felt how little force it takes to keep a canoe gliding through calm water? Or the forces might be immense—how much force do you think it would take to start an ocean liner sliding down off its wooden supports into the water? But big or small, forces are everywhere, interacting with you in lots of ways. Let's see if you can recognize some of the ways forces affect your life. Do any of the situations mentioned in the books on these two pages sound familiar?

Moving Heavy Things
by Jan Adkins.
Boston: Houghton Mifflin, 1980.

People have been lifting and carrying enormously heavy things since long before the Pyramids were being constructed. How do they do it? This book both tells and shows some little-known secrets of the moving business. Did you know that a strap around your forehead can make carrying a canoe easier? How would you knot a rope to hoist or lower an unconscious person to safety? This well-illustrated handbook makes tricky lifting problems simple. Once you've read it, you'll never mind a heavy load again.

MOVING HEAVY THINGS

JAN ADKINS

Burton's Zoom Zoom Va-ROOOM Machine
by Dorothy Haas.
New York: Bradbury Press, 1990.

Have you ever dreamed of inventing a wonderful new device that would make you rich and famous? Burton invents things all through this novel, although spies lurk and enemies glare. Burton and his friends confuse all the schemes of the bad guys; Burton's family (all inventors, too) have successes and surprises of their own; and best of all, Burton's newest invention will soon be carrying kids all over the world. Of course we can't tell you much about Burton's secret invention, but here's a clue: what has skateboard wheels and rocket wings?

Other Good Books To Read ▲▲▲▲▲▲▲▲▲▲▲▲▲▲▲▲▲▲▲▲▲▲▲▲▲▲

▲ *Which Way Is Up?* by Gail Kay Haines. New York: Atheneum, 1987.

What is gravity, anyway? This book with its well-drawn pictures and simple, clear explanations will help you understand once and for all the scientific meaning for words like *up, down, weight, mass,* and many others. Even Einstein's gravitons are introduced.

▲ *The Way Things Work* by David Macaulay. Boston: Houghton Mifflin, 1988.

You'll come back to this wonderful book again and again to see how more pieces of technology work. The telephone, the computer, the jet airplane, the tape recorder, the robot—it's an endless list. Macaulay's drawings do even more than his words to make the explanations clear.

▲ *The Hidden World of Forces* by Jack R. White. New York: Dodd, Mead & Company, 1987.

Forces are at work all around us. They make heavy jets stay up, they let a knife cut a sandwich, they help us grasp a glass of water and lift it to our faces. The universe is full of matter invisible forces control. This book makes the invisible understandable.

How Do You Measure Motion?

What changes when something moves? How can you tell how fast something is moving? You can move, and objects all around you can move, but how can movement be measured? In this lesson you'll explore motion, speed, velocity, acceleration, and how to measure movement on Earth.

Who'll Be First to the Finish Line?

Imagine dashing into cold ocean water with a group of 1,200 swimmers. You are beginning a triathlon and will be racing with the other triathletes nonstop for almost nine hours. The finish line is 225 kilometers (about 140 miles) away! Will you be the new champion?

Triathlons are three- part races that last all day. Women and men competing in a triathlon race toward the finish line by swimming 4 kilo-

Athletes bike 180 kilometers (about 112 miles) during a triathlon.

meters (about 2.5 miles), then bicycling 180 kilometers (about 112 miles), and finally running a full marathon of 42 kilometers (26 miles). The winner is the first person to finish all three events.

Top triathletes can complete these races in about nine hours. Remember, there are three parts to a triathlon—swimming, biking, and running. How much do you think triathletes' speeds change when they switch from swimming to bicycling and from bicycling to running? Can you swim as fast as you run or run as fast as you bike?

Minds On! Get together in groups of four to try to predict how much faster each of you can run than swim and how much faster each of you can bike than run. ●

Before entering a triathlon, athletes check the exact distances to be covered and the time the race should last. Knowing the usual speeds of other competitors in a race may help an athlete find a winning strategy. Athletes must also be certain they know the direction they should travel on the course. They can't win if they get lost!

Minds On! Scientists who study moving objects need to make accurate measurements of time and distance. Accurate time and distance measurements are also needed to determine the winner in many sports contests.

In your **Activity Log** page 2, list several different contests where the distance that something moves, rather than the time it takes, determines the winner (for example, the shot put).

In your **Activity Log**, list several sporting events in which the winner is the person who moves a measured distance in the shortest time (for example, a 100-meter dash).

During a fire drill, moving the distance from your classroom to an exit in a short period of time is important for your safety. List in your **Activity Log** several other examples of everyday tasks where time and distance are important. ●

Hundreds of swimmers begin racing at the start of a triathlon.

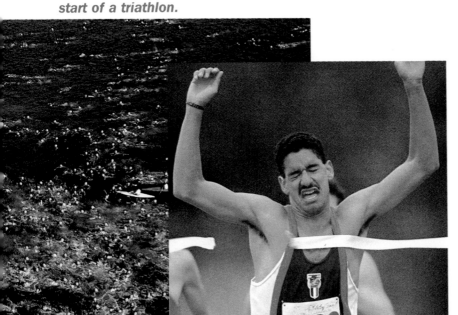

The winner of a triathlon is the first person to cross the finish line and break the tape.

Activity!

Science Triathlon

"How long will it take us to get to the store from your house? Should we take the short cut? If you ride your skateboard, can you keep up with my bicycle?" You answer questions like these every day. You probably can estimate travel time, distance, direction, and speed very well. But sometimes you need a more exact measure of an object's speed. In this activity, you'll calculate several average speeds in a Science Triathlon.

What You Need

stopwatch
meterstick
masking tape
Activity Log pages 3–4

What To Do

1 Use masking tape to mark a starting line on the floor. Measure 10 m from the starting line and mark this as the finish line. This will be your race-course. Choose a racer, a timer, and a recorder.

2 The racer should stand a few meters behind the starting line. At the start signal, the racer begins to walk at a normal speed to the finish line. When the racer crosses the starting line, the timer times the race to the finish line.

3 Record the number of seconds it takes the racer to walk 10 m in the data table in the **Activity Log**. Repeat this "walk" 2 more times and record these data.

Add these 3 times together and divide the sum by 3 to find the average time it takes this racer to walk 10 m. Record.

4 Switch roles. Now determine how long it will take a new racer to run 10 m. The racer should run from several steps behind the starting line to the finish line when the start signal is given. Run the course 2 more times. Calculate and record the average time.

5 Switch roles again so that everyone has a new role. Complete the science triathlon with a special race. The racer must touch the toe of one foot to the heel of the other foot on each step down the 10-m racecourse. Do this 3 times. Calculate and record the average time.

What Happened?

1. Which race had the shortest average time? The longest?
2. Use the average times you calculated to find the speed for each race. You can do this by dividing the distance moved (10 m) by the average time it took to cover the distance.

$$\text{Speed} = \frac{\text{distance moved}}{\text{average time}}$$

What was the speed in m/s for the walking race? For the running race? For the walking-toe-to-heel race?

What Now?

1. How long would it take to complete a nonstop Science Triathlon by walking 10 m, running 10 m, and toe-to-heel walking 10 m? What do you predict would be the average speed for the entire 30 m? Test your prediction by calculating the total time required and then dividing the total distance of 30 m by this time. Now have one team member complete the entire race. Measure the time it takes to complete the entire race and divide 30 m by this time to find the actual average speed for this race. How does this speed compare to your calculated average speed?
2. Use your data to estimate how long it would take to walk 100 m. To run 100 m. Test your predictions.
3. Design an experiment to calculate the average speed of someone riding a bicycle. How many m/s do you think a bicycle travels?

EXPLORE

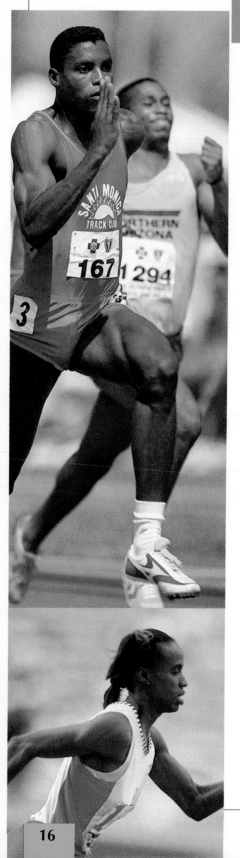

Measuring Motion

In the activity on the previous two pages, you studied several patterns of change of position. You measured the distance each racer moved and how long it took the racer to move that distance. You saw how the times changed when the racer changed his or her method of racing. You then calculated each racer's average speed.

Recall that average speed is equal to the total distance an object travels divided by the total time it takes to travel that distance. This can be written mathematically as follows.

$$\text{average speed} = \frac{\text{total distance}}{\text{total time}}$$

How does a scientist measure speed? A scientist will ask the same two questions you asked, "What distance did an object move? How much time did it take the object to move that distance?" By using these two pieces of information, a scientist calculates an object's average speed the same way you did in your Science Triathlon.

Minds On! How many ways can you tell that a car is moving? The most common way is simply to look at it. If a car is located to the left of you now, and a few seconds later it is located to your right, you know it has moved or you have moved. But do you always need to use your eyes to detect motion?

Imagine you're sitting in a car with a blindfold over your eyes. Could you tell if the car started to move? What would you feel if the car started off very quickly, turned a corner, or came to a sudden stop? Would the sound of the car's engine be different when it started moving? If the car's windows were open, would the air hitting your face feel different when the car started to move? What are all the different ways that you can sense motion? ●

The average speed of a runner is equal to the total distance run divided by the total time it takes to run that distance.

Long before there were baseball pitchers throwing fastballs or astronomers studying the motions of planets, people wanted to know how things moved. Humans living 100,000 years ago were motion experts. Hunters heaving a rock or a spear at wild game needed an accurate throw to get food.

Today's physicists are just as interested as those early hunters in how things move. **Physicists** (fiz´ ə sists) are scientists who study the structure and interactions of matter, as well as the changes in position that matter undergoes.

Matter is the "stuff" that makes up everything in the universe. Skyscrapers, ants, planets, and pollen grains are all composed of matter. Physicists have found that matter moves in predictable ways.

Physicists often measure the motion of matter, or speed, in meters per second. Everyday measures of speed such as how fast a car or airplane is traveling are given in kilometers per hour in most of the world. (A kilometer is 1,000 meters, about 0.62 mile.) Only one country, the United States, still uses the English units of inch, foot, yard, and mile to measure distance. When using English units, speed is usually given in feet per second or miles per hour.

Travel Agents—Time, Distance, and Direction Experts!

Physicists aren't the only people who need to be motion experts. Travel agents also need to be motion experts.

"What's the best way to make the following trip? I need to fly from Durham, North Carolina, early Wednesday and arrive in Tulsa, Oklahoma, by 11:00 A.M. Wednesday. Then, I need to be in Oklahoma City the next day for a 2:00 P.M. meeting. Should I rent a car at the airport or fly from Tulsa to Oklahoma City?"

Travel agents answer questions like this every day. Their job is to find the fastest, most convenient, and most economical means of travel for people who travel for business or for fun. They must have a knowledge of time, distance, and direction.

Travel agents spend much of their time working with computers. Their computers link them with airline, train, and hotel information networks so they can give their clients several different travel options.

When they're not working on their computers, travel agents may be taking free trips to learn about vacation resorts. They're working during these trips, but they also get to do some sightseeing!

Scientists investigating an object's motion will also want to know in what direction the object is moving. When both the speed and direction of an object are known, the object's **velocity** (və los´ i tē) can be defined.

Physicists are careful to distinguish between speed, which describes how fast an object is moving, and velocity, which describes both speed and direction. Nonscientists often use velocity and speed incorrectly to describe the same motion. For example, a car traveling on a curvy road

In 1990, the winning Indy race car traveled about 807 kilometers (500 miles) in 2.69 hours.

In 1911, the winning Indy race car traveled about 807 kilometers (500 miles) in 6.67 hours.

with its cruise control set at 88 kilometers (about 55 miles) per hour would stay at a constant speed of 88 kilometers per hour. However, this car's velocity would vary, though its speedometer always read the same. The car's velocity changes every time the car changes direction on a curve.

How do you use measures of speed and distance in everyday life? Knowing your speed and the distance you need to travel allows you to estimate how much time it will take to reach a certain destination. Suppose you wanted to travel from Atlanta, Georgia, to Indianapolis, Indiana, to see the famous Indy 500 automobile race. How long would it take to get there in a car traveling at an average speed of 80 kilometers (about 50 miles) per hour?

By checking a map, you learn that Atlanta and Indianapolis are about 800 kilometers (500 miles) apart—the same distance that the Indy 500 cars will go during the race. To calculate the time you would need to allow for travel, you divide the distance you will go by your average speed: 800 kilometers ÷ 80 kilometers per hour = about 10 hours. It would take you a bit more than ten hours of driving to complete this trip even if you did not stop for food or fuel.

How long would it take the winning Indy 500 race cars to travel the same distance, about 800 kilometers, at their top speed? The answer changes every year. Race cars are constantly being redesigned to go faster while maintaining safety. Sometimes bad weather or accidents slow the average speed of the race cars. In 1911, the first year that the Indy 500 was held, the winning car averaged about 120 kilometers (about 75 miles) per hour. In 1990, the winning car averaged 300 kilometers (186 miles) per hour. Use what you've learned about speed and distance to calculate how long it took these cars to complete the race!

Cars like this race about 807 kilometers (500 miles) at the Indy 500 race.

Have you ever stopped at the top of a steep hill, then coasted down on a skateboard or bicycle? Were you going at the same speed at the bottom of the hill as you had been near the top? Describe how your speed changed as you went down the hill.

The moving objects you've studied so far in this unit have all been moving at a constant speed. How can you tell for sure if you're moving at a constant speed or if your speed changes? One way to do this is to measure your change in position (how far you move) during a standard period of time (such as one second). To see how this works, do the Moving Marbles activity below.

The girl on the bike is pedaling along at a steady rate on flat ground. Her average speed is five meters per second. If her speed is constant, she'll travel five meters in the first second, another five meters in the next second, another five meters in the following second, and so on until she puts on the brakes to slow down or pedals faster to speed up. An object traveling at **constant speed** moves the same distance during each second of travel.

But what if the girl on the bicycle stops at the top of a steep hill? How will her speed change when she starts down? In the first second, she moves a short distance down the hill. She isn't moving fast—only one meter per second. During the next second, she picks up speed and is moving at two meters per second. If the hill flat-

Activity!

Moving Marbles!

What You Need

2 metersticks, masking tape, 2 school books, stopwatch, marble, *Activity Log* page 5

Tape 2 metersticks together so they form a V-shaped track as shown. Place this track on a long table or desk. Prop the first 10 cm of the track up on 2 school books. Place the marble in the higher end of the track. Let it roll down the track while your partner uses a stopwatch to call out when 1 s has passed, 2 s have passed, and 3 s have passed. Measure the distances when your partner calls out the times and record in your *Activity Log*. Repeat 2 more times. Average the distances the marble moved during each of the seconds. Record these data in your *Activity Log*. Subtract the average distance moved at 1 s from the average distance moved at 2 s. Subtract the average distance moved at 2 s from the average distance moved at 3 s. Record these numbers. Did your marble move the same average distance during each of the seconds?

tened out at this point, she could continue to coast at two meters per second for a while. But since she's on a steep hill, her speed continues to increase. After several more seconds, she's moving at six meters per second. Coasting down a steep hill on a bike is an example of acceleration. Scientists define **acceleration** as the rate of change of an object's velocity.

You saw in the Moving Marbles activity that the marble moved different distances each second. It was

accelerating. How might you tell that the girl riding the bike down the hill was accelerating?

You probably think of something speeding up when you hear the term acceleration. This is only partly true. Scientists define all changes in speed or direction as acceleration. An object that is slowing down has negative acceleration. This is why scientists use the term velocity very carefully. Remember, velocity describes both the speed

and the direction of a moving object. When an object changes directions, its velocity changes even if its speed does not.

In this lesson, you won't be asked to calculate an object's acceleration. However, it's important for you to be able to answer yes or no to the question, "Is this object accelerating?"

6 m/s   5 m/s   4 m/s   3 m/s   2 m/s   0 m/s
                                                                    1 m/s 1 m/s
                                                          2 m/s 3 m/s   3 m/s   3 m/s   3 m/s

You've learned about motion, speed, velocity, and acceleration of humans. What about the animals on Earth? Animals can reach amazing speeds and achieve rapid acceleration. Here are some maximum speeds of living organisms. How do the maximum speeds of animals compare with the maximum speeds of humans?

Amazing Motion in the Animal Kingdom

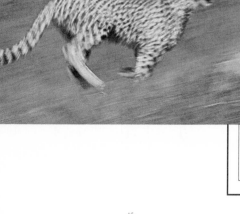

Organism/Conditions	Speed (kilometers per hour)
homing pigeon - level flight, no wind	152
hummingbird - level flight	37
himmingbird - power dive	103
African elephant	39
African rhinoceros	48
cheetah	71
greyhound	64
California sea lion - under water	16
Pacific bottlenose porpoise	30
racehorse	64
dragonfly	97
human - running short distance	36
human - running 1.6 kilometers (1 mile)	24
human - swimming	6.75
human - riding a bicycle	68

Expression			Speed - in kilometers per second, minute, or hour	
"slow as a turtle"			0.8 km/h	
"quick as a fox"			48 km/h	
"move at a snail's pace"			5.0 cm/minute	
"faster than a speeding bullet"			275 m to 320 m/s	
"a blazing fastball"			165 km/h	
"a mile a minute"			96.5 km/h	
"escape velocity"			40,000 km/h	
"runs like a deer"			56 km/h	
"like a streak of lightning"			300,000 km/s	
"like the speed of sound"			335 m/s	

Just in Time

Do you sometimes use interesting expressions about how fast things are moving? These expressions often contain comparisons to animals. How slow is "a snail's pace"? How fast does a deer run? The actual speeds of objects used in some expressions like these are given.

Write a funny story that uses all (or most) of these sayings about speed. Feel free to invent your own expressions of speed for the story, too!

A stopwatch can be used to time the motion of elephants, cheetahs, ostriches, and swimmers.

Sum It Up

In this lesson, you've learned how to determine the speed of an object. When you calculated speed in your Science Triathlon, you divided the distance the racer moved by the time it took him or her to move that distance. You discovered, too, how speed differs from velocity; velocity includes the object's direction of motion. If an object's velocity is changing, then the object is accelerating. Speed, velocity, and acceleration describe the patterns of change of motion by showing various kinds of change in an object's position.

Critical Thinking

1. Why is it called *average* speed?
2. What's the difference between speed and velocity?
3. What's your average speed if it takes you 30 minutes to walk to a friend's house that is two kilometers away?
4. Think about riding in a car from your home to school. How would you determine your average speed? When would the car accelerate?
5. Can speed ever be negative? What about acceleration? If so, give an example.

The release of energy from inside Earth caused forces to occur that led to the eruption of Mount St. Helens on May 18, 1980.

What Is Force?

Every day you experience several different forces, but you may not call them forces. You may say, "This book was pushed across the desk," or "I pulled my brother to school in a wagon." In this lesson, you'll learn about several kinds of forces and what causes them to occur.

Mount St. Helens before the May 18, 1980 eruption

Mount St. Helens after the May 18, 1980 eruption

Suddenly, the north side of Mount St. Helens rippled like water. Rocks and ice crashed down the sides of the volcano into the lake below. An enormous blast of scorching gas filled the air with ash traveling faster than the speed of sound. Two geologists flying over the mountain witnessed an amazing release of energy from inside Earth.

This release of energy caused tremendous forces to occur. In a matter of minutes, these forces caused the eruption and landslides that tore off the top 400 meters (about 1,300 feet) of Mount St. Helens. Its snow-covered peak was scarred by a crater 600 meters (about 2,000 feet) deep and 2,100 meters (about 6,900 feet) wide. A deadly blanket of hot, smoking ash soon covered a huge area around the mountain. Ash blocked out the sun in nearby towns, making noon as dark as night. The blast tossed 18-wheel logging trucks into the air, splintered ancient trees, and knocked down whole forests.

Matter is pushed and pulled about by the force of this tornado.

Volcanic eruptions, floods, earthquakes, hurricanes, tornadoes—in all of these spectacular events, matter is pushed and hurled about. These events unleash forces that shape and reshape Earth. Natural disasters are easy to study because they make obvious changes on Earth. However, scientists don't fully understand all the other forces shaping our planet.

Until the 1960s, few scientists had studied the enormous forces that occur within Earth that form mountains, move continents, and produce ocean basins. These forces are hard to study because the changes they cause occur deep underground over a very long period of time.

The landmasses we call continents don't appear to be moving, but they are. Geologists, scientists who study the structure of Earth, have discovered that continents and oceans float like rafts on top of 15 huge plates of rock that cover Earth's surface. Plates can move from one to ten centimeters per year, carrying entire continents or ocean basins with them. The forces required to move these plates are enormous. Scientists are still investigating how these forces are produced.

Where different plates collide, mountains are pushed up, volcanoes form, and earthquakes occur. Old areas of Earth's surface are sometimes buried deep under other plates, and new land forms in rifts or cracks between the plates. The eruptions of Mount St. Helens and the volcanic mountains in the northwestern United States are examples of what happens in an area where two plates are colliding.

Of course, not every force in the world is strong enough to move mountains. To feel different strengths of forces, do the Try This Activity on the next page.

When two plates collide, one plate can slide under the other. Part of the plate material moves down and melts. This melted material rises and when it reaches the surface, it produces a volcano.

Plates are blocks of Earth's crust and upper mantle.

Activity!

Experience a Force

Now you can experience a force.

What You Need
your hands, hand lotion, *Activity Log* page 6

Place your hands together lightly. Rub your hands back and forth quickly. Is it hard to move them this way? How do they feel when you stop?

Press your hands together tightly. Rub them back and forth. How do they feel when you stop?

Apply hand lotion to your hands. Press your hands together tightly and rub them back and forth. Write your observations in your *Activity Log*.

Activity!

Slipping and Sliding

In this activity, you'll pull an object across a table to see if changing the surface between the object and the table changes the force needed to move it across the table.

What You Need

smooth, level desk or table
3 small school books (all the same size)
2 self-sealing plastic food bags
2-m length of string
2 pencils
roller skate (optional)
sheet of sandpaper (at least as wide as the book covers)
masking tape
Activity Log pages 7–8

What To Do

1 Place 2 books in 1 bag and 1 book in the other bag. Seal the bags. Place both bags on a smooth table and tie the string around them. Leave 1 m of string between the bags. Move the bags until the string between them is tight and the bag containing 1 book is hanging off the edge of the table.

2 Let go of the bag hanging off the table. Record your observations in your *Activity Log.* Repeat this step 2 more times. What do you observe?

3 Tape a sheet of sandpaper onto the table, rough side up. Place the bag containing 2 books on top of it and let the bag containing 1 book hang off the table. Release the bag hanging off the table. Record your observation in your *Activity Log.* Repeat this step 2 more times.

4 What would happen if the books were sliding across the table on rollers? Write your prediction in your *Activity Log.* Place 2 pencils underneath the bag holding the 2 books. Let the bag holding 1 book pull them across the table. Record your observation in your *Activity Log.*

What Happened?

1. What supplied the force to slide the books across the table?
2. What had to happen for the books to slide across the table?
3. In what ways do the books slide differently if you set them on sandpaper? On pencils? Why do you think this is the case?
4. Are any forces affecting the sliding books besides the pull of the book?

What Now?

1. Can you think of other ways to make it easier to slide the books across the table? What would happen if you put them on a small cart or a roller skate? Test one of your ideas.
2. Can you think of a toy or a game that uses a sliding object? Describe the game. Could you still play the game if the sliding object were coated with rubber cement? Coated with oil?

EXPLORE

What Can We Find Out About Forces?

A **force** is a push or a pull that one object exerts on another object. It takes a force to start a lump of matter moving, stop it from moving, or change its velocity.

Friction is a force that opposes motion between the surfaces of two objects that are touching. Friction depends on the kinds of surfaces between the two objects and on the amount of force pressing the two objects together. Friction causes moving objects to slow down and eventually stop. It always acts in the direction opposite to the movement of an object.

Friction also occurs between two touching objects that are just sitting still. In this case, the frictional force between the two objects is just great enough and in the right direction to balance out any other forces that are acting on the objects at that time. The total force on the two objects is zero, and the objects won't start to move.

The more friction that exists between the bow and the violin strings, the easier it is to set the strings in motion.

There's no acceleration. The more force pressing two objects together, the more friction there is between those two objects.

You've done two activities that demonstrated how friction affects moving objects. When you rubbed your hands together hard in the activity on page 27, you felt your palms get hot. Friction produces heat. In the Explore Activity, you found it's harder to pull a book across a piece of sandpaper than across a smooth table. The rough surface of the sandpaper increased the friction between the book and the table. The book moved more slowly across the sandpaper than across the smooth table. These activities demonstrated two of the main effects of friction: warming up moving surfaces and slowing down moving objects. Now do the following activity to use friction to make music.

Activity!

Friction Music

Ben Franklin made music with friction. You can try his experiment.

What You Need
drinking glass with stem (half full of water), lemon juice, *Activity Log* page 9

Make sure the glass you use has no dents or chips on the rim. Hold the glass firmly on the table with one hand. Wet one of the fingers of your other hand and rub it around the rim of the glass in a circular motion. As you rub around the rim, press on it very gently at first. Slowly increase the pressure until the glass produces a clear, bell-like tone. *Safety Tip:* Hold the glass steady, and don't press so hard that you break it!

If you have trouble making the glass ring, wash your hands with soap and rinse them with water to remove any soap film. Dipping the tips of your fingers in a few drops of lemon juice will also help to increase the force friction between your fingers and the rim of the glass.

After you can make the glass ring, change the amount of water. Does the sound change when you raise or lower the water level? Can you change the sound by rubbing faster or slower? By pressing harder or softer? Can you and your class play a tune? Record your answers in your *Activity Log.*

Music/Art Link

Friction Can Make Beautiful Music

Sounds produced by the friction of two objects rubbing together can be irritating or pleasing. Squeaking chalk across a blackboard makes people cringe. Crickets attract their mates by rubbing their front wings together to make chirping sounds. But rubbing a bow across the strings of a violin or strumming a guitar string can start the strings vibrating and make music.

The quality and amount of sound produced when two objects rub together partly depends on the amount of friction between them. Recall that when you dipped your fingers in lemon juice you increased the friction between your fingers and the glass. Bows for stringed instruments are made by attaching hairs from the tail of a horse to a wooden bow. Horsehairs are smooth. Violinists rub rosin on the hairs of their bow to increase the friction between the bow and the strings. The more friction there is between the bow and the strings, the easier it is to set the strings in motion when the bow slides across them. The vibrations of the violin's strings make the musical sounds you hear.

In 1763 Benjamin Franklin invented an instrument called the glass harmonica. It consisted of glass bowls mounted on a spindle that was turned by a foot pedal. By moving his fingers from one bowl to the next, he could play complete musical pieces.

Friction and the Environment

Reducing friction is good for the environment and good for your wallet.

What would you do if you learned a simple way to reduce friction that would cost you nothing, would help decrease air pollution, and could save money? Would you be willing to try it?

All you need to do is to get the automobile owners you know to inflate the tires on their cars to the maximum safe pressure recommended.

Badly underinflated tires produce more friction and increase the amount of gasoline a car burns by as much as six percent.

In the United States, manufacturers are required by law to produce cars that get an average of 44 kilometers (about 28 miles) per gallon of gasoline. Since most people drive their cars about 24,000 kilometers (about 15,000 miles) per year, car owners buy about 2,070 liters (about 545 gallons) of gas a year at a cost of about $818.

Underinflated tires produce more friction than properly inflated tires and make it harder for the car to move along the road. When tires are underinflated, they wobble from side to side. This increases the friction between the road and the tire. The extra friction will cause fuel mileage to drop to 41 kilometers (about 26 miles) per gallon. This may not sound like a big change, but it means that the driver will have to spend about $52 per year more to drive the same distance. Because the car is burning more gasoline, it will also put an additional 665 pounds of CO_2 (carbon dioxide) into the atmosphere. CO_2 is one of the "greenhouse gases" that scientists are studying to see if they produce long-term changes in Earth's climate.

Improperly inflated tire.

Properly inflated tire.

What forces are involved in a karate kick and punch?

Minds On! What is giving a push or a pull in these pictures? Forces are acting in every case. How many pushes and pulls can you identify for each of the pictures? ●

What forces are involved in a golf swing?

What forces are involved when a child on a swing drags both feet on the ground?

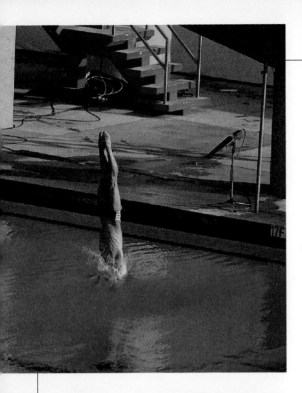

Forces in Your World

You need to know two things to determine the effect of a force on an object—the direction of the force (which way it's pushing or pulling) and how strong the force is (its magnitude).

Why does a diver jumping off a ten-meter platform fall toward the water? To answer, you need to know all the forces acting on the diver. What's the direction of the force? How strong is it? Are there any other forces acting at the same time?

One force you'll need to consider is gravity. Gravity is the force that pulls us toward the ground and holds water in the bathtub. Gravitational forces hold the moon in orbit around Earth and hold the planets in orbits around the sun.

The diver falls toward the water because gravity is a force acting between her and the water and because there is no longer a force pushing up on the diver, as there was when she was standing on the diving platform. **Gravity** is a pulling force that every object exerts on every other object. The force of gravity depends on the masses of the objects and the distance between them. The greater mass an object has, the more pulling force of gravity it will exert. Earth has more mass than the diver, so it exerts a greater pulling force of gravity on the diver than the diver exerts on Earth. Therefore the direction of pull of the diver is toward Earth. Gravity always pulls objects smaller than Earth toward the center of Earth. If Earth has more mass than an object, it will exert a greater force of gravity on the smaller object than the smaller object will exert on Earth. So, for any falling object less massive than Earth, including the diver, "down" is the answer to the question "What direction?"

As the distance between two objects

decreases, the pull of gravity between them increases. As the distance increases, the pull of gravity decreases.

You've probably been asked how much you weigh. You most likely answered in pounds. You may recall that scientists define weight as the force of gravity acting on a mass on Earth's surface. The unit of force used by scientists is the newton, and the symbol for newton is N. Weight is a measure of force, so it's expressed as newtons.

You need a measuring device to tell how strong a force is. Scientists often use spring scales to measure the magnitude of a force. A medium-sized apple hanging in a tree pulls down on the tree limb with a force of about one newton. The diver shown is being pulled downward by gravity with a force equal to her weight in newtons.

Scientists have tested the strength of Earth's gravity and found it to be just about the same all over the world. So anywhere on our planet that the diver performs, Earth's gravity will pull her down with about the same magnitude of force. But gravity will pull a person of greater mass with a greater pull.

Identifying the direction and strength of gravity, the main force acting on the diver, is easy. But answering the physicist's last question— "Are any other forces acting?"—is trickier. There are always several forces acting on all matter in motion near the surface of Earth. Many are hard to notice. However, one force always should be accounted for—the force of friction.

There's friction between the diver and the air. The diver's body pushes the air out of the way as she falls toward the water. This type of friction is called air resistance or drag. Do the Try This Activity to discover some properties of air resistance.

TRY THIS

Activity!

Air Resistance

You can feel friction between the air and an object.

What You Need
1 large piece of stiff cardboard
Activity Log page 10

Stand in a clear area and hold the piece of cardboard away from you. Swing it through the air. Did you feel the resistance of the air against the cardboard?

Design another experiment with the cardboard to feel the force of air resistance. You may wish to cut or fold it. Write directions for your new experiment and the results you get in your *Activity Log.*

Air resistance isn't a strong force for divers leaping from a ten-meter platform. Most divers never notice friction between themselves and the air. Astronauts, however, are especially interested in friction between the skin of their spacecraft and Earth's atmosphere.

Friction heats the skin of satellites reentering the atmosphere to several thousand degrees. Spacecraft returning to Earth must have heat shields. Otherwise, the heat generated by friction with the air would damage or destroy the spacecraft and its contents.

Heat-resistant tiles cover the fuselage of this spacecraft. These tiles shield the spacecraft from the heat generated by friction as the spacecraft reenters Earth's atmosphere.

Dynamic Diving on the Moon

If astronauts someday build a swimming pool on the moon, a diver could do much fancier dives than are possible here on Earth! On the moon, divers would fall ten meters from the platform to the water much more slowly than on Earth. With more time before hitting the water, spectacular dives would be easy! How is this possible?

Gravity exerts about the same amount of force everywhere on Earth's surface, but other places in the universe have different amounts of gravity. On the moon, the force of gravity is only one-sixth as strong as on Earth. The force of gravity is proportional to the mass of the objects. Earth is about six times more massive than the moon. Since the pull of the moon's gravity is weaker than the pull of Earth's gravity, falling objects accelerate toward the moon's surface more slowly than they would on Earth. The moon doesn't have an atmosphere, so air resistance wouldn't be a problem, either.

Can you think of other amazing feats you could do on the moon? Can you think of things that might be harder or more awkward to do on the moon?

Do You Have To Be Touching To Push or Pull?

You touch directly most of the things that push and pull you around. When you shove a refrigerator or zoom off on roller skates, you have a physical link to the thing you are pulling or pushing. You know gravity is a force that works without touching. Is it possible to exert another type of force without touching something? The Moving Magnets activity below will help you discover an answer.

This train floats above the track due to the magnetic force from the train and the magnetic force from the track. The train "floats" because these magnetic forces push each other away. Is there a lot of friction between the train and the track?

Activity!

Moving Magnets

What You Need
3 ring magnets, wooden pencil, *Activity Log* page 11

Stick the pencil through the hole in one of the magnets. Hold the pencil so the sharp end is pointing toward the ceiling. Place another magnet on the point of the pencil, and slowly lower it toward the bottom of the pencil. Are the magnets exerting a force on each other? Describe the force you feel. Remove the top magnet, but don't take the bottom magnet off the pencil. Turn the top magnet over and put it back on the pencil so its opposite side faces the bottom magnet. Slowly lower the top magnet as before. Do the magnets exert a force on each other this time? Is it the same kind of force you felt before? Describe the differences in the forces you feel in your *Activity Log*. Can magnets exert a force when they aren't touching each other? How can you tell? Can magnets exert both a push and a pull? What determines whether magnets push against each other or pull apart? Experiment by putting 3 magnets on the same pencil in different ways. Can you make 2 magnets "float" above the bottom magnet? Sketch the positions of the magnets when they are floating or sticking together. Are there similarities or differences between the magnetic forces and the force of gravity?

Friction Forces: Design and Engineering Aspects

Friction makes things hard to move. Transportation engineers and designers develop oils and lubricants to reduce friction in car engines and other moving parts. They also use wind tunnels to test the friction between high-speed air and car bodies. Streamlined vehicles slip through the air with less friction, so they use less gasoline and therefore cause less air pollution.

Transportation engineers and designers also do research on ways to increase friction! The force produced by the engine of a car couldn't push the car down the road without some friction between the tires and the road. Drivers find that they need more friction when they try to climb a steep hill on ice or stop quickly on badly worn tires. Think of what happens when you try to walk fast or run on ice.

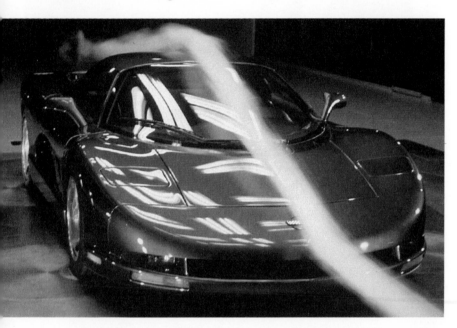

Engineers test new car designs in wind tunnels to determine the amount of air resistance between the car and the air.

Literature Link

Moving Heavy Things

"The cunning ways friction has been reduced would please the great Leonardo da Vinci. Monument builders move marble, granite, and slate blocks on their bases with ice cubes, adjusting positions and then allowing the unwieldy weights to melt into place. Sheet metal workers move half-ton flats of sheet copper and stainless steel by levering them up and rolling baseballs beneath them."
(excerpted from *Moving Heavy Things* by Jan Adkins)

What heavy things might you want to move more easily by reducing friction? Think of a very heavy thing, and draw a way to move it that reduces friction to a minimum. Show your drawing to a classmate. Have him or her write a sentence telling what's happening in your drawing.

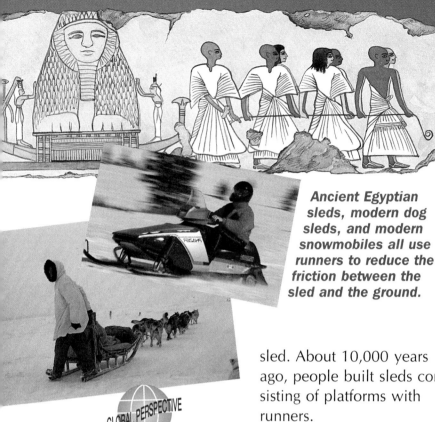

Ancient Egyptian sleds, modern dog sleds, and modern snowmobiles all use runners to reduce the friction between the sled and the ground.

GLOBAL PERSPECTIVE

The Evolution of Sleds

The first vehicle designed by humans wasn't a cart with wheels, but a sled. About 10,000 years ago, people built sleds consisting of platforms with runners.

Sleds allowed people to drag heavier loads than they could carry. Egyptians used sleds to move giant stones for the pyramids. They sometimes greased the runners for easier sliding. What force were they trying to reduce?

The Inuit (in' ü it) people are Native Americans who live in snow-covered northern Alaska and Canada. They transport heavy loads such as the bodies of seals, whales, and other wildlife to their villages.

Inuit designers over 1,000 years ago designed an efficient sled that could be pulled by dog teams. It's lightweight, has low-friction runners, and can carry heavy loads over snow and ice. The basic design is still in use. One thing has changed, however. Snowmobiles, rather than dogs, provide the force to pull many Inuit sleds today!

Sum It Up

In this lesson, you've learned that forces push and pull matter and that motion occurs only if the position of an object is changed. Friction acts to oppose motion and causes objects to slow down or stop. Another familiar force is gravity. Objects exert gravitational force on all other objects. The strength of the force of gravity between any two objects depends on their masses and the distance between them. Friction, gravity, and other forces interact and are important considerations for transportation designers and engineers, who work on new means of moving matter from one place to another.

Critical Thinking

1. What is friction? Is the force of friction greater between two children on a sled and the snow or between only one of the children on the same sled and the snow? Why?
2. Would it be possible to walk if there were no friction? Explain.
3. What forces are acting on a ball just after it is thrown?
4. Explain why astronauts weigh less on the moon.
5. Why is the pull of gravity on the moon less than the pull of gravity on Earth?

Can an Object Start or Stop Moving Without Help From a Force?

Starting and stopping, slowing down and speeding up—you probably experience these actions every day. Do you ever wonder what causes an object to start or stop moving? What might happen if people couldn't start or stop moving when they needed to? In this lesson, you'll find out how objects at rest can be made to move and how objects in motion can be made to stop.

Wildfire gallops onto the race-course carrying her jockey. They are competing in a steeple-chase—a contest of fence-jumping and speed. The horse and jockey who clear all the fences in the shortest time will become champions.

Wildfire approaches the first barrier—a fence 1.5 meters (about 5 feet) tall. The jockey gives a slight nudge to the horse's side. The horse springs forward, jumping the fence with room to spare. They make a slight turn and line up for the next hurdle.

Wildfire changes her stride as horse and jockey approach the next barrier, a wall with two rails on top. The horse is a little off balance and senses she cannot make a clean jump. Will she hit the rail and fall?

The jockey urges her to hurdle the wall, but Wildfire refuses. At the last possible moment she drops her head, braces her front legs, and stops short of the wall, uninjured.

But her jockey does not stop. He keeps moving straight toward the barrier, flies over Wildfire's lowered head, and sails over the wall alone. Gravity pulls the jockey toward Earth's center, and he lands with a thump. Luckily, he's not badly hurt, but he and Wildfire won't win today's race.

Spills like these often happen during steeple-chases. Why do objects keep going forward when the platforms they are riding on stop? Do the activity on the right to experience this.

You've just read about a jockey clearing the fence even when the horse stopped, and you've observed the motions of water balloons after they left your hand when you stopped running. How are these situations similar?

Both the jockey and the water balloons were riding on a moving platform (the horse and your hand). Both platforms were moving forward in a straight line. The horse was galloping toward the fence and you were running toward the finish line. Each of the platforms suddenly stopped. What happened to the motion of the jockey and the balloons?

If the horse stops moving, what happens to the jockey?

TRY THIS
Activity!

Moving Balloons

You'll use balloons to test motion. What can you discover?

What You Need

masking tape, meterstick, 2 balloons, water, *Activity Log* page 12

Mark a "start" and "finish" line with masking tape on the pavement 10 m apart. Tape a "warning" line 1 m in front of the finish line. Fill the balloon with water and tie a knot in the open end. Hold it by the knotted end out to the side of your body at shoulder height. At the start line, begin to run toward the finish line at a constant speed. Let go of the balloon directly over the warning line. Where did the balloon hit the ground?

Get another water-filled balloon. Set the balloon in the palm of your hand. Go to the start line, raise the balloon away from your body to shoulder height and run down the course again. This time, stop suddenly just as you reach the warning line. What happens to the motion of the balloon? Record your observations in your ***Activity Log***.

Activity!

Jet Racing Cars

You've seen that if matter is moving, it tends to keep on moving— like the jockey and the water balloons. If matter isn't moving, it will tend to stay where it is—at rest. How can you make matter that is at rest start moving?

What You Need

balloon-powered jet car
4 nickels
meterstick
lightweight cardboard
  8 1/2" x 11"
masking tape
scissors
Activity Log pages 13–14

What To Do

1 Make a balloon inflation gauge by cutting the sheet of cardboard into a "U" shape. The opening of the "U" should be 12 cm wide.

2 Mark a starting line by sticking the masking tape on a smooth, level floor or table surface 2 m long. Place the meterstick so that one end is even with the starting line.

3 Have one person blow up the balloon until it just fits into the opening of the inflation gauge. Have the same person blow up the balloon every time, and use the inflation gauge so there will be the same amount of air inside.

4 Assemble the balloon and car as shown in the diagram. Set the car on the starting line and let the air rush out of the balloon. Record your observations of how far the car traveled in your *Activity Log*. Repeat 3 more times and calculate the average distance in your *Activity Log*.

5 Use a piece of tape to attach a nickel to the top of the jet car. Repeat steps 3 and 4. Does it go as far or as fast? How does the average distance compare with your first trial?

6 Tape another nickel to the car. Repeat steps 3 and 4.

7 Now test the car 4 times with a load of 3 nickels, then 4 times with 4 nickels. Measure the distances the car travels, calculate the average distances, and record them in your *Activity Log*.

What causes this jet car to accelerate?

What Happened?

1. Which accelerated faster—the jet car carrying 4 nickels or the jet car with no extra mass placed on it? Which of these had the greater average distance?
2. Why is it important to use the inflation gauge every time to be sure you blow up the balloon to the same size?

What Now?

1. Would it be possible to get the jet car carrying 4 nickels to accelerate as fast as the jet car that has no extra mass placed on it? How could you do that? Design a new balloon inflation gauge to try this.
2. Two identical pickup trucks are entered in a drag race. The trucks' engines, tires, and bodies are exactly the same, but one of them is carrying a load of bricks in the back. Which truck will probably win the race? Why?

EXPLORE

Why Does Matter Sit Still?
Why Does Matter Keep Moving?

A net force must be applied to both the pebble and the boulder to start them moving.

To answer these questions, let's review your readings and explorations so far. Recall the steeplechase contest and the water balloon race. The motion of the jockey and the motion of water balloons demonstrated a basic property of all matter: Moving matter tends to keep moving in a straight line and at a constant speed unless acted upon by a net force. But what about matter that isn't moving? Is a big lump of matter that is sitting on the ground and not moving (like the big boulder shown in the picture) likely to start moving all by itself? What about a much smaller lump of matter, like the pebble in the girl's hand?

The answer to both questions is no! Matter tends to keep doing what it's already doing. This is true whether the lump is big (like the boulder) or small (like the pebble).

How Is It Possible to Move Matter?

To start matter moving, a net force must be applied to it. Recall from Lesson 2 that a force is a push or a pull that one object exerts on another object. What is a net force? You can experience a net force by doing the Pulling Forces activity below.

TRY THIS

Activity!

Pulling Forces

You'll be able to demonstrate a net force using washers in this activity.

What You Need

metal washer, 2 rubber bands, 2 newton spring scales, pencil, paper, goggles, *Activity Log* page 15

Work with a partner. Tie each rubber band to opposite sides of the washer. Attach the spring scales to the free ends of the rubber bands. Place your setup on a sheet of paper on a flat surface. Trace around the washer.

Each person should pull on a spring scale at the same time in opposite directions with the same amount of force (the same number of newtons). *Safety Tip:* Do not pull too hard. Record your observations in your *Activity Log.*

Now each person should pull on a spring scale with a different amount of force, but still in opposite directions. Record your observations in your *Activity Log.*

Balanced forces are equal in size but opposite in direction. When you pulled on the washer the first time, the forces you exerted on it were balanced. The washer won't move from its original position when the forces acting on it are balanced forces.

But what if forces are unbalanced? Unbalanced forces can occur when one force is larger than the other. Unbalanced forces can also occur when one force is not directly opposite the other force. When you pulled on the washer the second time, the forces you exerted on it were unbalanced, and the washer moved.

What will happen if you pull on the washer with equal forces that aren't in opposite directions? Try it.

A **net force** on an object exists when the forces acting on it are unbalanced. A net force will cause an object to start moving, speed up, slow down, stop moving, or change direction. Another way of saying this is that a net force will cause a change in the position of an object or a change in the velocity of an object. Recall that velocity describes both the speed and direction of an object.

Think back to the very beginning of this unit. Remember the tug-of-war contests. In which pictures on pages 8 and 9 do unbalanced forces exist?

Why Are Some Objects Harder To Move or Harder To Stop Than Others?

Look back at the pictures of the boulder and the pebble in the girl's hand on page 44. Would it be as easy for you to move the giant boulder as it is for the girl to throw the pebble? Why? The pebble and the boulder are both rocks. Can one rock be much harder to move than another? Why are bricks and barbells more resistant to being moved than cotton balls and bananas?

The two dogs pulling on the shoes are pulling with equal and opposite forces. These are balanced forces.

The two dogs pulling on the rope are pulling with unequal but opposite forces. These are unbalanced forces.

45

Minds On! Let's look at some rules about matter. One example of each rule is given. Work in groups of three to come up with two or three more examples of each rule. List these examples in one person's *Activity Log* page 16, and have all three group members sign the group's work.

1. Moving matter tends to keep moving in a straight line and at a constant speed. (When a horse stops suddenly, its jockey still moves forward.)

2. Matter at rest tends to stay at rest. (Rocks don't move without a push or pull by something.)

3. An unbalanced force or a net force is required to change the speed or direction of moving matter. (Air streaming out of the balloon caused the jet car to move forward. The forces on the jet car were then unbalanced and the jet car began to accelerate.)

4. The more matter an object contains (the more mass it has), the harder it is to change its speed or direction of motion. (A jet car carrying four nickels hardly moves when the balloon's air is released.) ●

n 1686, Sir Isaac Newton combined these different rules about how matter moves into a single statement we now call Newton's First Law of Motion. The First Law of Motion is—

An object at rest tends to stay at rest and an object in motion tends to stay in motion in a straight line and at a constant speed, unless acted upon by a net force.

Newton's statement of the First Law of Motion is also known as the Law of Inertia. **Inertia** (in ûr´ shə) is the property of matter that resists changes in speed or direction of motion. The more mass an object possesses, the more inertia that object possesses, therefore the larger the net force that will be needed to change its velocity. Remember that velocity includes both speed and direction. A change in velocity can be an increase or a decrease.

Inertia is a basic property of all kinds of matter.

From the smallest subatomic particle to the largest galaxy, every speck of matter possesses mass and therefore possesses inertia. The amount of mass each object possesses is a measure of that object's inertia.

In the Jet Racing Cars activity, you saw how more massive objects (the jet car with mass added) had more inertia and did not accelerate (change velocity) as much as the less massive object (the jet car without mass added) did when the same amount of net force was applied. You would have needed to apply a larger net force to the jet car with more mass added to get it to accelerate as much as the jet car with no mass added.

Is this man carrying real boulders or fake boulders?

What Controls How Much Inertia There Is in Matter?

The amount of inertia present in a lump of matter depends partly on size. If you have two barbells made of exactly the same kind of metal, the bigger barbell will have more inertia and be harder to lift.

However, size alone doesn't determine an object's inertia. Look at the picture of the boulder being used in a movie. It looks as if it should have a large amount of inertia and would therefore be very hard to pick up (change its velocity). You've probably already figured out how the man is able to move what you see in the picture with very little force—the boulder is a fake. It's made out of papier-mâché, not granite, as it appears.

The trick boulder shows another important fact about inertia: the amount of inertia that an object possesses depends on both the material the object is made of and the size of the object.

A baseball has more mass than a foam ball of the same diameter; a steel ball the size of a baseball has more mass than both balls. The sizes of the foam ball, baseball, and steel ball are all the same. Their masses are different because the steel ball has more matter in it than the baseball or the foam ball.

Minds On! Have you ever picked up an empty foam ice chest? Only a small amount of net force is needed to change a foam box's velocity from zero (when it is on the ground) to several meters per second.

However, if you fill an empty foam ice chest to the top with ice and soft drinks, it becomes harder to pick up. What will you need to do to pick up a full ice chest? Discuss your answer with your neighbor. ●

Sir Isaac Newton developed his ideas about inertia and the laws of motion over a period of years. Read the following pages to learn more about Isaac Newton's work and the way our scientific knowledge changes and is made known.

Sir Isaac Newton

Mo-Tzu

Aristotle

Scientific Development

Have you ever put off writing a report for school until you were forced to do it? That's what Sir Isaac Newton did with his discoveries of the Laws of Motion and the theory of gravitation. Newton completed his research in 1665 when he was only 23 years old. He didn't write a final draft of his findings for 20 years! *Principia Mathematica*, a book describing Newton's findings, wasn't published until 1687!

Newton's work might have been lost had it not been for his astronomer friend, Edmund Halley. Realizing how important Newton's research on motion would be to other scientists, Halley nagged Newton to rewrite his 20-year-old notes. Halley was so intent on having the book published that he paid the printing costs himself.

After Newton's work was published, scientists did experiments to test his conclusions. Their experimental results supported Newton's observations. Older ideas about motion were rejected in view of Newton's findings.

Aristotle's views on motion had been taught in European universities for almost 2,000 years, but his ideas were disproved in light of Newton's findings. Experimental evidence overturned centuries of reliance on the authority of the Greek philosopher. Aristotle believed that a rock thrown horizontally continued moving because air streamed in behind it and forced the rock forward. Scientists testing Aristotle's statement found no evidence of a forward force. Newton's first law, "an object at rest tends to stay at rest and an object in motion tends to stay in motion in a straight line and at a constant speed, unless acted upon by an outside force," replaced Aristotle's thoughts on motion.

But what if Isaac Newton had not published his discoveries? It's quite possible that you would be studying the law of inertia of Mo-Tzu (mô´ tsü´) as well as the law of gravitation of

PHILOSOPHIÆ
NATURALIS
PRINCIPIA
MATHEMATICA·

Autore *J S. NEWTON*, *Trin. Coll. Cantab. Soc.* Matheseos
Professore *Lucasiano*, & Societatis Regalis Sodali.

IMPRIMATUR·
S. PEPYS, *Reg. Soc.* PRÆSES.
Julii 5. 1686.

LONDINI,

Jussu *Societatis Regiæ* ac Typis *Josephi Streater*. Prostat apud
plures Bibliopolas. *Anno* MDCLXXXVII.

Principia Mathematica
described Isaac Newton's
scientific discoveries.

Abu 'l Fath Al-Khazini
(ä´bü l fäth äl kä zē´ nē).
Chinese philosopher Mo-Tzu wrote in the book *Mo Ching:* "The cessation of motion is due to the opposing force...If there is no opposing force...the motion will never stop. This is as true as that an ox is not a horse." This is another way of stating Newton's first law. It was published about 2,000 years before Newton was born.

An 18th century physics book showed this demonstration of Newton's third law of motion.

Scientists are commonly judged both by the quality of their own discoveries and by how those discoveries are used by later generations of scientists. Mo-Tzu is not well-known. Neither is Abu 'l Fath Al-Khazini, an Arabian scientist who stated a law of gravitation 500 years before Newton lived. Their discoveries in physics could have been the starting point for further research but were not, because they weren't published worldwide. That is our loss. Think of how far our knowledge of physics might have advanced by now if the Law of Inertia had been widely known 2,000 years before it was!

Lacking any hint that these discoveries had already been made, Sir Isaac Newton rediscovered the Law of Inertia and revolutionized the science of physics. His work laid the groundwork for the discoveries Albert Einstein made at the beginning of the 20th century. But if Edmund Halley hadn't encouraged him to write up his results, Newton probably wouldn't have received credit for his great scientific insights, any more than Abu 'l Fath Al-Khazini and Mo-Tzu did. What's more, we might still be waiting for someone else to rediscover these physical principles—someone who would find support from a large group of other scientists ready to cooperate in understanding them and furthering the scientific insight they provided. A scientific discovery can be thought of as a lighted candle—if a candle is lighted but no one is using its light to look at something, then the light is being wasted.

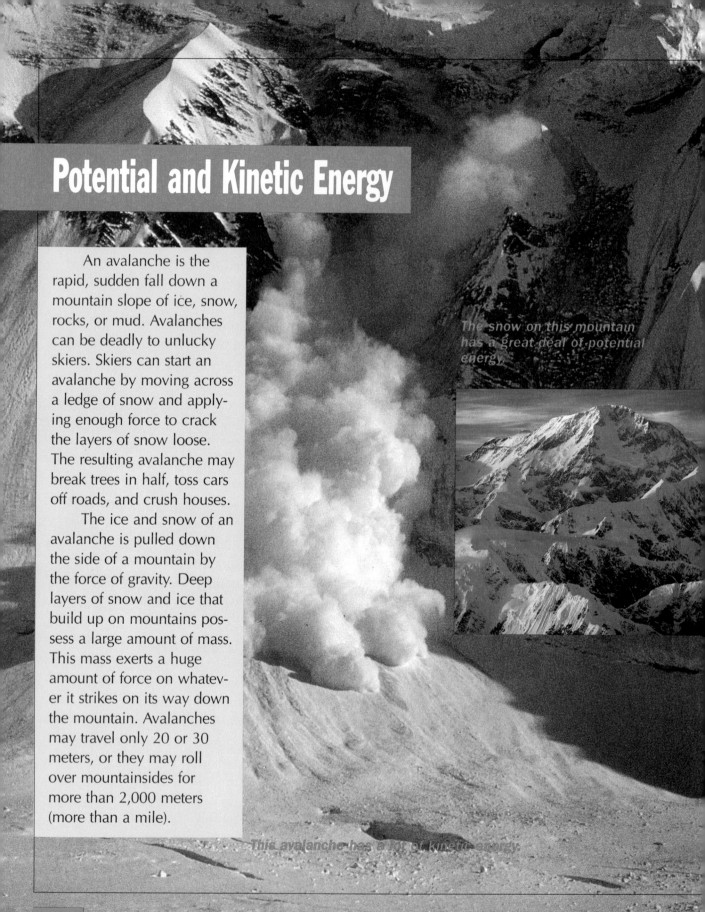

Potential and Kinetic Energy

An avalanche is the rapid, sudden fall down a mountain slope of ice, snow, rocks, or mud. Avalanches can be deadly to unlucky skiers. Skiers can start an avalanche by moving across a ledge of snow and applying enough force to crack the layers of snow loose. The resulting avalanche may break trees in half, toss cars off roads, and crush houses.

The ice and snow of an avalanche is pulled down the side of a mountain by the force of gravity. Deep layers of snow and ice that build up on mountains possess a large amount of mass. This mass exerts a huge amount of force on whatever it strikes on its way down the mountain. Avalanches may travel only 20 or 30 meters, or they may roll over mountainsides for more than 2,000 meters (more than a mile).

The snow on this mountain has a great deal of potential energy.

This avalanche has a lot of kinetic energy.

Scientists have a way of describing how much force is being exerted and predicting how much damage that force can do when snow is moving down the mountain. If scientists can estimate the mass and velocity of the snow present in an avalanche, they can calculate its kinetic energy. Kinetic energy is energy of motion. **Kinetic** (ki net´ ik) **energy** is a measure of how much force a moving object exerts as it moves a specific distance. An avalanche of a massive snow pack moving very fast down a steep slope will have a large amount of kinetic energy. The more kinetic energy the avalanche has, the more damage the avalanche can do.

As this mass of snow begins to move downhill, it breaks into blocks.

But geologists want to predict how much damage an avalanche might do before it happens. They can do this by calculating the potential energy of a snow pack. **Potential energy** is energy that an object has due to its position. Potential energy is a measure of how much force an object at rest is capable of exerting if it starts to move.

The amount of potential energy stored in an object depends on two factors: how much mass the object possesses and how high above Earth it is located. A massive, icy layer high on a mountainside has more potential energy than a light, snowy layer on a gentle hillside. The more potential energy the ice has, the more damage it can do if it starts to move.

Geologists and other earth scientists study potential avalanche areas each season. They measure the height of the layer of snow and ice on steep slopes, and they calculate its mass. They can then calculate the potential energy of a snow and ice pack in an avalanche-prone area.

On the basis of their measurements and calculations, earth scientists sometimes deliberately start small avalanches before big, dangerous ones can occur. They do this by setting off explosives where there is danger of a big avalanche.

A well-planned explosion will exert just enough force to break loose the ice crystals that hold the pack of snow and ice in place. In other words, the force of the explosion causes matter at rest (the snow pack) to begin to move. This matter has a great amount of inertia. The net force from the explosion must be very large to overcome the inertia of the snow pack. Once the inertia of the snow pack is overcome, the snow starts to slide downward because of the force of gravity. The moving snow exerts force as it travels down the slope. Another way of saying this is that the potential energy contained by the snow, while it was at rest on top of the mountain, is converted to kinetic energy as it slides downhill during the avalanche.

How Does the First Law of Motion Apply?

This child will continue to move along the water slide until the force of friction slows him down.

You run up to the water slide, leap forward, and slide ten meters across the lawn on your stomach. It's a great way to spend a hot afternoon! You're taking advantage of the First Law of Motion: moving objects continue moving in a straight line and at a constant speed unless acted upon by some unbalanced force. The unbalanced force of friction between your stomach and the water slide will slow you down gently and bring you to a stop.

Coming gently to a stop instead of continuing to move in a straight line can be a matter of life and death at other times. About 40,000 people in the United States die each year in automobile crashes. When a car moving 80 kilometers (about 50 miles) per hour hits a tree, the car crumples and stops moving, but the floor of the car where the seats are attached doesn't stop as quickly as the front bumper. If the passengers are not wearing seat belts, they'll continue to move forward at the same speed, just as the First Law of Motion predicts. They'll stop very suddenly (like the front bumper) when they crash into the dashboard or windshield.

The passengers will come to a less sudden stop if they're wearing seat belts. Seat belts and air bags save lives by applying an unbalanced force to passengers during the time the car crumples, stopping them from continuing in straight-line motion. By holding them in their seats, the seat belts stop the passengers from crashing through the windshield headfirst. Race car drivers using specially designed seat belt systems often walk away unhurt from crashes that occur at over 320 kilometers (about 200 miles) per hour.

Air bags safely prevent drivers and passengers from continuing to move forward at a constant speed in a straight line toward the windshield.

Safer Cars

Air bags and antilock brakes are two new inventions that help drivers and passengers avoid serious injury and death in car crashes. Both of these devices make cars safer by helping to avoid the problems caused by the fact that objects in motion (cars and passengers) tend to travel in a straight line unless acted upon by an outside force. In other words, air bags and antilock braking systems help you deal safely with Newton's First Law of Motion. Here's how they work. An air bag is a large fabric balloon stored inside the steering column or dashboard of a car. It's connected to collision sensors built into the front of the car and in the passenger compartment. When the sensors detect a change in motion of the car equivalent to the car hitting a brick wall at about 20 kilometers (12 miles) per hour, the sensors send a signal to the air bag. (This speed is about as fast as you can run.) The bag then inflates with nitrogen gas to protect the driver's and the passenger's heads and chests.

An air bag can be used only once. It inflates in less than 50 milliseconds—about half the time it takes you to blink an eye. It cushions your head and chest and prevents you from hitting any hard surface inside the car. In less than one second after impact, the bag starts to deflate. If it has prevented a car occupant from continuing in straight-line motion (as Newton predicted) and slamming face first into the windshield during an accident, it was a good investment in safety.

AIR BAG
MODULE

CRASH SENSOR

DIAGNOSTIC MODULE
W/INTERNAL
CRASH SENSOR

KNEE BOLSTER

When the crash sensors detect a large decrease in motion, they send a signal to the air bag to inflate.

Antilock braking systems (ABS) are designed to help drivers avoid having an accident by preventing the car from skidding. Many accidents occur when cars go out of control on wet or icy pavement. If the driver pushes down on the brake pedal too hard in a car with standard brakes, the wheels stop turning and the tires begin to skid.

When a tire is skidding, it can't apply enough force to the road to stop the car quickly or change the direction in which the car is moving. Just as Newton predicted, a skidding car continues moving in a straight line. If a tree or another car happens to be in the way of that straight line, there is very little the driver of the skidding car can do except hope that the seat belts are secure and the air bag system works.

Cars equipped with ABS are much less likely to skid when the driver applies the brakes during an emergency. The ABS work by having a sensor at each wheel measure how fast the wheel is changing speeds. If the sensor determines that the wheel is about to lock up and cause a skid, a small computer takes control of the braking system and reduces the pressure being applied to that brake. The wheel doesn't skid, and the driver is still able to steer the car even during an emergency.

Scientists and engineers are working to make cars safer all the time, but no car safety device is perfect. For now, the best advice for any driver or passenger is, "Buckle your lap and shoulder seat belts, and drive carefully." If the car stops suddenly, let the safety belt and the air bag stop your straight-line motion— not the windshield.

When this car drives over the patch of ice, the force of friction between the tires and the road is decreased. The car will begin to skid.

Air bags and seat belts act to control the harmful effects of inertia. But sometimes inertia's effects are exactly what is wanted. Many of the structures that engineers design take advantage of the inertia of certain materials. The more massive an object is, and the more inertia it has, the more it resists being moved. When you want something to stay in place or to hold back a great amount of energy, you make it very massive. Inertia holds earthen dams in place, allowing us to hold water in lakes and control floods. Massive rocks are used to line shipping channels and make jetties. The inertia of the rocks prevents them from being washed away.

Minds On!

Work in groups of four to come up with a list of several examples of structures or products that use inertia to hold back force or protect consumers. Write your lists in your **Activity Log** on page 17. Share your list with the other groups in your class. ●

Sum It Up

In this lesson, you've learned that net forces change the state of motion of an object. A net force on an object exists when the forces acting on it are unbalanced—that is, when the forces acting on the object interact in opposite directions with unequal force. Unless an unbalanced or net force acts on an object, the object will tend to keep doing whatever it is already doing. If the object is at rest, it tends to remain at rest. If the object is moving, it tends to continue moving in a straight line and at a constant speed. You've also learned that inertia is the property of matter that resists changes in the speed or direction of motion. More massive objects have more inertia. When you under-

stand how forces act together on matter, you can answer the questions that began this lesson—"Why does matter sit still? Why does matter keep moving?"

Critical Thinking

1. In your own words, tell what Newton's First Law of Motion means.
2. What is the relationship between mass and inertia?
3. Is it possible for an object to have several forces acting on it and still not change its motion? Why or why not?
4. Is it possible for an object to continue to move if there is no force on it in the direction in which it is moving?
5. What do seat belts in cars have to do with the First Law of Motion?

What Controls Acceleration?

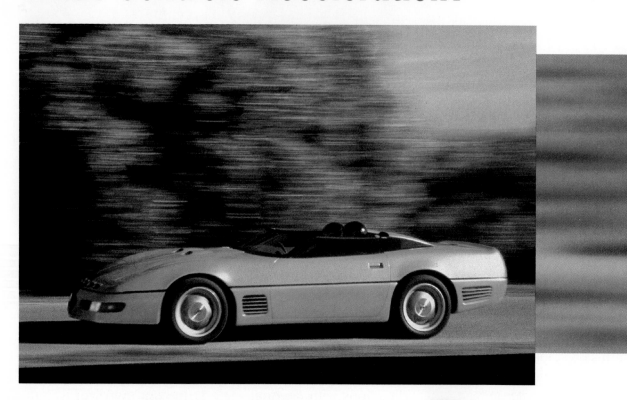

—moving faster and faster and faster—

—slowing down more and more and more—

—dodging to the right, darting to the left—

Moving faster, slowing down, and changing directions are all examples of acceleration. Why does a baseball accelerate after it leaves the pitcher's hand? Why does a soccer ball slow down when it hits a fence? In this lesson, you'll explore the kinds of things that affect an object's acceleration.

Propellers roar and tires screech. An airplane and a sports car race side by side down a deserted runway. The car pulls even with the airplane. The fearless hero jumps from the car to the airplane, captures the criminal, and . . . the movie ends.

Could a fast car really catch an airplane before the plane takes off, or is the scene just a movie trick? Is there a scientific way to compare the speeds of an airplane and a car and predict what will happen? One way to approach this question is to use what you've already learned about measuring an object's motion. In order to figure out if the car can really keep up with the plane, you need to know how far the airplane rolls down the runway and how fast it's moving when it lifts off the ground. In other words, you need to know about the plane's change of position and the plane's acceleration.

Minds On! Can a car accelerate as fast as this airplane? Absolutely! Many sports cars can reach speeds of 160 kilometers (about 100 miles) per hour in 6,000 meters (2,200 feet). Drag-racing cars can accelerate to 400 kilometers (about 250 miles) per hour in 4,000 meters (about 1,465 feet).

By applying your present knowledge of how objects move, can you tell if a chase scene is really happening the way it appears in a movie?●

Twin-engine airplanes like the one shown need to roll about 6,000 meters (2,200 feet) down the runway in order to reach their takeoff speed of 160 kilometers (about 100 miles) per hour. A car must be able to reach the same speed within the same distance in order for someone to leap from it to the plane.

Activity!

Rolling Along With a Constant Force

Let's explore what causes a change in an object's acceleration.

What You Need

roller skate
string, 1 m
newton spring scale
3 2-L plastic soft-drink
bottles/caps
smooth surface—1 m long
2 L of water
2 L of sand
Activity Log pages 18–19

What To Do

1 Fill a 2-L bottle with water. Leave the second 2-L bottle empty. Fill the third 2-L bottle with sand. Screw the caps on all the bottles.

2 Place the bottle of water on the skate as shown. Attach the skate to the spring scale with a piece of string. Gently pull on the spring scale until you apply just enough force to start the skate and bottle moving very slowly.

3 How many newtons of force did you use to move the bottle of water? Record the data in your *Activity Log.*

4 Remove the bottle of water and place the empty bottle on the skate. Attach the spring scale as before and pull just hard enough to start the skate and empty bottle moving very slowly. Compare the amount of force needed to move the empty bottle to the amount of force needed in step 2. Record your comparison in your *Activity Log.* Leave the empty bottle on the skate. Hold the skate still with one hand. Pull the spring scale until it shows the same amount of force that you used to move the bottle of water in step 2. Keep pulling on the scale with the same amount of force you used to move the bottle of water. Now, let go of the skate. Record your observations in your *Activity Log.*

What Happened?

1. Which has more mass—the empty bottle or the bottle of water?
2. Which takes more force to accelerate—the empty bottle or the bottle of water?
3. When you apply the same amount of force to each bottle, which one accelerates more, the empty bottle or the bottle of water?

What Now?

1. The bottle of sand has more mass and therefore more inertia or resistance to change in motion than either the empty bottle or bottle of water. How much force do you think it would take to accelerate the bottle of sand?
2. Set up an experiment to test your prediction of the amount of force needed to move the bottle of sand. Was your prediction correct?
3. Why do bicycle racers use very low-mass bicycles? Would a bicycle with a large amount of inertia help win a race?

EXPLORE

A Relationship—Pushes and Pulls, Mass, and Acceleration

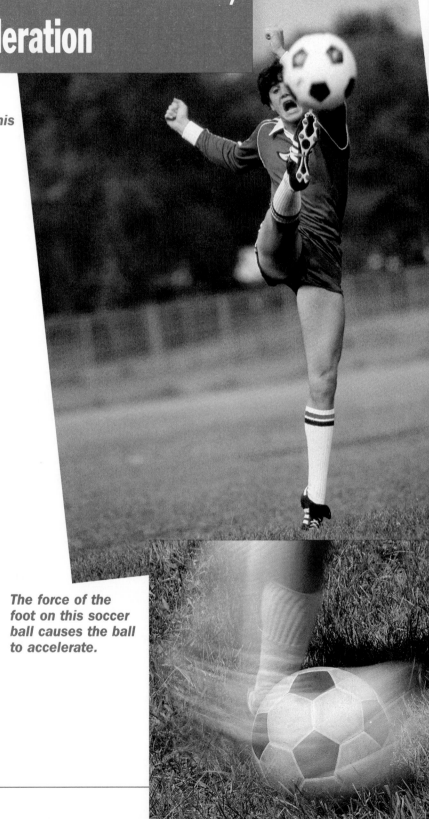

A large force applied to this soccer ball will cause a large acceleration of the soccer ball.

In the Explore Activity, you saw that more massive objects require more force to accelerate. The water-filled bottle required more force to accelerate than the empty bottle did. The water-filled bottle had more mass than the empty bottle. The sand-filled bottle had more mass than the water-filled bottle. The sand-filled bottle required more force to accelerate than the water-filled bottle. If you think about it, you experience this relationship every day.

Since we expect matter to move in predictable ways, we plan our actions to suit our predictions about motion. You wouldn't play a game of tennis with a bowling ball or try to knock down a brick wall with a feather.

The force of the foot on this soccer ball causes the ball to accelerate.

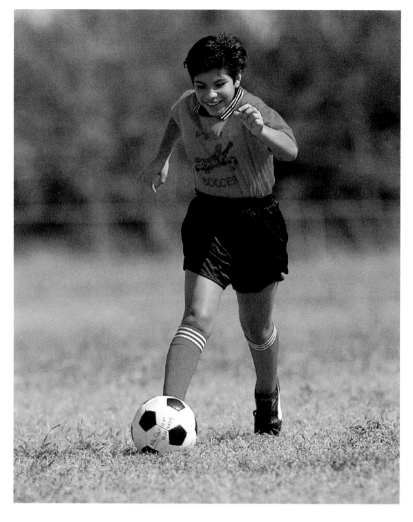

A small force applied to this soccer ball will cause a small acceleration of the soccer ball.

Yet feathers and bowling balls are both matter. Recall that all matter is composed of atoms, and atoms are composed of electrons, protons, and neutrons. All matter moves according to the Laws of Motion discovered by Sir Isaac Newton.

Also recall that a force is a push or a pull that one object exerts on another object. Newton's Second Law of Motion states the relationship among pushes and pulls, mass, and acceleration. The Second Law of Motion states—

The acceleration of an object depends on the net force acting on that object and on the mass of that object.

If the mass of an object does not change, the acceleration of the object will increase when a larger force is applied. For example, when you tap a soccer ball with your toe, it hardly moves. Kick it hard, however, and the soccer ball flies down the field.

If the force exerted on two objects is the same, the acceleration of the object with the larger mass will be less than the acceleration of the object with the smaller mass. Race cars are built from very light materials. If two cars are identical except for their masses and the same amount of force is applied by the cars' engines, the race car with the lower mass will accelerate faster than the race car with the greater mass.

When engineers design an automobile, they can use the relationships among mass, force, and acceleration given in Newton's Second Law to predict how the car will perform. During the design stage, engineers may decide to build a car using low-mass or high-mass materials, or they may put a larger engine in the car to produce more force.

An animal, however, doesn't have the option of redesigning itself to improve its ability to accelerate. Once an animal is grown up, its abilities to run, jump, and change direction don't change very much. Yet an animal's speed and mobility can mean the difference between life and death.

Have you ever tried to catch a grasshopper? When a grasshopper sitting on a blade of grass sees you approaching, it uses its big hind legs to spring into the air and fly away. Every time it lands, it uses its hind legs to produce the force required to send it flying off in a different direction.

Grasshopper legs can't produce a large amount of force. But grasshoppers have to be able to escape from bigger, stronger, faster animals including birds, toads, and people. The rela-

This baseball pitcher is exerting a force to accelerate the baseball. The catcher's mitt is well padded to absorb the force of the accelerating baseball.

tionships among a grasshopper's mass, the force it can produce, and its rate of acceleration help to explain how it can avoid being captured.

Grasshoppers are hard to catch because of their

great ability to accelerate. They have a small amount of mass, so the small amount of force they can produce with their legs and wings is enough to accelerate them to top speed very quickly. Having low mass also allows grasshoppers to change directions almost instantly. Recall that changing direction while moving is also acceleration.

Many other animals also depend on changing

directions quickly to help assure their survival. Fleas, frogs, and houseflies are all super accelerators. All of them are low in mass, can go from a standstill to top

speed very quickly, and can change directions in a flash. They're living proof that races are not always won by the fastest competitor. Sometimes the best accelerator wins.

This grasshopper uses its hind legs to produce the force that accelerates it forward.

Momentum

I f you play baseball or hockey, you probably wear a helmet and pads. These protect you if you're hit by the ball or puck. But tennis players don't need to wear pads or a helmet. Tennis balls travel as fast or faster than baseballs, but getting hit by one usually doesn't cause serious injuries. Why do baseballs and hockey pucks hurt when they hit you? You can use Newton's Second Law of Motion to answer this question. First, a baseball has more mass than a tennis ball. Also, changing the speed of a baseball from a large value to zero (or slowing down) requires a large negative acceleration. The force your body must exert to cause this negative acceleration increases as the mass of the

ball increases. The greater force required to stop a baseball compared to a tennis ball is enough to cause severe injury. This is why baseball catchers wear padded catcher's mitts. The padded catcher's mitt absorbs most of the force from the moving baseball. The catcher's hand doesn't need to exert all of the force to slow down and stop the baseball, and the catcher won't experience pain or injury to his or her hand.

But acceleration is hard to measure. Sometimes what you really want to know about a moving object is "Is it going to cause damage if it hits me at that speed?" In other words, how much "bashing power" does it have?

Do the next activity to learn about "bashing power."

Activity!

Does It Bounce or Does It Bash?

Which do you think has more "bashing power"—a table-tennis ball or a golf ball moving at the same velocity? Do this activity to find out.

What You Need

golf ball, table-tennis ball, large, empty coffee can— open on one end, rubber band, 2 paper tissues, goggles, *Activity Log* page 20

Hold a table-tennis ball in one hand and a golf ball in the other. Hold both balls 1 m above the floor. Release both of them at exactly the same time. They'll hit the floor at the same instant. Are they traveling at the same speed when they hit the floor? How can you tell?

Place a paper tissue on top of the open end of a large, empty can. Hold it in place with the rubber band so that it's tight like a drumhead. Hold the table-tennis ball 1 m above the can and drop it so that the ball hits the middle of the tissue. (If the ball doesn't hit the center of the tissue, try again.) What happens?

Place a new paper tissue on top of the open end of the can as you did before. Hold the golf ball 1 m above the can and drop it so the ball hits the middle of the tissue. (If the ball doesn't hit the center of the tissue, try again.) What happens this time? Which ball has more "bashing power?" Record your answers in your *Activity Log.*

"Bashing Power" is Momentum!

Scientists have a term that means "bashing power." They call it momentum. **Momentum** (mō men′ təm) is defined as the product of an object's velocity times its mass. You probably already know that getting hit by a massive object (like a car) or getting hit by a fast-moving object (like a baseball) will hurt. An object's "bashing power" depends on its mass times its velocity, or its momentum. Think about momentum as you debate about bicycle helmet laws on page 65.

Momentum is defined as the product of an object's velocity times its mass.

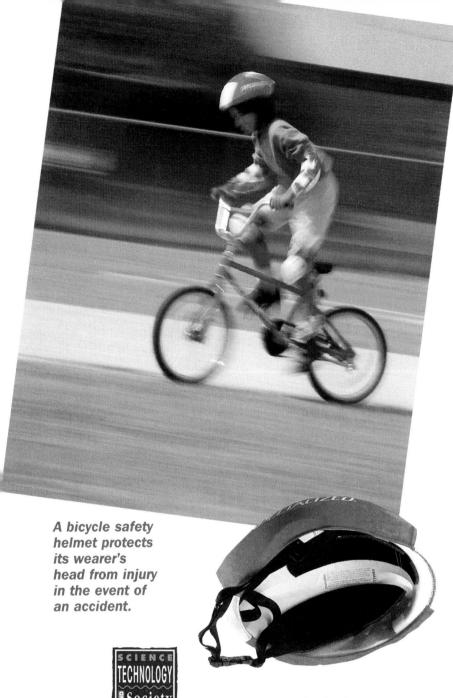

A bicycle safety helmet protects its wearer's head from injury in the event of an accident.

Bicycle Helmet Laws

How much momentum do you have as you ride a bicycle down the street? Your mass doesn't change as you ride along, but often your velocity increases (you accelerate). As your velocity increases, your momentum increases—you have more "bashing power."

What happens if you fall from your bicycle with this greater "bashing power?" You would probably injure yourself! Approximately 1,000 Americans die each year as a result of bicycle accidents. The cause of death is head trauma in 75 percent of these accidents.

Lawmakers in some areas of the United States have passed bills requiring all bicyclists to wear helmets or pay fines—as much as $100 per violation. The makers of these laws realize that the greater "bashing power" a bicycle rider's head has, the greater the risk of injury to the head.

Many bicycle riders don't want to wear helmets. They think helmets are hot and uncomfortable. These "anti-helmet" bicycle riders feel that laws shouldn't require them to wear safety helmets if they don't want to.

What do you think? Get together with several of your classmates who have different opinions on bicycle helmet laws. Have a debate about the pros and cons of bicycle safety helmet laws.

The Momentum of Space Junk

Would you believe that a piece of aluminum the size of a pencil eraser could cause as much damage to an orbiting space shuttle as a bomb? It's true! Over a million tiny pieces of "space trash" consisting of flecks of paint, plastic, and small pieces of metal from old satellites are orbiting Earth at very high velocities. Many pieces are in orbits where they may hit the space shuttle or other satellites. The momentum of this trash is so large that space scientists and astronauts are worried about the potential danger it poses.

This is a scanning electron micrograph of a crater in the louvers of a space satellite. The satellite had been exposed to space for about 50 months. Scientists found six holes per square foot of the louvers. These craters were caused by very high velocity impacts with paint flakes.

Pieces of space trash in orbit may hit orbiting satellites like this one.

Most of the pieces of space trash are very small—no bigger than this letter "o." But these small pieces of junk are moving at extremely high velocities— about 11,200 meters (about 7 miles) per second. These objects have a small mass, but because of the high velocities at which they are moving, they have an enormous amount of momentum.

In 1983, the windshield of a space shuttle was hit by a fleck of paint smaller than the dot over this letter "i." This paint particle gouged a small crater in the window. If the window had broken, the spacecraft might have been destroyed during reentry.

The National Aeronautics and Space Administration (NASA) is concerned about the dangers caused by space trash. NASA is sponsoring research on ways to avoid damage caused by these tiny bits of orbiting junk. Someday we may launch a space-traveling, garbage-collecting satellite to make space travel safer!

Literature Link

Burton's Zoom Zoom Va-ROOOM Machine

How do people come up with ideas such as a space-traveling, garbage-collecting satellites? Usually ideas such as this come from a need that someone has identified.

"Where do ideas come from, anyway? Burton didn't know. They just happened.

Sometimes he saw a problem that cried out for an answer, like poor Clinton's misery. That had resulted in the Automatic Dog-Washing Machine.

Sometimes he just wished things didn't have to be the way they were—like having to make his bed every morning. And so his No-Hands Automatic BedMaking Machine came to be.

Sometimes his ideas grew out of things he seemed to see in snow swirling in the wind or in the shadowy lines of a tree.

There were more ideas around than Burton could possibly use. It was only when he saw a really great one that he glommed onto it and set to work. He worked fast, never able to catch up with his excitement.

There was no way Burton could have guessed the astonishing idea that was waiting for him to find it that particular day." (excerpted from *Burton's Zoom Zoom Va-ROOOM Machine* by Dorothy Haas)

Have you ever invented anything? Whether you have or not, where do you think ideas come from? Brainstorm with one or two classmates to decide on a problem that needs a solution. Then come up with several ideas to solve it. The ideas don't have to be practical or even possible. Just make them creative.

Applying the Second Law of Motion

How has Newton's Second Law of Motion changed the way we live? Let's look at some more creative ideas in the fields of medical and sports engineering.

Roger jogged three kilometers this afternoon. Lots of people do that, but Roger does it while wearing two artificial legs made of carbon fiber, the space-age metal titanium (tī tā' nē əm), and a new type of plastic. These strong, low-mass materials of which his artificial legs are made have helped Roger lead a much more active life.

Roger's legs were badly injured in a car crash. It was necessary to amputate them. He was fitted with a pair of wooden legs and learned to walk again. But the wooden legs were heavy. After walking a few blocks, he would need to rest. The Second Law of Motion helps explain why Roger's new legs are so much easier to use than the more massive older set.

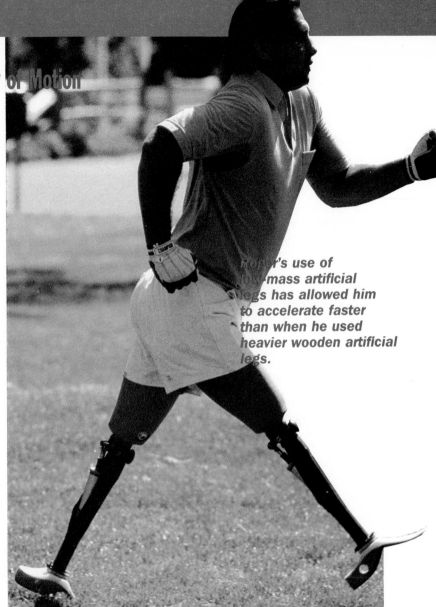

Roger's use of low-mass artificial legs has allowed him to accelerate faster than when he used heavier wooden artificial legs.

When you are walking or running, the muscles of your thighs and hips apply a force to your lower legs. This causes your lower legs and feet to accelerate. The more massive your foot and lower leg is, the more force is required to move them forward quickly.

Roger's thigh and hip muscles can produce only a limited amount of force. When these muscles are applying their maximum force to a large mass, they get tired quickly. By switching to artificial legs made of less massive materials, Roger was able to reduce the mass that his muscles had to accelerate with each step. Using low-mass artificial legs allowed Roger to accelerate faster than when he used the heavier wooden legs with the same maximum amount of force.

Reducing the mass of sports equipment can also improve other athletes' performances. Imagine how hard it would be to run a 10-kilometer (6.2-mile) race with a brick strapped to each of your shoes! Competitive runners wear low-mass racing shoes for the same reason that Roger benefitted from low-mass artificial legs.

Runners can accelerate more quickly in low-mass shoes. In a long race, low-mass shoes are less tiring to wear. Running shoes need to provide a balance between low mass and adequate protection for the runners' feet, however. Sports shoes are designed to protect the runner's feet from injuries and to spring off the running surface, allowing the runner to bounce a little on each stride. If the mass is too low, foot protection is sacrificed.

Looking Back

Remember the race between the airplane and the sports car? The sports car accelerated at about the same rate as the airplane. Now can you use the Second Law of Motion to explain how they accelerated at about the same rate?

Sum It Up

In this lesson, you've been studying Newton's Second Law of Motion and learning how forces, mass, and acceleration act in relationship to each other. Newton's Second Law of Motion states that the acceleration of an object depends on the force applied to it and on the mass of the object. You've seen Newton's Second Law at work when you exerted a force to accelerate a roller skate with different amounts of mass on it. You've also studied the relationship among force, mass, and acceleration in the real world—in cars and planes, in sports, and in insects and other animals jumping to save their lives. Momentum is the product of mass times velocity. Momentum can be thought of as "bashing power." You experienced the effects of mass times velocity or "bashing power" when you dropped a golf ball and a table-tennis ball onto a paper tissue. The harmful interactions that take place when one massive object hits another can be prevented or reduced by the use of helmets, seat belts, and air bags. Whether the forces, masses, and accelerations that are acting together on an object are great or small, Newton's Second Law always governs what happens.

Critical Thinking

1. In your own words, explain Newton's Second Law of Motion.

2. Why do some sports cars accelerate quickly?

3. If a tennis ball and a baseball are moving at the same velocity, which has more momentum? Why?

4. A baseball player found that she could hit the ball farther when she used a heavier bat. However, when she tried an even heavier bat, she didn't hit the ball as far. Why do you think this happened?

5. Why does it take more force to pedal a bicycle to get it started moving than when you are already bicycling along a level street?

What Are Action and Reaction Forces?

Action and reaction pairs. What do these words have to do with forces? What interaction occurs between two objects that causes an action and a reaction? If you push your hand against the wall, does the wall push back against your hand? In this lesson, you'll explore how forces always exist in action and reaction pairs.

Struggling to control the fire hose, a team of firefighters advances toward a solid wall of flames. The fire and smoke are dangerous, but so is the force exerted by the fire hose. No single firefighter is strong enough to control the force exerted by this large fire hose. The hose pushes backward against the firefighters. They must work as a team to push the hose forward toward the fire. If the wiggling hose escapes their grasp, it may whip around and seriously injure a member of the team.

Dangling over the edge of a cliff, a rock climber's safety depends on her climbing skill and on the rope to which she is attached. The upward force exerted on the climber by the rope is saving her from falling. Climbers inspect their ropes carefully before each use. What might happen if a sharp rock sliced partway through the rope? Do the next activity to look at action and reaction forces.

The firefighters must work as a team to push the hose toward the fire.

Activity!

Wheeling Away!

Let's experience pairs of forces.

What You Need

desk chair on wheels, 2–L plastic bottle, sand, *Activity Log* page 21

Sit on the desk chair and push against the wall with your foot. Did you and the chair change positions? How far did you travel? In what direction did you move? Can you name the pairs of forces?

Return the chair to its original position, and this time push harder against the wall. When you push against the wall, do you feel the wall pushing back against your foot? Now move the chair away from the wall. Clear a large space in front of and behind the chair. Fill the 2–L bottle with sand. Sit in the chair with both feet a few inches off the floor and hold the sand-filled bottle in front of your chest. Using both hands, push the bottle away from your body and release it.

Safety Tip: Be sure no one is close enough to be hit by the bottle!

How did you apply a force to the bottle? Did the bottle apply a force to you? Did the chair move when you released the bottle? Record your observations in your *Activity Log.*

Minds On! Have you ever filled a balloon with air and let it go? What happened? Does it take a force to fill a balloon with air? How can you tell? Does the air inside a balloon exert a force against the rubber sides of the balloon? How can you tell? Do the rubber sides of the balloon exert a force against the air inside? How can you tell? Why does the balloon fly around the room when you let go of the open end? What forces are acting on the balloon and on the air? ●

According to Sir Isaac Newton, seeing an apple falling from a tree stimulated his thinking and led to his discovering what we now call Newton's Laws of Motion.

You already know about Newton's First and Second Laws. These laws explain how unbalanced forces affect the motion of matter. Now you'll explore Newton's Third Law of Motion.

This climber exerts a downward force on the rope.

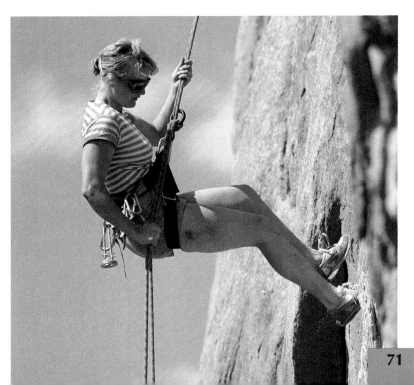

Activity!

Launching a Balloon-Powered Rocket

Let's build and test a rocket that uses a balloon for its engine.

What You Need

balloon
long thin plastic bag
plastic drinking straw
4 m of string
masking tape (2 pieces, each
   about 8 cm long)
meterstick
Activity Log pages 22–23

What To Do

1 Tie one end of the string to the back of a chair or desk. Push the string through the drinking straw. Tie the other end of the string to a second chair. Move the chairs apart until the string is level and tight.

2 Tape the plastic bag to the straw as shown. Blow up the balloon and hold the end closed. Don't tie a knot in the end!

3 Pull the straw and plastic bag to one end of the string so that the open end of the plastic bag is at the knot in the string. Place the balloon inside the plastic bag and let go. What do you observe? Use the meterstick to measure the distance traveled.

4 Have the same student blow up the balloon again. Place the balloon inside the plastic bag and fly the balloon-powered rocket along the string again. Repeat this process 4 more times. Measure the distances traveled with the meterstick. Record your measurements and observations in your **Activity Log.** Calculate the average distance traveled.

What Happened?

1. How far did the balloon rocket travel along the string? What was the average distance traveled by the balloon rocket?
2. What pushes the air out of the balloon? Would the straw travel along the string if you attached a paper bag full of air to the straw and then let go? Why or why not?
3. What do you think caused your balloon-powered rocket to move in the direction it did?

What Now?

1. How can you measure the average speed of the balloon?
2. Help your teacher organize a balloon rocket race. How could you make your balloon-powered rocket go faster? Can you make it travel completely across the room?

EXPLORE

73

Equal and Opposite Forces

Gases expanding

Nozzle opens ;
expanding gases escape

Newton asked himself, "Where do forces come from?" He realized that forces always come in pairs that are equal and act in opposite directions. The apple he may have seen hanging from a tree was pulling down against the limb of the tree. The limb, on the other hand, was pulling up against the weight of the apple. These upward and downward forces were opposite and equal. Newton decided that a force applied to any object must be applied by another object. Newton was able to then state his Third Law of Motion—

Whenever an object exerts a force on a second object, the second object exerts an equal and opposite force on the first object.

The force of the expanding gases escaping through the nozzle of the rocket is the action force.

This law can be stated in terms of action and reaction forces—**for every action force, there is an equal but opposite reaction force.** It's important to note that the "action" force and the "reaction" force are acting on different objects.

Both balloon-powered rockets and rockets traveling in outer space provide good examples of equal and opposite action-reaction forces. The stretched balloon pushes on the air, forcing it out of the open end of the balloon. This is the action force. An equal and opposite reaction force occurs inside the balloon as the air pushes back on the balloon. This reaction force pushes the straw forward along the fishing line.

Rocket boosters attached to the space shuttle push it into orbit in the same way. When the space shuttle's rocket boosters are started, they burn fuel and produce large amounts of hot gases that rush out of the back of the booster. That's the action force. The reaction force of the gases pushing back on the booster is equal in strength but opposite in direction. This reaction force sends the shuttle and rocket boosters upward.

Let's look back to some of the examples given in the first part of this lesson and see how the Third Law of Motion explains what's happening.

Remember the fire hose shooting water on the burning building. The nozzle of the fire hose is pushing in the opposite direction from which the water is moving. The water pushing against the nozzle produces an action force. The nozzle pushing back against the water produces the reaction force. The reaction force is exactly equal in strength but pointed in the opposite direction of the force of the hose. Firefighters are able to hold the nozzle still by pushing it toward the building with all their strength.

Action-reaction forces

They're using their muscles to produce a force that balances the reaction force. As long as the forces are balanced, the net force on the hose is zero, and the nozzle doesn't move.

Pairs of action and reaction forces are present whether matter is moving or sitting still. Forces always act in pairs. Look back at the picture on page 71 showing the rock climber dangling in mid-air. She isn't moving up or down. She is exerting a downward action force on the rope equal to the weight of her body and equipment. The rope is exerting an upward reaction force on the climber. The upward force of the rope on the climber is exactly equal to the downward force exerted by the climber on the rope. However, until an unbalanced force acts on the climber, she will not move up or down.

Action-reaction forces

Mollusk Movers

Action and reaction forces are found in nature as well. Mollusks make up the largest group of water animals. Mollusks are generally slow moving creatures like snails, slugs, scallops, squids, and clams. But several types of mollusks use very specialized action-reaction forces to move around quite rapidly.

Scallops are two-shelled mollusks that look similar to clams. Scallops can change their locations or escape danger by rapidly opening and closing their shells. When a scallop closes its shells, water is forced out from between the shells. The action force is caused by the force of the shells on the water. The scallop then shoots backward. This reaction is caused by the force of the expelled water on the scallop's shells.

This scallop is using action and reaction forces to escape from the sea star, a predator.

Squids are another type of mollusk that use an even more remarkable scheme for high- speed swimming. Squids are fast-moving hunters that live in the sea. They use their tentacles to swim forward or backward and to grasp the fish they eat. But if a squid is trying to catch a fish to eat (or avoid being eaten by a much bigger fish), it shoots a high-velocity stream of water out of a tube in its body (the action force). The reaction force is caused by the force of the expelled water on the squid. The result of this reaction force is acceleration in the direction opposite to the high-velocity stream of water. Can you see a similarity between the squid and the fire hose?

Squids use action-reaction forces to accelerate rapidly. The funnel tube can be reversed for acceleration in the opposite direction.

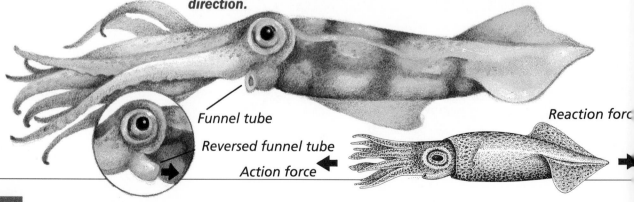

Funnel tube

Reversed funnel tube

Action force

Reaction force

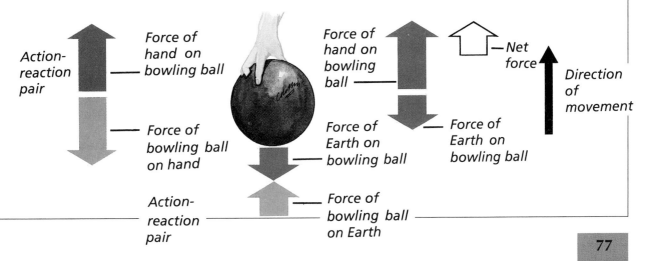

If You Provide the Action, What's the Reaction?

All sporting events involve action and reaction forces. Some are very obvious, and some are a bit harder to identify. For example, when you're roller skating and you push against the wall, you're exerting an action force on the wall. The wall exerts an equal and opposite reaction force on you that will accelerate you away from the wall. You can't see the wall moving in the opposite direction, but there is a very small motion of the area of the wall that you pushed against. Another example would be hitting a baseball. You exert an action force with the bat on the ball, but the ball also exerts an equal and opposite reaction force on the bat.

Work in groups of three or four to list as many action-reaction forces in sporting events as you can. Record these sporting

What are the action and reaction forces in these sporting events?

events in your **Activity Log** page 24. Trade lists with other groups and discuss these sporting events in class. Remember—action-reaction forces act on different objects!

Each of the action-reaction pairs shown is equal. The net force on the bowling ball is in the upward direction, therefore the bowling ball is accelerated upward.

Action-reaction pair — Force of hand on bowling ball

— Force of bowling ball on hand

Action-reaction pair — Force of bowling ball on Earth

Force of hand on bowling ball —

Force of Earth on bowling ball —

Net force

Direction of movement

Force of Earth on bowling ball

Why Do We Need To Know About the Third Law of Motion?

The Third Law of Motion can help you predict what will happen when you apply a force to an object. This happens daily in your life. For instance, when you push the door to your classroom open, the door will exert a force on your hand. That's why it takes some work to push the door open. You need to overcome the force the door exerts on your hand.

The Third Law of Motion is also important for many technical jobs, such as engineering, architecture, and mechanics. People who work in these fields need to know about action and reaction forces so they can plan how to control all possible forces when doing their jobs.

How does knowing about Newton's Third Law of Motion aid a bridge designer? Do the following activity to find out.

TRY THIS Activity!

Design Your Own Bridge!

Use your knowledge of action and reaction forces to build a model bridge from playing cards.

What You Need
deck of playing cards, masking tape

Work with 2 other students to build a support structure for a bridge that is strong enough to support 2 large textbooks, using only playing cards and masking tape. Rules for building your bridge: You may use no more than 10 playing cards to construct your bridge. You can't use any wood, steel, or other sturdy material to make your bridge stronger. You may use masking tape to hold the structure together.

How you construct the bridge is completely up to your design team. Be creative! Experiment with your design and build something original! Whose bridge will be the strongest? Who will have the most unique design? Which team will use the fewest playing cards to hold up the books? Build yours and find out!

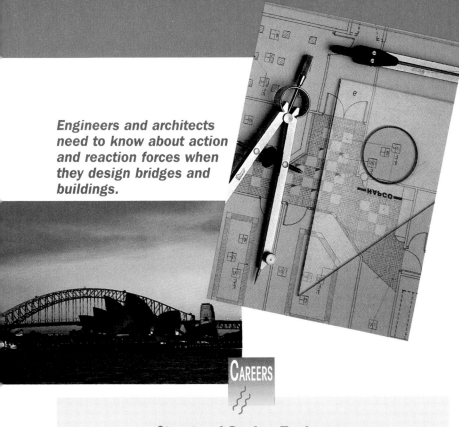

Engineers and architects need to know about action and reaction forces when they design bridges and buildings.

CAREERS

Structural Design Engineers

The Third Law of Motion is very important to structural design engineers. Part of the job of structural design engineers is to design frameworks and foundations for buildings and equipment. If these engineers didn't understand applications of the Third Law of Motion, many engineering decisions would be a matter of guesswork.

To become a structural design engineer, you must study mathematics, physics, and engineering in college.

Having a curiosity about forces and motion helps!

Part of the job of structural design engineers is to study what causes structural failures of equipment. The engineers then work out solutions to prevent future breakdowns. Good engineering designs make buildings and equipment safer and more reliable to use. With their knowledge and experience, structural design engineers really make a difference in people's lives!

of action forces and reaction forces—"For every action force, there is an equal and opposite reaction force." Remember, action and reaction forces act on different objects. You experienced these forces interacting on matter in your activity with the balloon and straw on a string. You've also explored and read about action and reaction forces in sporting events, space travel, and underwater life. In fact, no two objects anywhere can interact without there being action and reaction forces.

Critical Thinking

1. In your own words, explain Newton's Third Law of Motion.
2. A girl climbs a rope during gym class. She exerts a force on the rope due to her weight. What other force or forces are involved in this situation?
3. What action and reaction pairs exist when catching a basketball?
4. What action and reaction pairs exist when sleeping in a bed?
5. What action and reaction pairs exist when a rocket accelerates into space?

Sum It Up

Newton's Third Law of Motion says, "For every force, there is an equal and opposite force." This law can also be stated in terms

Tug-of-War Contests Revisited

Do you recall the tug-of-war contests shown at the beginning of this unit? Let's apply what we've learned throughout this unit to see who will really win these contests!

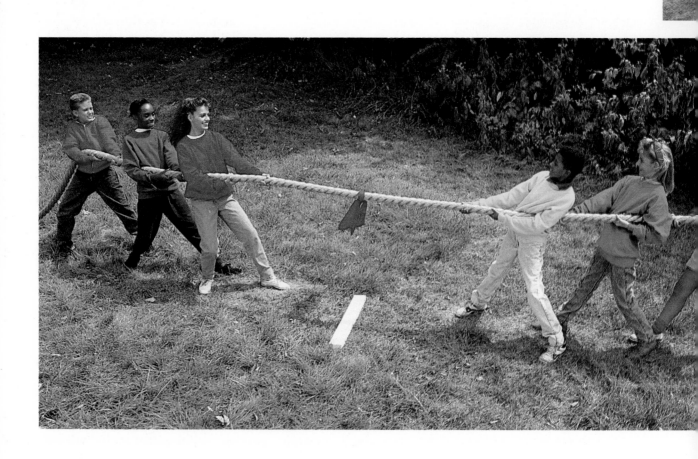

Is the force exerted on the rope by the team on the left balanced by the force exerted on the rope by the team on the right? What will have to happen in order for one of the teams to win this tug-of-war contest?

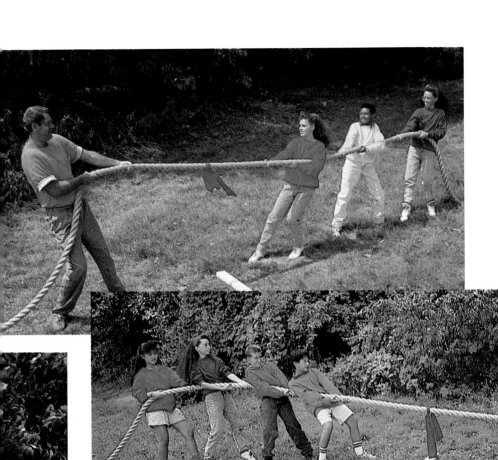

Is the force exerted on the rope by the adult balanced by the force exerted on the rope by the children? What will have to happen for a winner to be declared in this tug-of-war contest?

Is the force exerted on the rope by the children balanced by the force exerted on the rope by the boulder? How could the children win this tug-of-war contest?

Is the force exerted on the rope by the children on roller skates balanced by the force exerted on the rope by the children in shoes? What will happen when both teams exert more force on the rope?

Environmental Costs

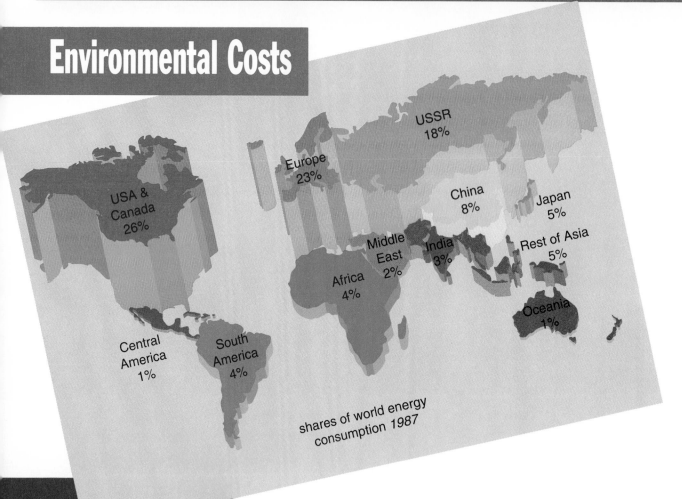

USSR
18%

Europe
23%

China
8%

Japan
5%

USA &
Canada
26%

Middle
East
2%

India
3%

Rest of Asia
5%

Africa
4%

Oceania
1%

Central
America
1%

South
America
4%

shares of world energy
consumption 1987

Burning coal produces energy that can be used to produce force. The environmental cost is air pollution.

You've looked at the forces involved in tug-of-war contests, and you've identified where these forces were working and how they interacted with each other and with matter. Now, let's think about other places where forces are important and how they are produced.

Today in the United States, we often use machines to produce the force needed to get us from one place to another or to process the food we eat. The machines use energy in the form of coal, oil, and gas to produce the force. Before many of these machines were invented, however, people used to rely on muscle power to do some of these jobs. Some countries still rely on older forms of producing force.

These countries use much less of the world's limited fossil-fuel resources to support each person. An average resident of India uses about 50 times less energy than is used by a United States resident.

What are the environmental costs of using so much energy? The costs include air pollution, oil spills, decreasing amounts of ozone in the atmosphere, decreasing numbers of forests on Earth...the list of environmental concerns is long.

Some of the solutions to these concerns lie in making informed decisions about the methods we use to produce force and do work. If you can use your muscles to walk to the library, should you ask someone to drive you there? If a system of mass transportation could be developed in your area, would enough people ride it instead of driving their cars? Walking or riding mass transportation helps to conserve fuel and thereby stretch Earth's limited fuel reserves.

Work with two friends to do the following Try This Activity. How can you use your knowledge of forces to help make a difference in the world?

TRY THIS Activity!

A New Way To Move

Work in groups of 3 to design a new method of transportation. This could be a new type of bicycle, a new type of car, a new type of boat, or whatever you decide. Try to make your new method of transportation use energy efficiently. Brainstorm to come up with several ideas, then choose the best idea and test it. Use what you now know about forces—frictional forces, gravitational forces, balanced and unbalanced forces, and action and reaction forces—to help with your design. Share responsibility for gathering background information and equipment, then work together to build your transportation model. Share your model with your classmates.

GLOSSARY

Use the pronunciation key below to help you decode, or read, the pronunciations.

Pronunciation Key

a	at, bad	d	dear, soda, bad
ā	ape, pain, day, break	f	five, defend, leaf, off, cough, elephant
ä	father, car, heart	g	game, ago, fog, egg
âr	care, pair, bear, their, where	h	hat, ahead
e	end, pet, said, heaven, friend	hw	white, whether, which
ē	equal, me, feet, team, piece, key	j	joke, enjoy, gem, page, edge
i	it, big, English, hymn	k	kite, bakery, seek, tack, cat
ī	ice, fine, lie, my	l	lid, sailor, feel, ball, allow
îr	ear, deer, here, pierce	m	man, family, dream
o	odd, hot, watch	n	not, final, pan, knife
ō	old, oat, toe, low	ng	long, singer, pink
ô	coffee, all, taught, law, fought	p	pail, repair, soap, happy
ôr	order, fork, horse, story, pour	r	ride, parent, wear, more, marry
oi	oil, toy	s	sit, aside, pets, cent, pass
ou	out, now	sh	shoe, washer, fish mission, nation
u	up, mud, love, double	t	tag, pretend, fat, button, dressed
ū	use, mule, cue, feud, few	th	thin, panther, both
ü	rule, true, food	th	this, mother, smooth
ů	put, wood, should	v	very, favor, wave
ûr	burn, hurry, term, bird, word,courage	w	wet, weather, reward
ə	about, taken, pencil, lemon, circus	y	yes, onion
b	bat, above, job	z	zoo, lazy, jazz, rose, dogs, houses
ch	chin, such, match	zh	vision, treasure, seizure

acceleration (ak sel´ ə rā´ shən): the rate at which velocity changes

action-reaction pairs (ak´ shən-re ak´ shən): two forces, acting on different bodies, having equal strength but opposite direction

air resistance (âr re zis´ təns): the force of air against a moving object; also called drag

average speed (av´ rij spēd): the total distance an object travels divided by the total time it takes to travel the distance

balanced forces (bal´ ənsed fôrs ez): forces, acting on the same body, equal in size but opposite in direction

constant speed (kon´ stənt spēd): no change in speed; acceleration is zero

drag: see air resistance

force: a push or pull one body exerts on another

friction (frik´ shən): a force that opposes motion between two surfaces that are touching each other

gravity (grav´ i tē): the mutual force of attraction that exists between all objects in the universe, force Earth exerts on all objects on or near it

hypothesis (hī poth´ ə sis): the proposed answer to a question or tentative solution to a problem; an educated guess based on observation

inertia (in ûr´ shə): the property of a body that resists any change in velocity

kinetic energy (ki net´ ik en´ ər jē): energy of motion; a measure of how much force a moving object exerts as it moves a specific distance

magnet: any object that has a magnetic field and is able to exert forces on other magnets

mass: the amount of matter in an object; the measure of the inertia of a body

matter: anything that has mass and takes up space

momentum (mō men´ təm): the mass of an object multiplied by its velocity

motion (mō´ shən): change in position

negative acceleration (neg´ ə tiv ak sell ə rā´ shən): a decrease in the rate of velocity

net force (net fôrs): force that results from unbalanced forces acting on an object; changes the motion of an object

newton (N) (nū´ tən): the unit of force; force required to accelerate a 1-kg mass at the rate 1 m/s/s

physicists (fiz´ ə sists): scientists who study the structure and interaction of matter, as well as the changes in position that matter undergoes

plates: rigid blocks of Earth's crust and upper mantle

potential energy (pə ten´ sh l): the energy due to position or condition; a measure of how much force an object at rest is capable of exerting if it starts to move

spring scale (spring skāl): a device used to measure force in newtons

total distance: the maximum time it takes to travel a certain distance

total time: the maximum separation of two positions

unbalanced forces (un bal ənsed fôrs ez): forces, acting on the same body, unequal in size and/or opposite in direction

velocity (və los´ i tē): the speed and direction of a moving object

weight: the force of gravity that Earth exerts on an object resting on its surface

INDEX

INDEX continued

CREDITS

Searching for Lost Tombs

Shirley Granahan

Before You Read

The tiny underground entrance opens to a long, narrow tunnel. It's dark, and the air is hot and humid. What's inside the tiny chambers that line the long hallways? Human skeletons! This may sound like a horror movie, but it's not. It's the discovery of an ancient Egyptian tomb. As you get ready to read this book, think about the following and take notes.

Where have you read or heard about ancient tombs? Where have you seen artifacts, objects made by humans, from ancient civilizations?

What kinds of things do you think ancient tombs contain? What do you think you can learn about ancient civilizations from the objects found inside a tomb?

Preview the book by looking at the table of contents, headings, photos, and special features.

What do you see in this book that you already know something about?

Write down two questions you have about tombs.

Look at the photos and captions on pages 18–19. What do you think you can learn from these artifacts?

Why do you think it might be important to study ancient tombs and the objects they contain?

List three facts or ideas that you think you'll discover in this book.

Contents

From
Beyond the Grave

A tall man stood in the middle of the hot desert in Egypt. He was just outside the entrance to a tomb thousands of years old. The man had spent several years searching for it with his team. His shoulders and arms ached from digging into rock and dirt. Finally, there it was!

Dr. Kent Weeks and his team of **archaeologists** had uncovered the entrance to a hidden tomb. They had dug up a small doorway. It was only a couple of feet high. That was much too low for the men to walk through. They would have to crawl in on their hands and knees.

The underground entrance opened onto a long, narrow tunnel. It was a very tight space. The air was hot and humid. Their clothes were soaked with sweat. Slowly, they moved ahead.

Archaeologists often search the deserts of Egypt to find clues to the past.

Kent Weeks scrambled across giant slabs of stone that covered the floor. These slabs had probably fallen from the ceiling years before. This made him nervous. Was the ceiling weak and in bad shape? Would more of it collapse? Could the ceiling crash down on top of them? In spite of that, Dr. Weeks kept crawling. He had to know what was inside the tomb. To find out, he had to reach the end of the tunnel.

Does this sound like a scene from *Raiders of the Lost Ark* or *Tomb Raider*? Actually, for this archaeologist, it's just another day at work. Archaeologists are scientists who dig up the past. They uncover tombs. They also dig up ruins of long-lost buildings, human bones, and more. They study all these things to learn about life in the distant past.

The archaeologists had to crawl through this narrow entrance to get into the hidden tomb.

Why Look for Tombs?

Archaeologists like Kent Weeks search for tombs because they're often the only things left behind by ancient people. Everything above ground may have been wiped out by war. Or destroyed by the weather or a natural disaster. Why are there so many tombs? Every culture has a way to take care of the dead. That's true of the past and today, too.

How people treated their dead also gives us clues to their beliefs. For example, some ancient cultures believed in an **afterlife,** or life in another world after death. They often placed items such as clothing, jewelry, and pottery inside graves and tombs. They believed the dead would use them in that other world.

This robot is called the Pyramid Rover. It searches places archaeologists can't reach.

These items, called **artifacts,** are sometimes found perfectly **preserved,** even after thousands of years. Examining artifacts helps archaeologists make guesses about how people lived long ago.

These workers must gently brush off dirt, layer by layer, so they don't damage the skeleton.

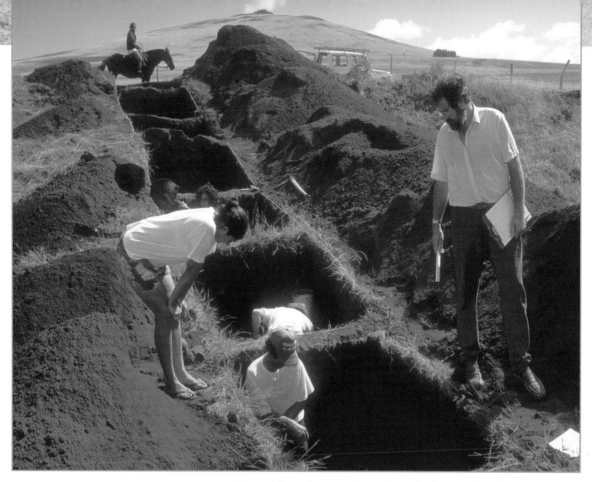

Even if modern technology helps archaeologists find a **site**, it still takes hard work to dig it up.

How to Find a Tomb

Archaeologists don't go digging just anywhere to find tombs. They know that tombs are found where people once lived. And people usually settled near good soil for farming. They also built towns and cities near rivers, lakes, and other water sources. So archaeologists search for places where ancient people might have found those things. Those places are where people probably lived, and died, long ago.

Archaeologists also read historical records, such as diaries or letters. Often, these records are hundreds, or even thousands, of years old. They might contain clues to help find tombs. Archaeologists also interview people who live in those places now. These people may have heard stories or **legends** about ancient tombs.

The Forgotten Tomb

The lost tomb that Kent Weeks uncovered turned out to be one of the most important discoveries found in Egypt. It's in an area called the "Valley of the Kings." It sits just outside the city of Luxor in southern Egypt. Dozens of buried tombs can be found throughout that area. The best-known tombs are located in the northern part of Egypt, inside the famous pyramids of Giza. Many ancient Egyptians are also buried there.

The tomb that Kent Weeks unearthed, or dug up, sits in the heart of the Valley of the Kings. When Dr. Weeks and his team crawled inside, it was actually the third time that archaeologists had entered the tomb in the past 200 years. In 1825, a British traveler named James Burton came to southern Egypt to explore the area. He discovered the tomb, but spent only a few hours inside.

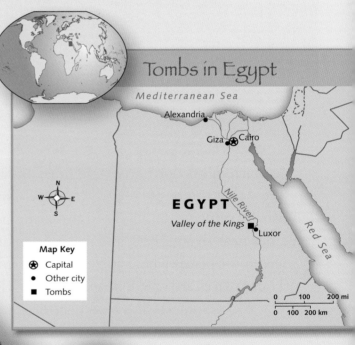

Tombs in Egypt

Mediterranean Sea

Alexandria

Giza · Cairo

EGYPT

Nile River

Valley of the Kings · Luxor

Red Sea

Map Key
- ✪ Capital
- ● Other city
- ■ Tombs

0   100   200 mi
0   100 200 km

The Great Pyramids of Giza are one of the most famous sights in the world.

Almost a hundred years later, archaeologist Howard Carter entered the tomb. He thought he had made a discovery. But when he stepped inside, he found bones and pieces of pottery scattered around. Carter thought that robbers had broken in more than a thousand years before. Believing the tomb was worthless, he lost interest. So he left, dumping rocks and sand over the entrance. The unknown tomb remained hidden for many years.

Years later, Kent Weeks came to Egypt from the United States to search for tombs and other ancient sites. In 1989, he learned that the Egyptian government planned to widen roads near the Valley of the Kings. Dr. Weeks knew from James Burton's notes that a tomb was hidden in the area. He also knew that road construction might cause the tomb to cave in. It had to be found soon, or it might be lost forever.

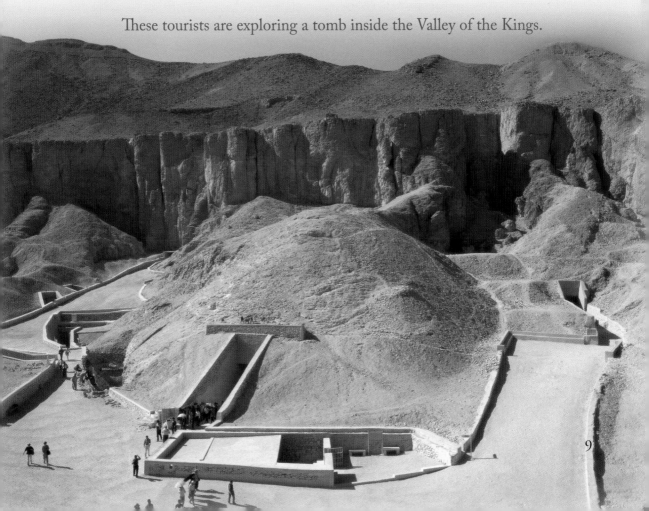

Dr. Kent Weeks

These tourists are exploring a tomb inside the Valley of the Kings.

9

Into the Tomb

So Kent Weeks went on a hunt for the lost tomb. His crew flew hot air balloons over the Valley of the Kings. They looked for signs on the ground below. After several months, they had an idea where the tomb might be located. The team started **excavating** the tomb later that year. It was hard, hot work. They used pickaxes to pound rocks. They used shovels and hoes to remove dirt. As they dug, they discovered that the tomb had been partially destroyed. It had been **raided** hundreds of years before by tomb robbers, who were probably searching for gold and other riches. Several floods had also damaged the tomb.

Inside the Tomb

Hallway

Chambers

Main Chamber

Main Entrance

Chambers

The site that Kent Weeks unearthed is bigger than other tombs that have been discovered in Egypt.

It took five years for the team to remove enough dirt and **debris** to enter the tomb. They finally crawled through the narrow tunnel in 1994. As they entered the tomb, they were shocked to find more than just one small room. In fact, there were several hallways. Each was hundreds of feet long. The hallways were lined with dozens of smaller rooms. There were more than 150 of these different **chambers.** This wasn't any ordinary find. It turned out to be one of the largest tombs uncovered in Egypt.

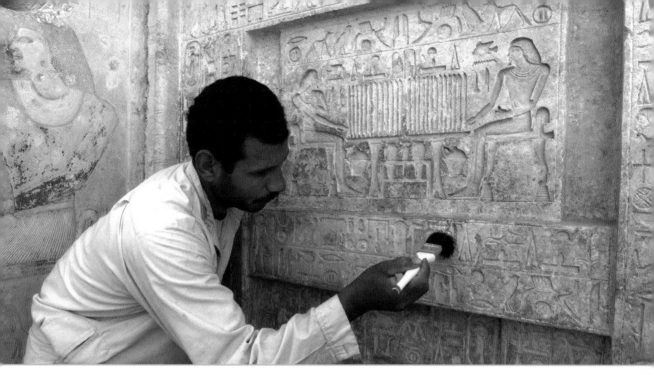

Hieroglyphs like the ones shown in this photo above represent letters, words, and ideas.

Archaeologists have given each tomb in the Valley of Kings a number. This tomb became known as Tomb 5, or KV5. That stands for Kings' Valley Tomb Number 5.

Dr. Weeks and his team began to explore Tomb 5. They discovered that the walls were decorated with colorful art and writing, known as **hieroglyphs.** Hieroglyphs carved or painted onto tomb walls tell stories about people's lives. Some are read across, others from top to bottom. Reading hieroglyphs is similar to reading a code. Historians had to figure out how to understand them.

Hieroglyphs on the walls of Tomb 5 mentioned several sons of Ramses II. He was Egypt's most famous ruler. Dr. Weeks became excited. These hieroglyphs could mean only one thing. Tomb 5 was the long-lost burial place of Ramses' sons!

Anicent Egyptian Alphabet

a w ch
i b d
p dsch
y f q
aa m
n k
ch
r g
s t
h
h sch tsch

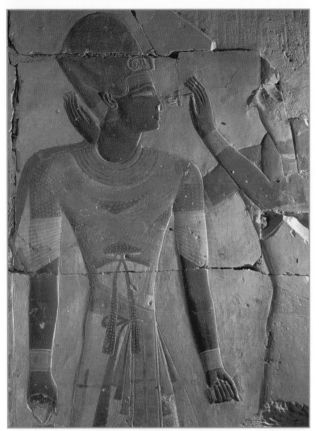

This ancient image of Ramses II was created while he was still pharaoh.

Egypt's Greatest Pharaoh

Ramses II was in his twenties when he became **pharaoh,** or ruler of Egypt, in 1279 BC. He ruled for a phenomenal 67 years. At a time when most Egyptians lived until the age of 30, Ramses II lived well into his 90s.

Ramses wasn't just a pharaoh. He was also father to more than 100 children. The massive tomb that he built for his sons tells us what a powerful and wealthy leader he was.

Work began on Ramses' own tomb as soon as he became pharaoh. Like most rulers, he wanted to make sure he would be buried in style.

While laborers were building the pharaoh's tomb, they also worked on a tomb for his sons. Tomb 5 was even bigger than the pharaoh's tomb. It would have to be. Because it was meant to hold the bodies and belongings of many more people.

Kent Weeks and his team found a number of bodies inside Tomb 5. They believe the bodies belong to Ramses' sons. One clue is a huge carving. It shows one of the sons, Amun, riding into battle.

An Archaeologist Speaks

"The tomb of Ramses' sons is really interesting because it includes the bodies of people who were not rulers. This is very different from the other tombs in the Valley of the Kings."

Dr. Joe Wegner
Museum of Archaeology
and Anthropology
University of Pennsylvania

Ramses built more monuments and tombs than any other pharaoh, including this temple in Abu Simbel.

13

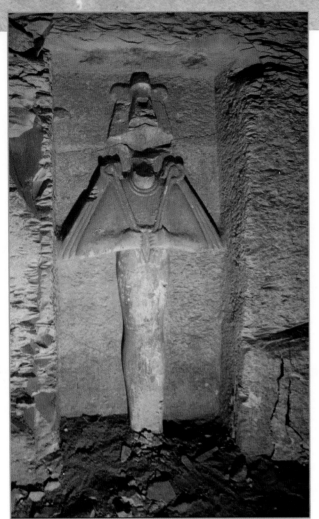

This statue of Osiris, god of the afterlife, stands at the end of a hallway in Tomb 5.

Journey to the Afterlife

As in many other tombs, Tomb 5's hieroglyphs describe the lives of ancient Egyptians. They also tell about the afterlife and religious beliefs.

Ancient Egyptians believed that a person's spirit took different forms. The two most important forms are the *ka* and the *ba*. The *ka* was energy. It gives a body life. That helps the body develop and grow. The *ba,* on the other hand, was character, or soul. Egyptians believed that when people died, their *ka* and *ba* came together in their tombs. They became **immortal** and could live forever in the afterlife.

Some of the hieroglyphs Kent Weeks found show Ramses presenting his sons to the Egyptian gods in the afterlife. One of the first artifacts that Dr. Weeks found was a huge statue of Osiris. He was the god of the afterlife. Egyptians believed that Osiris and his family would be there to welcome people as they entered the next world. Dr. Weeks' crew also found **shabtis.** Those are little wooden or clay statues. Ancient Egyptians believed that they would come to life and become servants in the afterlife.

These Egyptian students are studying a mask in a museum. Ancient rulers were often buried with masks to make it easier for the *ba*, or soul, to recognize the body when it entered the tomb.

What's the Difference?

Rich and poor Egyptians were treated very differently when they died. The photo on the left shows the tomb of a ruler. The photo on the right shows a worker's grave. Describe some of the differences between the two photos.

Mad About Mummies

In addition to artifacts, Dr. Weeks also found bits and pieces of **mummies.** Preserving dead bodies as mummies was also connected to ancient beliefs. Egyptians mummified corpses so they would last for an eternity in the next world. Ancient Egyptians also mummified cats and other animals. They wanted to make sure people's pets would live in the afterlife, too.

When you picture a mummy, you might think of a bandaged creature from a horror movie. But a mummy is really just a dead body that's been treated so it won't rot.

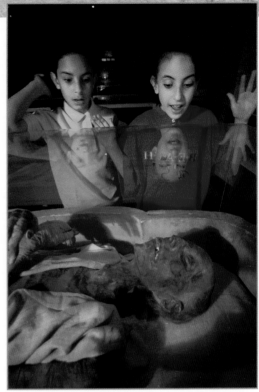

Ramses' corpse is one of the best-preserved mummies ever found.

Canopic jars held a mummy's liver, stomach, intestines, and lungs.

How to Make a Mummy

Making a mummy was a complicated process. It took about 70 days and had several steps.

1 First, ancient Egyptians cleaned the body. Then, they used a long, hooked instrument to reach up through the nose and remove the brain. They didn't think the brain was important. So after they scraped it out, they threw it away.

2 Next, Egyptians cut a slit in the left side of the body to remove the liver, stomach, intestines, and lungs. These were stored in canopic jars to be buried with the mummy.

3 The heart was left in place because Egyptians believed that it was the center of intelligence. It would be needed in the afterlife.

4 The next step was to stuff the body and cover it with pounds of salt called **natron.** The salt slowly sucked fluids out of the body to dry it out. After 40 days, priests washed away the natron. Then the body was stuffed with padding.

5 Finally, the body was wrapped in layers of soft linen strips. Sticky tree sap glued the strips together. Now the mummy was ready for burial.

Life Along the Nile River

All the things that people would need in the afterlife were buried with the mummies. Clothing, makeup, wigs, food, pots, plates, cups, and musical instruments were all there. Even toys and games. The more belongings people placed inside their tombs before death, the better off they believed they'd be in the afterlife.

Dr. Weeks and his crew unearthed thousands of objects in Tomb 5. They found pottery, wooden furniture, and beaded jewelry. They even found a stone receipt for an oil lamp delivery.

Most of the artifacts had been smashed by tomb robbers. Or they had been shattered by floods that swept into the tomb. Archaeologists are still working to piece together the different items. But even so, these artifacts have already shown them a lot about life in Egypt.

Pharaohs were buried with riches, like this shield and gold ring.

Ancient Egyptians loaded up their tombs with all sorts of things, even foods like figs and bread.

18

For example, the team found clothing and sandals. The clothes were made out of linen. This makes a lot of sense because linen is very light and airy. It was the perfect cloth for Egypt's hot climate. The sandals were made of leather or straw. In life, sandals protected people's feet against sand and stones on the desert floor.

Tomb paintings help archaeologists learn about everyday life. This one shows ancient jewelry and furniture makers.

In tomb paintings you can see that both men and women wore necklaces, bracelets, and other jewelry. Rich Egyptians wore expensive gold or silver. Poorer people wore copper and **faience.** Faience is colorful beads made of baked clay.

It's been more than ten years since Kent Weeks and his team first excavated Tomb 5. They're still uncovering new chambers and new artifacts every year. Their amazing finds are rich with information. They tell us what it might have been like to live along the Nile River when Ramses ruled.

An Archaeologist at Work

Dr. Peter Piccione is a professor at the College of Charleston in South Carolina. He also spends a lot of time in Egypt digging for tombs and artifacts. In 2005, he excavated sites in an area known as Western Thebes. We talked to Dr. Piccione to find out what it's like to search for lost tombs.

Why did you decide to become an archaeologist?
I wanted to learn about different parts of ancient Egyptian life and put them together. Instead of saying I'm an archaeologist, I call myself an **Egyptologist.**

What project are you working on now?
I'm clearing out the tombs of a father and son. Both were priests, or religious leaders, in ancient Egypt. Their tombs were first discovered in the early 1900s. We're going back to clean them out and copy the carvings and paintings on the walls. Scenes on tomb walls tell us about the person's life. You can use them to build family histories.

Western Thebe

Do you use any high-tech tools or methods in your work?
We're using satellites to photograph the tombs of noble people in an area called Western Thebes. Satellite images are extremely precise and exact. We can use this information to make maps and guides for all the tombs. They'll be available on a Website for people to visit to find out all about the tombs in Western Thebes.

What kinds of interesting things have been found in Egyptian tombs?
Egyptian rulers wanted to have servants and soldiers with them in the afterlife. The earliest Egyptians buried the bodies of actual workers with their king when he died. We don't know if the workers were sacrificed or if they willingly took poison so they could be placed in the tomb. We just know that they were all buried at the same time. This was long before tombs were built in the Valley of the Kings. Eventually, the Egyptians used statues instead of real people.

Have you had any unusual experiences while excavating a tomb?
Not really. The only scary thing happened in a tomb that was deep underground. I went inside with another archaeologist. She went into one of the chambers ahead of me. I heard her scream, "The ceiling is moving!" I raised my flashlight and saw thousands of bats hanging above. They were flapping their wings and it really did look like the ceiling was moving. We immediately took off. As we quickly hiked out of the entrance, several Egyptian guards came up to us. I couldn't remember the Arabic word for "bat," so I drew a picture. They laughed at us. They were used to seeing bats and thought we were silly.

What do you like best about your work?
I love to discover an idea that's thousands of years old and bring it to life again. It's kind of like virtual time travel. It's fascinating to find out how people lived, what they thought, and what they believed long ago.

Western Thebes

Map Key
⊛ Capital
• Other city
■ Tombs

Mediterranean Sea

Cairo ⊛

EGYPT

Nile River

Red Sea

Western Thebes ■
Luxor

0   100   200 mi
0   100   200 km

The Army of the Dead

Tombs aren't found only in Egypt. They're uncovered all over the world. One of the most amazing tombs was discovered in China.

On an ordinary spring morning in 1974, three farmers walked across a field near Xi'an (SHEE AHN), China. Over the past few months, very little rain had fallen. So the farmers were looking for a good place to dig a well. They picked a spot less than a mile from a hill. The farmers began to dig, in search of water.

One farmer's shovel suddenly hit something hard. He peered into the dark hole to see what he had found. To his surprise, he discovered the head of a clay man. The farmers reported their find. A team of archaeologists came to Xi'an to have a look. They dug further into the ground. They soon realized that the head was part of a life-size statue.

The statue was dressed in the uniform of a soldier. The archaeologists had heard rumors about clay figures buried with one of the great emperors of China. Could this be the location of his lost tomb?

A Tomb in China

Map Key
- ✪ Capital
- ■ Tomb

Great Wall · Beijing ✪

CHINA ■ Xi'an (Sian)

N · E · W · S

| 0 | 400 | 800 mi |
| 0 | 400 | 800 km |

The archaeologists brought out their shovels and began to dig. The team had no idea they were about to unearth one of the most fabulous finds of the twentieth century. As they dug, they uncovered an underground pit. In this pit, were hundreds of clay soldiers. These soldiers stood ready for war, complete with horses and weapons. It had taken the archaeologists two years to discover a great army of the dead.

The figures were made of baked clay, or **terra-cotta,** from the Italian words *terra*, which means "earth," and *cotta*, which means "cooked."

Qin Shi Huang Di

An Army for an Emperor

During the next 21 years, archaeologists uncovered more than 1,000 soldiers and horses in three different pits. They believe there are 8,000 statues. But they have yet to unearth them all.

The statues were made between 246 BC and 206 BC. Each one is different from the next. Some soldiers wear long shirts called **tunics.** Others have thick armor. All are buried in the tomb of Qin Shi Huang Di (CHIN shur hwang DEE). He was the first emperor to rule in the country now known as China.

The ancient Chinese, like the Egyptians, believed in an afterlife. There, they would need the same things after death that they needed in life. But why was this ruler buried with soldiers and swords instead of bracelets and bread?

More than 2,000 years ago, the country of China didn't exist. Instead, that area was made up of a dozen different kingdoms that were sometimes at war with each other. But one ruler changed all that. He was only 13 years old when he took the throne of one of those kingdoms. Over time, he created a powerful army and conquered nearby **territories.** By the time he was 38, he ruled six kingdoms. In 221 BC, he declared himself emperor.

An Archaeologist Speaks

"The emperor's tomb has a map that shows the empire that he ruled in life. The ancient Chinese believed that he would go on to rule this land in the afterlife, too."

Dr. Joe Wegner

While the emperor's soldiers conquered China, his laborers built his tomb. He believed that he'd need a massive army in death—just as he had in life. The objects found in his tomb don't tell archaeologists as much about daily life as those in Egyptian tombs. Instead, they give a feeling of what it must have been like to go to war in ancient China.

Artists sculpted the terra-cotta army, giving each statue a different set of facial features. Archaeologists believe the statues were modeled after actual soldiers in the emperor's army.

The emperor dressed in clothes made of colorful silk.

When archaeologists first uncovered the terra-cotta army, they found many statues broken into pieces. Decades later, they're still putting pieces back together.

25

Building a Clay Army

Archaeologists believe that it took about 40 years and 700,000 people to complete the enormous tomb. It's the size of a small city. There's a palace and courtyards. It's even bigger than Tomb 5 in Egypt. In fact, it's the largest discovered tomb in the world.

Just imagine how huge this project must have been. It required enormous amounts of money and workers. The tomb tells something about the ruler who had it built, just like the tombs in the Valley of the Kings. For one thing, it also required a powerful leader. In his way, Qin Shi Huang Di was just as commanding as Ramses II.

Sculptors made weapons for his terra-cotta army. In all, archaeologists found about 10,000 axes, spears, swords, and arrows. Some were made of clay. Others were made of bronze.

The terra-cotta army didn't need only weapons. They also needed **chariots.** Chariots were used in battles, but also for fast-moving races.

This bronze chariot is one of two found inside the tomb. Over time, the shiny metal turned a shade of gray.

Archaeologists have found a number of wooden chariots inside the emperor's tomb. Each one was big enough to carry two soldiers plus a driver. Unfortunately, they have decayed over time.

The archaeologists also found two enormous chariots made out of bronze. The larger of the two has a covered carriage. That was very unusual. Carvings of clouds and dragons decorate the inside. And there are traces of silk cloth, which was probably used to make cushions. The chariot is one of the biggest bronze artifacts ever uncovered anywhere on Earth.

All of these objects give archaeologists a sense of the things the army needed when they went to war. Imagine marching into battle wearing thick armor, and carrying a sword or spear, with soldiers right behind you riding in chariots.

What's the Difference?

Ancient Chinese and Egyptian tombs both held statues that were modeled after soldiers or workers. People believed that these statues would come to life and serve their rulers in the next world. But the statues looked very different. What do you think these figures tell about their cultures?

Chinese Soldier

Egyptian Worker

An Uncovered Burial Chamber

Much of the emperor's enormous tomb has been excavated. But there's still one area yet to be found. It's the burial chamber that holds his body. Finding it is tricky though. Some archaeologists believe that the emperor booby-trapped his tomb. Supposedly, bows and arrows are rigged to shoot anyone who tries to enter.

Even though the burial chamber hasn't been uncovered, the terracotta army is still one of the most stunning finds of the past hundred years. Millions of tourists travel to Xi'an, China, each year to view the awe-inspiring army. Meanwhile, excavations continue, and new artifacts are found all the time. Who knows what else archaeologists will uncover, and what else they'll learn about life in ancient China under the first emperor?

What Will Our Tombs Say About Us?

In some ways, we're a lot like ancient people. Today, many still bury bodies in graves or in tombs called **mausoleums.** Mausoleums are very different from ancient Egyptian and Chinese tombs, however. They're above ground, not hidden below. They're also much smaller, and paintings and hieroglyphs don't cover the walls.

We're like ancient people in other ways, too. Many still leave things for the dead at their graves. Family members often leave flowers and, sometimes, food, such as a bowl of rice. People are often buried with things they enjoyed while they were alive—a favorite outfit, for instance.

Like the ancient Egyptians, many people still treat bodies before they're buried to preserve them. But we don't make mummies. Instead, some use chemicals to **embalm** a body and keep it from rotting.

Someday, archaeologists may dig up our graves. We may not have magnificent tombs like the ones in Egypt or China. And we may not take precious jewels or chariots with us. But the way people are buried today will show archaeologists of the future a lot about how we lived and what we believed.

Keep Going!

Here are some ways to share what you've learned, find out more, and develop your talents. Maybe you'll come up with your own idea.

THINK AND WRITE

From crawling through narrow, dark tombs to uncovering ancient human remains, archaeologists have fascinating but challenging jobs. Why do you think an archaeologist's work is important? How do people today benefit from understanding what life was like long ago? Write your thoughts on this topic and share them with the class.

TALK TO THE EXPERTS

Find out firsthand what it's like to study ancient cultures and uncover ancient artifacts by interviewing experts in these fields. Use resources in your community or Websites to locate specialists. Here are some ideas:

- Contact a nearby history museum and arrange an interview with an Egyptologist or another expert on ancient civilizations.
- Interview a professor of ancient languages or ancient history at a local college.
- Communicate on-line with archaeologists and scholars from around the world at **www.asor.org/outreach/AskArch.htm.**

DIG DEEPER

Did you have any questions before you read the book that are still unanswered? If so, what are they? What questions came up in reading? Here are some Websites where you can start looking for answers. When you find them, write them down and tell where you found them.

Kent Weeks' Theban Mapping Project
www.thebanmappingproject.com

Secrets of the Pharaohs
www.pbs.org/wnet/pharaohs/

Dynasties of China—Qin Dynasty
www.travelchinaguide.com/intro/history/qin/

WRITE LIKE AN EGYPTIAN

Ancient Egyptians used pictures, called hieroglyphs, to record stories and ideas. In one form of hieroglyphics, a picture stands for a whole word. In another, each picture represents a letter. Go to a Website such as

members.aol.com/egyptnew/hiero.html

or find a book that shows what the hieroglyphs stand for.

- Use the symbols to write your name. You can turn it into a fancy nameplate, as ancient Egyptians did.
- Try your hand at writing a whole message. Exchange messages with a classmate. Can you figure out each other's messages? What do they say?

GLOSSARY

afterlife \af ′ tər līf\ *n.* life after death

archaeologist \är kē ä′ lə jist\ *n.* a scientist who studies the remains of ancient cultures

artifact \är′ ti fakt\ *n.* a man-made object used in everyday life, such as a bowl or piece of jewelry

canopic jar \kə nō′ pik jär\ *n.* a container used by ancient Egyptians to hold bodily organs during the process of making a mummy

chamber \chām′ bər\ *n.* a room

chariot \char′ ē ət\ *n.* a two-wheeled cart pulled by horses

debris \də brē′\ *n.* the remains of something that's been broken or destroyed

Egyptologist \ē jip tä′ lə jist\ *n.* a person who studies ancient Egypt

embalm \im bälm′\ *v.* treat a body with chemicals to preserve it and keep it from rotting

excavate \ek′ skə vāt\ *v.* dig up

faience \fā äns′\ *n.* clay that has been baked and glazed; a kind of ceramics

hieroglyph \hī′ rə glif\ *n.* ancient Egyptian writing in the form of pictures

immortal \i mor′ təl\ *adj.* alive forever

legend \le′ jənd\ *n.* a story or myth that comes from the past

mausoleum \mô sə lē′ əm\ *n.* an aboveground tomb

mummy \mə′ mē\ *n.* the dead body of a human being that has been preserved in a specific way for burial

natron \nā′ trän\ *n.* salt that was used to dry out and preserve mummies

pharaoh \fer′ ō\ *n.* an ancient Egyptian ruler

preserve \pri zərv′\ *v.* keep safe or free from harm

raid \rād\ *v.* attack

shabti \shäb′ tē\ *n.* a small statue that represented a servant and was buried in an Egyptian ruler's tomb

site \sīt\ *n.* a place. An archaeological site is a place with buildings or artifacts left by people long ago

terra-cotta \ter ə kä′ tə\ *n., adj.* baked clay

territory \ter′ ə tor ē\ *n.* an area that belongs to and is run by a government

tunic \tü′ nik\ *n.* a simple, long shirt with or without sleeves that falls to your knees

---

Pronunciation Key

\ə\ among \ər\ m**u**rder \a\ **a**sk \ā\ **a**pe \ä\ h**o**p, c**a**r \ch\ **ch**op \e\ **e**nd \ē\ gr**ea**sy \g\ **g**et
\i\ h**i**d \ī\ **i**ce \j\ **j**et \ŋ\ ki**ng** \ō\ n**o** \ô\ s**aw** \oi\ t**oy** \oo\ b**oo**k \ou\ **ou**t \th\ **th**ank \th\ **th**en
\ü\ b**oo**t \y\ **y**ou \zh\ A**s**ian

Index